In Memoriam

Lillian Elizabeth Randolph

1908—1965

This book is dedicated to the memory of Lillian Elizabeth Randolph.

Her violent and premature departure from this life left a painful and irreplaceable void for her family, heartaches for her friends, and a lingering sadness for the community.

> One can remember without being consumed.
> One can recall without being macabre.
> Tragedy should not overwhelm our existence,
> Nor should it be dismissed and forgotten.

Lillian's Legacy

Marriage and Murder in Rural Iowa

By

Carroll R. McKibbin

ISBN: 1-4033-9252-8 (e-book)
ISBN: 1-4033-9253-6 (Paperback)

Library of Congress Control Number: 2002095572

This book is printed on acid free paper.

Printed in the United States of America
Bloomington, IN

Photo: Getty Images

1stBooks — rev. 03/03/03

Contents

Acknowledgements

I am grateful to the many people who contributed to this book. The topic was painful for many, especially family members. And yet, with few exceptions, the people I contacted gladly provided the information included in this study. We share a common bond in caring about Lillian, and a mutual desire to provide a record of the events surrounding her death.

I would prefer to provide a list of contributors and thereby acknowledge specifically those who supported my efforts. It would be a lengthy roster of nearly one hundred and fifty people. However, a number of them asked that their names not be mentioned. In fairness to all, and in an effort to reduce speculation on sources of information, I decided to make this general expression of appreciation.

To those who would not talk with me, I have tried to understand. To those who did meet with me, some for many hours over a number of days; to those who allowed access to documents that are not normally public information; to those who sent me materials, such as letters, diaries, and personal accounts; to those who sent me information by e-mail, in one instance over 100 pages over a year's time — to all of you I wish to express my deepest appreciation. Along the way I have gained a number of enduring friendships. That is an unanticipated and major satisfaction.

Carroll R. McKibbin

Introduction

"Speak the truth and shame the Devil."

Francois Rabelais

Guthrie Center is as much a part of me as the blood that runs through my veins. Hometowns can be like that. Memories of throngs of town folk and farmers jabbering on downtown sidewalks on Saturday evenings while dark brown June bugs, inspired by the muggy Iowa summer, attempted futilely to scale the massive front window of Cronk's Cafe. Of car-seated patrons at band concerts honking their horns in approval of a rendition of "Mexicali Rose," overpowering the applause of the audience seated on the grassy slope of the courthouse lawn. Of the horse races at the county fair where the crowd favorite was "Charles T," a locally raised sorrel with a white foreleg. And of murder.

In American folklore gangland killings only occur in big cities like Chicago and New York. Rural towns like Guthrie Center are supposedly the innocent and law-abiding backbone of America. These are the people who, far removed from urban violence and crime, produce the amber waves of grain and supply the Private Ryans. The good people of Guthrie Center were shocked when the brutal ways of organized crime struck in their midst.

Local law enforcement officers, inexperienced in matters of homicide, grappled with the case. No charges were ever filed, even though local public opinion identified immediately the main evildoer. The court of public opinion may have informally solved the crime, but the formal criminal justice process did not. That is a part of *Lillian's Legacy*.

Unsolved homicide investigations are never officially closed. When all leads have been exhausted, they are designated "cold cases" and only periodically reviewed. There is no public record of such cases. As a matter of policy, police agencies do not allow public scrutiny of their files. That policy is logical for an active investigation, but when many years have passed and key witnesses and suspects have died, it makes less and less sense. In a democracy the public has an obligation to remedy evil, but that responsibility is rendered more difficult when the details of cases are permanently sealed in police files. That concern is also a factor in *Lillian's Legacy*.

Lack of information stokes the fires of rumor mills. That is what occurred in Guthrie Center, where enduring and malicious rumors damaged reputations and forced ruptures in the life of the community. There were stories of several people fleeing to Nebraska, Arkansas, and California with "hush money," including one who allegedly lured the victim into a fatal trap. There were whispers of criminal investigators, both local and state, being bribed by the chief suspect. Gossip spread of exchanges of large amounts of cash, as well as fanciful tales of the victim supposedly seen running from her abductors. Truth has but one version. That is another feature of *Lillian's Legacy*.

The events of this study began at a time when the modern women's movement was gaining momentum. Many of the reasons for that campaign are reflected in the circumstances described in this study. The victim was a battered wife who suffered at the hands of two husbands. Her avowed purpose in life was to create a home for her four children. Those who knew her best saw her life as devoted to children and church. She was educated and talented, but had few options beyond futile attempts to placate a husband. She was dominated and controlled via physical abuse, psychological torment, and financial pressure. In the end she was dependent upon the mercy of a husband and the protections of society. Both failed her. That is an important message and a large part of *Lillian's Legacy*.

The full story of the events of this study could not be told while the chief suspect was alive. He lived among those who knew. They were fearful or intimidated or both. Many still are, although he has been dead for a number of years. I assumed that his death would encourage witnesses and other knowledgeable people to reveal their information. I was partially correct. Two years after his death I began research on this project. Sources of information include: Interviews with many family members and friends of the victim and the chief suspect, witnesses and other knowledgeable people, reporters who covered the case, and law enforcement officers; dozens of newspaper accounts and relevant books; public records at the courthouse in Guthrie Center and at several public agencies in Des Moines, including some previously confidential files; and letters and diaries of the victim and the primary suspect. Wherever possible I have used the exact words of those involved to explain perspectives and events. There is no fiction in *Lillian's Legacy*. I have endeavored to provide as true an account as possible. Statements placed within quotation marks, with occasional grammatical license, are *verbatim* references to transcripts, letters, diaries, newspaper articles, books, public records, files, and interviews.

For the aforementioned purposes and by the described means I am providing for public scrutiny an account of the before and after events of the murder of Lillian Randolph. In that way I have tried to contribute to *Lillian's Legacy*.

Chapter I

A Faustian Wedding

"I would be happy with anyone who would be good to me and my children."

Lillian Chalman

Guthrie Center was buzzing. Telephone chatter and back fence gossip ricocheted about town. Howard Randolph had married a stranger, someone from "up north." The few known details passed quickly among the two thousand inhabitants. Apparently she was from Minnesota and her name was "Lillian." There are few secrets in a small town, and people were curious and eager to know more about the newest addition to their community

Unlike the new Mrs. Randolph, the people of Guthrie Center had known Howard Randolph many years. Indeed, he was the best known man in this small Iowa town, tucked away among rolling hills of cornfields fifty miles to the west of Des Moines. Howard ran a large business operation, had the most money, and lived in the nicest house. Most families in the community had a least one member employed by him in one of the many positions that his egg, poultry, creamery, and general farming enterprises provided.

Howard was twelve when he moved to the area with his mother and three brothers in 1920. Richard Randolph, his father, died suddenly on the family farm near the southern Missouri town of Summersville, where Howard was born and the Randolph family had lived for a number of years. Bessie Randolph, a widow at the age of thirty-six, took her four sons, Roosevelt, Donald, Howard, and Earle to live at her parents' farm three miles west of Guthrie Center. There, Bessie set up a household for her family in the upstairs of the Columbus and Alferetta Simmons home.

Bessie Randolph was a crusty and stubborn but sympathetic woman who set an example of hard work for her sons. She had an extreme sense of frugality that went so far as avoiding the flushing of toilets to save water. Howard acquired his mother's work ethic and frugality, including her penchant for saving water. When sharing accommodations in his adult years, he requested often that the bath water of others be saved for his use.

The Randolph boys attended a country school near the Simmons home and routinely walked the three miles to Guthrie Center for errands and

1

amusement. On the farm they enjoyed hunting, fishing, and trapping. All four graduated from Guthrie Center High School, something of an achievement in the days when farm children first had to take examinations to qualify for admission to a high school, and then meet its requirements to receive a diploma.

Of the Randolph boys, only Howard stayed in Guthrie Center. Donald spent most of his adult years in International Falls, Minnesota; Earle never married and ran a news stand in New York City; and Roosevelt operated a resort near Greenfield, Iowa, twenty-five miles to the south of Guthrie Center. Bessie re-married, this time to John Eaton, and moved to Monteith, only a few miles south of Guthrie Center. She lived there until John died, and then moved to Guthrie Center and ran a rooming house on Main Street.

Howard Randolph graduated from the local high school in 1926. Many years later several surviving schoolmates still remembered him vividly. Mildred Holmes Denny recalled Howard as an Honor Roll student who helped his slower classmates with their assignments, but otherwise was aloof and "not very sociable." Elberta Harkins did not recall Howard as an Honor Roll student, but did remember him as being "shrewd," a word that many people recall as a dominant part of Howard's personality. Maxine Goochey, who was Howard's first wife and two years behind him in school, remembered him as a capable student more noteworthy for his ambition than his academic achievements.

After high school Howard Randolph attended Chillicothe Junior College in Missouri, taking mostly business courses, before returning to his hometown two years later. Howard resumed his relationship with his high school girlfriend, Maxine Goochey, and in 1930 the 22-year-old Howard and Maxine, three years his junior, were married. The young couple made their home in Guthrie Center, where Howard was selling insurance out of a Buick, the first of thirty-one that he would own in his lifetime.

An important evening activity of Howard in those early years of marriage was reading law books that he borrowed from local attorneys. He had a keen interest in legal processes. Howard saw the law as a tool for his ambitions and used it frequently in years to come. Attorneys and courtroom battles became a major part of his existence, and a part that seemed to provide enormous pleasure to him. Maxine recalled that "he was never happier than when he was in a law suit." She also offered, "All he was interested in was money, and he didn't care how he got it."

Howard moved from insurance into the poultry business when his uncle, Charlie Gilson, hired him as an incubator operator at his plant in Bagley, a small town twelve miles to the north of Guthrie Center. After a short period of employment with his uncle, Howard decided to return to his hometown and operate a poultry business of his own. Rumor has it that Howard borrowed the necessary money from his uncle to establish his new business enterprise, but never repaid him. Thus was launched another enduring feature of Howard's reputation: taking advantage of others.

Howard moved his poultry business from place to place in Guthrie Center until in 1937 he constructed a modern facility with a long loading dock on the north side of Prairie Street, between Third and Fourth Streets, one block south of the main business district. Across the street he bought a warehouse and converted it to a chicken slaughtering and dressing operation. He added cream and butter to his expanding business enterprises when he purchased the Farmers' Cooperative Creamery, one block south on Third Street. Howard's "Corn and Clover" butter, eggs, cream, and chickens were soon found in grocery stores throughout the Midwest, and later throughout the United States and into foreign markets.

By the later 1930s Howard Randolph's marketing operation extended to the East Coast, where New Jersey underworld figures were squeezing legitimate produce dealers out of business. One dealer filed suit against the mob in an effort to hold onto his business. Howard was called to New Jersey as a witness in the case and, taking opportunity over principle, testified against the plaintiff. The erstwhile dealer lost his business as a result. He committed suicide. The case enhanced Howard's growing reputation for placing money over principle, and commenced the new feature of connections with unsavory figures. Employees and business associates became increasingly aware of Howard's connections with criminal elements.

A former employee in Guthrie Center recalls seeing an unknown, suspicious visitor who drove a black Cadillac with Illinois license plates and occasionally visited Howard's office, where the two of them talked behind closed doors. Another former employee, who worked at Howard's office in Harlan, Iowa, recalls visitors from Kansas City who were "out and out crooks." A former business associate in Runnells, Iowa, stated that he was sure that Howard Randolph had criminal contacts in Chicago, New York, and Kansas City, and that Howard often mentioned the names of Lew Farrell and Florin DePaglia, reputed underworld figures in Des Moines. A former bookkeeper in Guthrie Center was suspicious of Howard's business methods because he sometimes took as much as $100,000 in cash on business trips to Chicago. A Randolph family member summed up Howard's underworld connections succinctly: "He was in with the big boys."

Howard was thirty-three and well within the draft age at the time of the attack on Pearl Harbor. When the war was over he told unknowing people he had been a combat pilot. In reality, he applied for and received a deferment because he was supplying eggs, chickens, and butter to the military. His business thrived during the war and eventually required larger facilities closer to railroad freight transportation. Thus he built a large red tile structure with a Quonset-style roof on lower Third Street near the tracks of the Chicago, Rock Island, and Pacific Railroad. Trucks backed up to the seventy-foot loading dock to deliver cases of eggs to be quick-frozen in a voluminous walk-in freezer. On the second floor of the new building an egg-breaking facility was constructed. Refrigerated box cars filled with brass-plated three-gallon cans of dried and frozen eggs were used to ship Randolph products to all regions of the country and into Mexico.

Randolph expanded his product line into beef in 1941 when he purchased a cattle ranch, now known as the "Bar-L," just beyond the southern city limits of Guthrie Center. Throughout the war and afterwards Randolph extended his farm holdings. Cattle raising, although a small portion of Randolph's commercial enterprises at the outset, was always Howard's favorite business endeavor. Many years later he sold all of his business enterprises but farming and cattle raising, applying high tech methods to the latter that gained him national recognition.

Howard's burgeoning business empire became officially "Randolph Foods" and its plant operations spread throughout Iowa. Eventually he owned poultry and creamery businesses in Guthrie Center, Des Moines, Sac City, Carroll, Harlan, Boone, Marshalltown, Lenox, and Russell. He also assembled a network of Iowa and Missouri produce dealers who contracted to sell their chickens, eggs, and cream to him. These independent contractors funneled their products into Howard's expanding operations and allowed him extensive control over produce prices, particularly in the egg market. In 1952 the Department of Agriculture officially charged him with manipulating the Chicago egg market by withholding shipments. Randolph's penalty was a one-year suspension of his trading privileges at the Chicago commodities market, the largest in the country.

Undaunted by the Feds and delving into his bag of illegal and shady practices, Howard used the social security numbers of others to continue his trading and returned to the national and international egg business in a big way. Within a few years he was again shipping large quantities of eggs. For example, in 1958 his companies sent more than *eighty boxcars* of eggs to Mexico City.

The first manager for Howard's cattle raising business was his father-in-law, Charles Goochey, an experienced farmer who moved from Minnesota to Guthrie Center to work for Howard. The business relationship did not last long, however, as Charles "could not get along with Howard," as Maxine Goochey Randolph recalled. And thus another feature of Howard's personality became evident: he had difficulty getting along with people, particularly those who worked for him at the managerial level. Whatever his genius was for developing a business empire, he was sorely lacking in human relations skills.

Marion Messersmith, a long-time friend of Howard recalled, "I saw a lot of good men come and a lot of good men go." In one instance when she had become a friend of the wife (Eileen) of one of Howard's managers, George Friday, she begged him not to fire George. Eileen told Marion, "I wish I had a tape recording of everything he promised us." But, true to Howard's business practices, there was no tape recording, there was no written document, and there was no record whatsoever other than the Fridays' painful memories. Despite Marion's pleas Howard fired George, leaving the impression with her that he received special satisfaction out of his heartless action. In another instance of Howard's joy of firing people, he dismissed Bob Gilson after he learned that Bob was part of a group including Marion who had gone out to dinner together. Apparently Howard considered Marion an exclusive possession. When an acquaintance of Marion's from Topeka, another "Howard," said that he had received a very good business offer from Howard Randolph, Marion urged him not to accept. But he did, became disillusioned like many others, and was fired, also like many others.

Over the years Howard Randolph fired dozens of managers. The typical pattern was to offer a managerial position to someone living outside the community. A number of extravagant, oral promises would be made to entice the potential employee. But after the new manager had relocated his family to the site of his new employment, many promises would go unfulfilled. The employee was faced with accepting employment on the *de facto* terms, quitting, or being fired. If Howard felt that he was not getting full compliance with his demands, the manager would be fired harshly and immediately. Acrimony among those who left ran high. Howard ended up being threatened, sued, and physically attacked on a number of occasions. None of that caused him to alter his methods.

A case in point is the business proposal that Howard once offered a local man, Dick Jorgensen. Using one of his typical business approaches, Howard slipped a note into Dick's shirt pocket outlining a business proposition. Howard proposed that Dick manage one of his farms and that they split expenses and profits fifty-fifty. Dick was sufficiently interested to look over the farm and accompanying house with his wife, Doris. When Doris discovered crayon markings on the interior walls of the house she told Dick that the walls needed cleaning, painting, or wallpapering.

Dick called Howard and told him, "Doris and I might be interested in your proposal, but something has to be done about the crayon marks on the interior wall of the house. I assume that the fifty-fifty arrangement would mean that you and I would split the costs of the painting or wallpapering."

"No," replied Howard. "The inside of the house would be part of your fifty percent."

"Well then," Dick responded, "does that not mean that you would pay for the cost of new gravel for the driveway to the house?"

"No," said Howard. "Since the driveway leads to the house, that would also be part of your fifty percent."

Dick terminated the phone conversation at that point, wondering when Howard's fifty percent would ever kick in. Dick and Doris discussed the proposition and decided that they did not want to deal with Howard's math. The next day Dick ran across Howard and told him he had decided to decline the offer.

"Wise decision," said Howard. "I admire you for that. I'll find another sucker."

Howard's rough-and-tumble methods did not go unnoticed by his business peers and associates. An egg and poultry dealer in Lenox, Iowa, who could not collect on a $4,000 debt of Howard's, decided that he would no longer do business with him and informed Howard accordingly. A short time later the man's business burned to the ground. Arson was suspected, and the dealer believed Howard was responsible. He reported his suspicions to the Iowa Bureau of Criminal Investigation, but no direct evidence connecting Howard with the fire was found. Another highly respected poultry and egg dealer in Manson, Iowa, who also served as the mayor of his community, reported to the Iowa BCI his concerns about the legality of Howard's business practices. Again there was no direct evidence of illegal behavior.

Howard Randolph's business was his life. He was consumed by it. The purchasing power of money was not his priority—he spent as little as possible. But he loved the challenge of besting people in business transactions, and money was the gauge of his triumph.

Chick Gonzales, the long-time owner of the Guthrie Center *Times,* recalled being invited by Howard to accompany him and two local business associates, Leo Hagen and K.H. "Kenny" Buttler, to an Iowa University football game on a fall afternoon in the late 1950s. The trip to Iowa City in the days prior to the interstate system required a drive of four hours. Chick, new in Guthrie Center at the time, sat in the back seat of Howard's pink Buick as the other three passengers conducted a high power discussion of the egg market all the way to the football stadium. After Howard parked near the stadium, he went to a nearby phone booth, explaining he had to make a few business calls. He told the others to go on to the game and he would join them later. They did so. Howard never joined them. When they returned to the parking lot after the game Howard was still on the telephone. He finally finished as the parking lot emptied. On the way home Howard described his latest business coup, never once asking about the game. When they reached Des Moines, Howard suggested they stop for dinner at his favorite restaurant, "Vic's Tally-Ho." They were hardly seated when Howard said he had to make a business call, and borrowed a dime from Chick for that purpose. Leo, Kenny, and Chick ate alone as Howard apparently closed another business deal. The dime was never repaid.

Two local high school athletes of the 1950s, Loren Squires and Paul Charter, went to Howard's office to solicit an ad for the football schedule poster. Howard, as usual, was busy on the phone, this time with a receiver in each hand. It was apparent that he was dealing with customers who were unhappy with the quality of eggs he had shipped to them. Numbers, promises, and offers were exchanged until Howard finally said, "OK, I'll let you have them for twelve cents a dozen," acting as though he had made a major concession. When he hung up, and knowing that the boys had been listening, he gleefully announced, "I only paid eight cents a dozen for them." He did not buy the five-dollar ad.

Howard Randolph's second highest priority, after business success, was women. When his first wife, Maxine, was asked to identify the favorite hobby of Howard, she responded without hesitation: "Girls." She recalled that his infidelity commenced almost immediately after their marriage in 1930. As his business empire expanded, so did his network of lady friends. There was one in Chicago, one in California in the San Fernando Valley, another in Minnesota, and several sprinkled about Iowa in Des Moines, Perry, Algona, Stuart, and for good measure, a couple in Guthrie Center. One of them, who now lives in California, laughed as she recalled, "He was never happy with just one woman. Heck, he had one in every town." Howard's reputation as a womanizer was well established.

Myrna Swain Bartlett began working for the Guthrie Center newspaper a few years after graduating from the local high school in 1934. Myrna, a very attractive young lady, apparently caught the attention of Howard Randolph. While in the newspaper office to place an ad, Howard spied the shy, pretty teenager and approached her about going to work for him.

"What do you make here?" he demanded of Myrna. "I'll double your salary."

Myrna was flabbergasted. Her employer, Vern Hall, was present, making the circumstances even more awkward. Howard seemed oblivious to Vern in awaiting Myrna's response. But she did not respond, and Howard left. A few years later, after Myrna had married and her husband, Norris Bartlett, was awaiting his call to World War II military service, Howard suggested that the young couple use his newly acquired Minnesota lake cabin for a vacation. The proposal was enticing, but the young couple knew Norris would soon be leaving and were distrustful of Howard in any case. They declined the offer.

The Bartletts' response to Howard's seemingly kind invitation was reflective of a growing opinion in Guthrie Center that Howard Randolph never made an offer out of pure kindness. He wanted something out of every relationship, and his primary motivations were money and women.

Howard's infidelity notwithstanding, a son, Richard, was added to the Randolph household in 1941. Howard quickly made a point of telling people he was not the father. His mother, Bessie, reinforced Howard's claim by telling others he was probably sterile from complications of childhood mumps. True or not, Howard's version became widely accepted among locals, although there was another opinion that he had a special interest in a young lady in Minnesota and was seeking a way to terminate his relationship with Maxine. In either case, their marriage did not last long after the birth of Richard. Maxine took her son and left Guthrie Center. She kept him from Howard throughout his childhood and adolescence. It was not until Richard finished a tour of duty in the Army more than twenty years later that Howard developed a relationship with him.

Money, power, and sex as motivating factors in human behavior have a limitless history. The first two applied to Howard Randolph in the traditional sense, and profoundly so, but not that of sex. His physical capabilities in that respect were questionable. One former lady friend recalls that Howard's relationships with women "were not romantic," apparently meaning they did not include the physical aspect of passion. But he liked to be in the presence of pretty women and have them fawn over him, perhaps attracted by a large roll of twenty-dollar bills he carried in his pocket. Power over others was a large factor in Howard's behavior. He gained obvious satisfaction in controlling people and moving them in and out of his life.

Howard Randolph was no Don Juan. Outside of money, and therein may be an easy answer, he seemed to have little to offer a woman. He dressed formally, nearly always wearing a suit and tie. His reddish-brown hair was combed into an Eddie Bracken-style pompadour. Indeed, from a distance he looked well dressed and neatly groomed. Up close was a different matter. A very different matter. He had legendary body odor, at least partially because his mania over saving water deterred the use of a bath or shower. The local joke was that his B.O. would take paint off a wall. After Howard visited an office or store, people muttered about the offensive odor and opened windows and doors. In his office he had the habit of working with his shoes off. The odor of his feet, combined with his normal B.O., drove employees to look for reasons to take a break outside.

Another disincentive for female attraction to Howard was his less than masculine features and nature. He was larger in the hips than in his narrow shoulders. His voice was soft and lilted. Like a girl, he liked to sit with his feet folded under him, especially when he sat on the floor. Men who physically challenged him considered him a coward. When he was confronted with possible violence, and that happened on a number of occasions, he offered no defense other than words. His response came in the form of legal recourse or financial leverage.

Howard made ostentatious displays of money when out of town. In those settings he provided gifts and travel for his lady friends, including a car, a fur coat, jewelry, and a variety of trips. In return, Howard was seemingly satisfied to be in the presence of attractive women who were responsive and obedient to him. He occasionally asked favors of them, such as running errands, making phone calls, or allowing him to use the social security numbers of them or their children in his business. But he was not sexually demanding of women in a physical sense. One called him "more of a touchy-feely guy who liked to look."

In Guthrie Center Howard was cautious about displays of his obvious wealth. He always had a new Buick, and that set him apart from many others in a land of Chevys and Fords. Otherwise he was known as niggardly. In other cities he was known by many as a man who carried a large wad of bills, bought people gifts, picked up the check, and displayed a certain charm. That was not the Howard that the people of Guthrie Center knew.

Locals were surprised when Howard, in his fiftieth year, constructed an opulent house at the south end of the municipal golf course. Until then he had lived in very modest quarters in the back of his gray stucco office on the corner of Third and Prairie. Why would he now be switching to a three-bedroom house? What did he have in mind? The community knew that Howard Randolph never did anything without a reason, particularly when there was a cost involved.

The motivation for building a new home became apparent when Howard remarried. For some reason he had decided to become a family man. But there was something too charitable about that to fit the local image of Howard Randolph. Surely there was something more to it; something connected with money or women. Local speculation was extensive.

Perhaps the new Mrs. Randolph was rich and Howard was after her money. Perhaps she was a stunningly beautiful, buxom, younger woman like Howard seemed to prefer. Perhaps there was a business or tax angle that he was exploiting. Whatever the motives of Howard in proposing to Lillian, it was a major surprise to the people of Guthrie Center that he was taking a bride. The reputation of Howard in the community was fixed and

9

negative. People asked each other, "Who and why would anyone marry Howard Randolph?" The community would soon have answers. They were not exactly what had been anticipated.

The new Mrs. Randolph was attractive and trim at 5'4" and 125 pounds, but she did not have the looks of a Hollywood starlet as some had imagined. She was neither rich nor young. She had struggled financially in Duluth and was only a year younger than Howard. And she had four children. That was particularly baffling. Why would Howard elect to become the stepfather to four children? It certainly did not fit his local image. Speculation continued about his *real* motives.

Lillian Hedman was born to a family of Swedish immigrants in West Duluth, Minnesota, on August 5, 1908. Her father, Gustaf Hans Hedman, had come to the United States from the small town of Bergsgarden, Sweden, when he was nineteen. He left behind his parents and five siblings. He never saw them again. In a letter to his family Gustaf wrote: "The fever of what was over the hills made me pack up and sail the Atlantic."

Gustaf was processed for admission into the United States at Ellis Island, and then took a train to Chicago, where he found employment at the Chicago Cottage Piano Factory. He soon moved on to Minnesota where the terrain and climate were more like his native Sweden, and where many other Scandinavians had settled. Gustaf Hedman resided in West Duluth for the rest of his life.

Gustaf worked as a lumberjack and in a local sawmill during the day, and spent his evenings taking a preparatory class for American citizenship. It was in that class that he met Anna Christina Magnusson, also a Swedish immigrant. Anna's parents had left her with grandparents in Smaland, Sweden, when she was only three-years-old so they could immigrate to the United States and establish a home. They had planned to send for her shortly thereafter, but it was nearly twelve years before Anna rejoined her parents in Stillwater, Minnesota. A few years later she moved to Duluth and met Gustaf.

Gustaf and Anna were married in 1899. They raised a family of seven, of which Lillian was the fifth born. Gustaf worked most of his adult years as the Milk and Dairy Inspector for the City of Duluth. Anna was a housewife who canned large quantities of food for the family of nine and washed laundry in a creek behind their West Duluth home.

Lillian enjoyed school, attending Longfellow Elementary School and Denfield High School in West Duluth. After receiving her high school diploma in 1927, she enrolled at Duluth State Teachers College with the encouragement of her parents. She lived at home while attending college and recalled fondly how her mother sometimes prepared a bowl of peanuts as a treat for her return home from classes.

Lillian's first teaching job was near Hibbing, Minnesota, at a country school where the benefits included lodging at a home next door. Lillian met other teachers in the area and occasionally invited some of them to the Hedman house for the weekend, where the young ladies slept three or four crosswise in a bed. Lillian had learned to play the piano by ear, and loved to entertain her company. She was particularly fond of hymns and favored "The Old Rugged Cross" and "Rock of Ages."

Lillian continued her teaching career at Homecroft School in a rural area to the immediate north of Duluth until she married Bob O'Hara, also a native of West Duluth. Bob owned a prosperous service station on Grand Avenue. Lillian told her daughters how she and Bob had lived in a "substantial house with a double circular staircase," and she had owned two fur coats when her neighbors were happy to have one to fight the cold Minnesota winters.

Lillian had two children with Bob: Henry, who acquired the nickname "Hank" shortly after his birth in 1938, and Ann, who was born three years later. At the same time that Lillian was creating her own family she lost her mother to cancer. Soon thereafter World War II began and Bob was inducted into the Army, leaving Lillian to care for two young children on her own. Tragedy was to follow. A fall in the basement of their home resulted in a brain injury to Bob that claimed his life. Robert O'Hara died on April 12, 1945, the same day as President Franklin Roosevelt.

Being a young widow with two small children was a daunting prospect, but at least Bob had left Lillian with the resources to continue her comfortable, middle-class existence. She also had the emotional support of her nearby family as she began her new life as a single parent.

After World War II Lillian became better acquainted with an old friend, Roy Chalman. Roy was of Norwegian extraction, Americanizing his family name from the original spelling of Kjellman. He had just concluded a lengthy stint in the Navy. The relationship of Roy and Lillian turned serious and they were married.

Roy moved into Lillian's house and became the stepfather of Hank and Ann. Another child, Wendy, was born to Roy and Lillian in 1948. Two years later the Korean War broke out and Roy was called back into the Navy, leaving behind two stepchildren, one of his own, and a pregnant wife. In 1951 a second daughter, Vicki, was born.

When Roy returned from the Navy he was a changed man. He drank heavily, and according to family members, was "a little crazy" at those times. Lillian, Hank, and Ann all suffered physical abuse at the hands of Roy. On one unfortunate occasion, Lillian called the police for assistance.

Roy also had a problem holding a job. After ten years of marriage Lillian had spent all that Bob O'Hara had left her, including life insurance, bonds, savings, and even the proceeds from the house she had to sell in an effort to support the family. An ill-fated business venture of Roy in Bennett, Wisconsin, combined with his persistent drinking and occasional physical abuse, convinced Lillian that she would be better off looking after her family on her own. She fled Wisconsin in the middle of the night with her children, going to the Minnesota home of her sister and brother-in-law, Helen and Clarence Erickson. She then filed for a divorce from Roy Chalman. Lillian was a forgiving and persevering woman. Years later she wrote that Roy was "a dreamer," but did not mention his financial irresponsibility and physical abuse.

Once again Lillian was on her own. Now a middle-aged woman with four children, and without the resources she had after the death of her first husband, she set about putting a life together for her family. Hank, who was now back in the household after living with his aunt and uncle, Lorraine and Jim Belluci, while the rest of the family was in Wisconsin, had a job and was paying for his room and board. Ann, at fifteen, was the source of a monthly Social Security check because her father had died and she was still a minor. Child support payments for Wendy and Vicki came from time to time from Roy. And Lillian was substitute teaching in the Duluth elementary school system on nearly a daily basis. With a $1,000 loan from her father she was able to make the down payment on a modest house in West Duluth and establish a home for her children.

Lillian Chalman and Howard Randolph had known each other casually for nearly twenty years when he proposed marriage in 1957. Howard had first become acquainted with Lillian through her youngest sister, Lorraine, and her older brother, Leonard "Buck" Hedman. Buck was something of an exile from West Duluth after being tried for inciting a riot in connection with a 1920 lynching of three black youths. Although acquitted of the charges, Buck decided to move away. He eventually became the owner of the Hedman Resort on the shores of Lake Winniebigoshish.

The gorgeous and shapely Lorraine worked for Buck in the summer and caught the eye of Howard who owned a nearby cabin. When they met Lorraine was only eighteen, while Howard was thirty-three and married. Her family, including Buck, were concerned about the attention Howard was showing to Lorraine. Those concerns, but not Howard's attention, ended when Lorraine married an old friend, Jim Belluci, when he returned from the Army after World War II. In the meantime, Howard had divorced Maxine, his wife of twelve years, and Lillian had become a young widow.

Howard continued his fishing trips to Minnesota and became acquainted with Jim Belluci. When visiting Duluth Howard made a point of entertaining Jim and Lorraine. On some of those occasions Lillian was also present, first on her own and later with Roy Chalman when she remarried.

During a 1957 trip Howard learned that Lillian had divorced Roy. He invited her to join him for dinner at a luxurious restaurant. Howard asked Lillian out a second time and included her children in the invitation. He lavished her family with meals, entertainment, and gifts in the days that followed. Before leaving Duluth, Howard invited Lillian to visit him in Guthrie Center. She accepted and arrived at his home with her three daughters in October of 1957. She later wrote that "the house was lovely" and "we were all impressed."

Howard proposed marriage to Lillian during the second day of her visit. He told her he would send Hank to Drake University in Des Moines, and when Ann graduated from high school he would send her to college as well. As for the nine-year-old Wendy and six-year-old Vicki, Howard promised to make them his "little princesses" and to treat them accordingly. Lillian, he said, would have her own automobile, a new fur coat, and the entire family would take a vacation in Hawaii the next summer. He also wanted to adopt her four children. They would become "Randolphs" and heirs to his considerable fortune.

Lillian was "flattered," as she later put it, but felt the proposal was very sudden. Although dazzled by the prospects as Howard had described them, she and Howard had not seriously dated and she had gone through a painful divorce only a year before. Moreover, she had developed a stable, albeit sometimes lonely, life. She responded to Howard that she would have to return to Duluth, reflect on his proposal, and discuss it with her family.

Instant security for her children and another chance to develop a full family life for them were compelling reasons for a forty-nine-year-old woman to accept Howard's proposal. The contrast between her meager, hard-working existence in Duluth and what Howard was promising in Guthrie Center were enormous. Although her personal relationship with Howard had neither length nor depth, she pushed herself to create the interest and feelings of the usual prospective bride. She wrote that Howard was "a perfect gentleman" and that she "had come to care for him." But perhaps her true feelings were more evident when she also wrote: "I would be happy with anyone who would be good to me and my children."

Gustaf Hedman expressed concern that Lillian would be moving away and marrying a man she did not know well. Helen, Lillian's oldest sister and with whom Lillian was particularly close, expressed her concerns in muted terms. She was the family diplomat and knew that Lillian greatly respected her views. She did not want to interfere with Lillian's chance for happiness. Helen also knew that she and her husband, Clarence, had wed abruptly twenty-four years before and were happily married. Her final words of counsel were: "The main thing is that you find happiness and companionship together."

Lorraine, who knew Howard better than anyone in the Hedman family and is Lillian's only surviving sister, remembers her surprise at the news. "Out of the blue he proposed to her. The marriage happened so fast." She also recalls having "mixed emotions" about Lillian becoming Howard's wife. The opportunity for economic security was obvious, but Lorraine knew that Howard's personality was "complicated" and had dimensions to which Lillian had not been exposed. She knew him as a calculating, "never spontaneous" individual who "always had a reason" and did not always keep his promises. She wondered why Howard had proposed to Lillian so suddenly, but she also did not want to stand in the way of Lillian's opportunity.

Lillian's family had always been close and supportive. In the end they told her to use her best judgment. If she decided to accept Howard's proposal, they would certainly wish her well.

Lillian's two oldest children, Hank and Ann, were not keen on being uprooted from their existence in Duluth, where they had been born and raised. Hank was out of school, had a job, and a serious relationship with a young woman, Margaret "Peggy" Frerichs, who would soon become his wife. Ann was a junior in high school and was not pleased with the prospect of being displaced. But the little girls, Wendy and Vicki, were excited about making the move. Wendy, now a mother of three, recalls, "I wanted a dad so bad. He (Howard) took us out in Duluth. He seemed so generous. He could be very charming. I was ready for him to be my dad." Even as a nine-year-old, Wendy was concerned for her mother's security. She recalls, "I wanted my mother to be taken care of." Ironically, that was precisely what her mother was trying to provide for Wendy and her siblings.

Lillian took several days to discuss Howard's marriage proposal with her children and larger family. During that time Howard called frequently and urgently, pressing her to say, "Yes." Eventually she did. Lillian Chalman and Howard Randolph began to make plans to be married.

Neither Howard nor Lillian wanted a big wedding. Lillian, a life-long and devoted member of the Lutheran Church, wanted to have the wedding ceremony performed by a Lutheran minister. Howard had been raised as a Quaker, but was not active in that faith. He consented to the Lutheran marriage. On January 30, 1958, Lillian Elizabeth Chalman and Howard Fitz Randolph were joined in marriage in a ceremony conducted by the Reverend L.G. Gabbert of the Immanuel Lutheran Church in Casey, Iowa. Lillian's son, Hank, served as Best Man, and his recent bride, Peggy, served as Maid of Honor. Following the wedding ceremony Lillian and Howard read a message from Lillian's sister, Helen, which was sealed in an envelope addressed: "Not to be opened until you are Mr. and Mrs. Howard Randolph." Along with the normal good wishes, Helen addressed a specific message to Howard: "I know that Lillian's greatest desire in life is kindness and thoughtfulness for her and her children...." She continued: "Please take Lil's burdens over and give her a life of peace and contentment—she is so in need of that as she has had a family responsibility for so many years it would be nice for her to have a good shoulder to lean on."

In Duluth Lillian's three daughters awaited the return of their mother and the approaching move to their new home in Iowa. The people of Guthrie Center shared their anticipation and a high level of curiosity. What would the new Mrs. Randolph be like?

Chapter II

Life With Howard

"Just a few months after our arrival we knew there would be trouble."

Wendy Holman

Shortly after her January marriage to Howard Randolph the new Mrs. Randolph and her family moved to Iowa. Howard gave Hank a job working at his Des Moines Foods plant in Iowa's capitol city, and he and his bride, officially "Margaret" but better known as "Peggy," found housing in Urbandale in the western suburbs of Des Moines. Lillian and the other three children moved into Howard's comfortable home. Ann enrolled as a junior in the Guthrie Center High School, while Wendy became a fourth grader and Vicki a second grader in the local elementary school.

The transition into the local schools, always difficult in mid-year, was particularly difficult for the two younger girls. They discovered that the elementary grades in Guthrie Center were more advanced than in Duluth. They felt like they had been promoted to a higher class in mid-year, and with no preparation. They struggled to keep up with their classmates. To make matters worse they also experienced taunting from their new classmates who called them "rich kids" because their new father was Howard Randolph. Some of the children even composed a new song to "welcome" Wendy and Vicki. The title of the mocking jingle was "Randolph the Bowlegged Cowboy," and was sung to the tune of "Rudolph the Red-Nosed Reindeer."

Although the children did not receive the warmest of welcomes at school, they did have a large and commodious house to live in. Ann had her own bedroom with a double bed next to the attached garage. Wendy and Vicki shared a bedroom with single beds in the southeast corner of the house, and Howard and Lillian occupied the master bedroom on the southwest corner of the front of the house.

The Randolph house needed cleaning and organization after several years of a bachelor's existence. Lillian, with help from her daughters, set about putting their new home in order. She had some ideas on decorating, but decided to ease into the new setting before discussing such matters with her new husband. Lillian had very clear thoughts about the organization of a household, believing, in her words, that the wife is "head of the house" and the husband is "head of the business," but was willing to allow such a division of responsibilities to evolve in her new household.

Lillian'a expectations in marriage largely involved support for her children, although she had personal considerations as well. She wanted a better life, meaning more resources and love and affection, for herself and her children. She had known Howard Randolph for a long time but not well. Their "courtship" had been lightning quick. Lillian referred to Howard as "Mr. Randolph" when in the presence of others, revealing a formality in their relationship rather than the endearing nature of a close and loving couple.

Good marriages involve a husband and wife giving to each other and experiencing mutual satisfaction in the process. The marriage of Lillian and Howard was more a matter of what each thought they could gain from the other. For Lillian those motivations were clear when she wrote: "I could be happy with anyone who could be good to me and my children." She recognized as well that a married couple is supposed to have a romantic bond, as she later wrote that by the time of their marriage "I had come to care for Howard," and added, "he was a perfect gentleman."

"Caring for" someone does not connote the same depth of feelings as "love," the normal emotion of a marital relationship. And although Lillian occasionally used that term when writing to Howard, it was more a matter of wishful thinking than reality. Their marriage had more the quality of a business transaction than a passionate love affair. He was accustomed to business transactions and may have been satisfied with a "business arrangement" with his wife. If he had a need for love and affection with his new family, it was directed primarily at Lillian's youngest daughters, Wendy and Vicki, whom he liked to refer to as "his little princesses."

Wendy recalls that the family thought the marriage was "kind of quick," but also remembers that "we were going to have everything we ever wanted." Vicki recollects that her mother was "vulnerable with four kids" and that Howard "had money and made lots of promises." Close friends of Lillian are quick to mention her interest in support for her family as a major motivation in marrying Howard. It is perhaps too trite to say that she married him for his money, but it is doubtful she would have agreed to become Mrs. Randolph and move to Iowa if he had been a man of modest means.

Just as Lillian was interested in the financial support Howard could supply to herself and her children, Howard was attracted to Lillian because she had children. He had a number of single lady friends who surely would have married him. But he seemed to be interested in becoming a family man. He was fifty years old, had no relationship with the son born to his

17

first wife, and had a fondness for children—particularly little girls. Lillian had two of those. Howard wanted children in his daily life. At the age of fifty and convinced of his inability to father a child, marrying a woman with small children was his only option. Indeed, an obvious priority for Howard in the marriage was to have children. It was as though he married to have children rather than a wife. In that respect Lillian was a vehicle to Howard's interest in being a father. Later, however, he would see her as a rival and impediment for the affections that he craved from "his" daughters.

Howard may have had other considerations in acquiring a family, such as some kind of business advantage. He had been previously suspended from the Chicago Board of Trade for illegal actions in the egg market before he proposed to Lillian. At that time he had asked several business associates and friends for their social security numbers in order to surreptitiously continue his egg trading. He even asked one lady friend for the social security number of her ten-year-old son for that illegal purpose. Thus it is possible that Howard had similar motivations connected with Lillian's children, whether he acted upon them or not.

Whatever his motivations may have been, a "deal" had been struck between Lillian and Howard. The *de facto* and unspoken marital contract was for Lillian to supply a family for Howard, and for him to provide for their support. Those were the apparent expectations of Lillian and Howard when they repeated their marital vows. Lillian hoped that love and affection would evolve between Howard and her, but there is no indication that Howard shared that expectation. His marriage to Lillian certainly did not curtail his relationships with other women. Indeed, the first Christmas after their marriage Howard sent a gift of jewelry to a lady friend in northern Iowa which was considerably more expensive than the modest gift he gave to Lillian. By the time of that first Christmas in Guthrie Center, some ten months after the marriage, Lillian and her children had already had their dreams of material comforts and happiness shattered. Wendy recalls that "just a few months after our arrival we knew there would be trouble." The first major disappointment, one that the daughters of Lillian remember vividly, involved the annual high school prom. This May event is the social highlight of the year for local high school students.

Ann, like other girls her age, wanted a suitable gown for the occasion, her first formal dance. Lillian approached Howard with a request for money to buy Ann a formal for the prom. "No," he responded. "It shouldn't be necessary," apparently indicating that the dress, at least in his opinion, was non-essential and a frill. Ann was crushed when she heard the news and began crying. Lillian tried to console her and said she would find the means to buy the dress, and did so by using the monthly Social Security check that she was receiving in Ann's name at that time.

Howard took the purchase of the formal as defiance of his decision that "it shouldn't be necessary." When he learned that Lillian had purchased the formal from a Social Security check, a means of support of which he had not been previously aware, he demanded that henceforth she turn the checks over to him. She followed his wishes. Howard began to deposit the monthly Social Security checks, intended for the support of Ann, into his personal bank account. Lillian, not wanting to confront her new husband at the outset of their marriage, allowed the deposits to continue for a time. Eventually, however, she became so desperate for money that she requested that the Social Security Administration in Kansas City mail the checks to the local sheriff's office, where she picked them up personally and converted them to cash before Howard could gain control of them.

While Lillian and her children could only wonder what the future might bring, Howard had already fulfilled his primary motivation in marrying Lillian when he adopted all four of her children on April 5, 1958, two months after the marriage. He was now the legal father of Hank, Ann, Wendy, and Vicki. Howard's contract of marriage, like most of his business transactions, had resulted in quickly achieving his objective, while the other party or parties to the agreement were left to wonder what their end of the bargain might bring. Prior to the adoption of Lillian's children, Howard did not have the legal rights of a father. Now that he did, Lillian, in a sense, had become superfluous.

The primary, and perhaps only, immediate satisfaction for Lillian in her marriage was living in the nice home that she had first seen in the fall of 1957. She saw a lot of the Randolph house because she was practically marooned there. Howard's pre-marital promise of a new car and driving lessons was one of his first promises to turn to dust. Hank and Peggy were living in Urbandale, a distance of fifty miles, and were inaccessible unless Hank drove to Guthrie Center or Howard drove her to their home, a rare occurrence. Howard was disinclined to supply transportation for Lillian for any purpose and was out of town a lot, sometimes for business reasons and sometimes for "personal affairs." The three girls rode a bus to school and did not return home until late in the afternoon. And thus Lillian spent a lot of time by herself. Her access to the outside world was largely by telephone. When Howard was home he actively discouraged her use of the phone. When he was away, which was often, she took advantage of his absence to renew the semblance of a social existence.

Lillian attempted to develop a friendship with a neighbor, Pauline Sheley. Pauline lived within walking distance of the Randolph house and Lillian had no other transportation. It was a convenient arrangement, but not one that Howard could accept. Howard had taken advantage of Pauline's husband, Fay, in a farming venture and there was hostility between them. Indeed, Fay had attempted to choke Howard in his office. An intervention by Sheriff Bennie Sheeder, called by Howard's secretary, Martha Dahlund, had saved Howard's neck—literally. At a later date an altercation developed between Howard and Fred Sheley, Fay's son. Howard told him, "When you least expect it someone will catch up with you." A few years later Fred was murdered in New Orleans and the Sheley family inquired as to whether it was possible that Howard Randolph might be responsible. The police replied, "No."

Lillian could not see why Howard's differences with Fay should interfere with her friendship with Pauline. When possible she would slip over to the Sheley house for a cup of coffee and a visit. When Howard learned that Lillian was continuing to see Pauline he went to the Sheley house, marched in without knocking, and in the presence of Pauline and her adolescent daughter, Pam, grabbed Lillian by the wrist, twisted her arm, and dragged her out of the house. Pauline and Pam were aghast. That was the end of Lillian's friendship with Pauline. She never returned to the Sheley home.

*****

Howard had business associates but no real friends. He brought his business colleagues to his house on occasion and had Lillian prepare meals for them. But she and Howard did not socialize as a couple. Lillian was becoming increasingly lonely in her isolated circumstances beyond the city limits, only minutes from town by auto. Lillian soon learned that she had to depend upon others for transportation, or walk.

Lillian was raised in the Lutheran faith. She joined the local Lutheran Church after her arrival in Guthrie Center and soon became active in church activities. She was thoroughly embarrassed that she seldom had money for the collection plate and tried to be supportive of the church in other ways. She joined the "Ladies Aid" organization of the church, as well as its "Homemakers' Club." She taught Sunday School and sang in the choir. Locals came to see her life as one of church and children, and not much else.

Lillian needed transportation for her various church activities. Infrequently Howard would give her and the children a ride, sometimes friends would provide transportation, but most of the time she and the children went by foot. The walk from the Randolph residence to the Lutheran Church was a mile and one-half, most of it on gravel roads. The trip consisted of a distance on the dusty gravel road that ran from their home past the west edge of the municipal golf course to an intersection with State Highway 64. There they scampered across the highway, like a mother duck and her ducklings, to avoid the dangers of cars traveling at speeds of 60 miles per hour or more. On the other side of the highway they walked on another gravel road that ran between the Union Cemetery on the south and an older cemetery to the north. Along the way they had to pass between two high concrete walls on either side of the road, with hardly enough space for two cars to pass. When they reached Twelfth Street they could walk on a concrete sidewalk for the remaining four blocks to the church.

In the summer the walk to church was hot and dusty, hardly suitable conditions for a mother and daughters in their "Sunday School clothes." In the winter they often walked into the teeth of a frigid northwest wind. When it snowed drifts would form between the concrete walls separating the cemeteries, allowing only enough space for one lane of traffic.

Lillian was proud and embarrassed. She was too proud to call people for rides to church, although she would accept rides from those who passed by and offered them. Marvin Shackelford, whose brother would one day be the husband of Ann, used to intentionally drive along the route that Lillian took to church so he could give her a ride. The local highway patrolman of the time, John Novy, did much the same. People at church would usually give Lillian and her children a ride home.

After Ruby Krakau moved to Guthrie Center in 1959, a year after Lillian's arrival, she became a good friend of Lillian and often provided church transportation. On hot summer days, when Ruby was unavailable, Lillian would sometimes cut through the cemetery on the way home and stop at Don Bates' Midway Service station on Highway 64 to share a bottle of Coke with her daughters. Don, who ran the business with the help of three sons, would usually tell one of his boys to "run Lillian on home."

Howard made a point of not being involved in Lillian's church activities. The Lutheran congregation and other townspeople took getting Lillian and her children back and forth to church as something of a community project. Howard was known to be strange and capable of being cruel. But locals seldom confronted him on such matters. Personal idiosyncrasies of neighbors become accepted, even if they are not liked. People would say, "Oh, that's just Howard."

Thus, as is the local manner of reducing confrontations and working around the shortcomings of others, townspeople would simply help Lillian and her children get back and forth to church. They tried to alleviate the impact of Howard's meanness by providing church transportation themselves, and allowing "Howard to be Howard."

Thus Lillian, as she trudged back and forth to church, found out the hard way that Howard was not going to keep his promise to buy her a new car. The promised family trip to Hawaii, presumably to take place in the summer of 1958, was "postponed" until the following summer, at least that was Howard's word on the matter. But in February of that year (1959) Howard

21

decided that they should go to Florida instead. Howard's new plans were communicated to Lil soon after she had been tipped off by the wife of a business associate of Howard that he had sent an expensive Christmas gift to a lady friend in northern Iowa. Lil was upset to learn that Howard had another woman in his life and she was doubly unhappy to know that he had purchased expensive jewelry for his mistress when she was increasingly hard pressed to keep the household running on the scant resources Howard made available to her.

She had been promised a family trip to Hawaii and was not pleased that Florida was now being substituted, but that was a minor issue compared to the others. Lillian was in no mood to go anywhere with Howard and told him exactly that. He told her that she "*would* go," and proceeded "to twist and pound on her arms," as she later wrote, until she fell to the floor. She was frightened. She relented. The family went to Florida. Wendy remembers the trip as a "good time," but never knew about the beating of her mother that preceded the trip.

Lillian became a grandmother in the summer of 1958 when Hank and Peg's daughter, Beth, arrived. She was delighted to have a granddaughter, but was increasingly worried about her son's financial circumstances. Howard was only paying Hank $1.15 per hour—less than half the median income for a man at that time. It was a struggle for Hank and Peggy to get by. That added to Lillian's worries.

Howard seemed to have a need, a craving, to be loved by children. He wanted his stepdaughters, particularly the two youngest ones to show love and affection for him. He seemed to think that being their legal father would automatically result in the close and loving relationship he sought, no matter how he treated them. He repeatedly accused Lillian of being an impediment to the development of love for him by his stepdaughters. Howard felt that there was a "lack of love," as he put it, from his new family. On March 2, 1959, hardly a year after their marriage, Howard, Lillian, Wendy, and Vicki sat down for a family counseling session in an effort to create more love and understanding in the family. The results, showing the influence of the little girls, were recorded first in the handwriting of Howard and then Lillian on a sheet torn from a 1947 appointment calendar. Howard wrote, spelling Lillian's nickname as "Lill" rather than "Lil" and in response to the children's desires, "Howard and Lill will love each other all the time. A kiss when HR goes to work and one when he returns." And then it was Howard's turn for his input and underlining: "Mother will tell the children that Daddy <u>loves</u> her. That will make them happy again and love <u>him</u> all the more." The children then wrote: "Daddy and mother will not fuss anymore." And finally Lil wrote of her desires: "And Daddy will <u>call</u> <u>us</u> or have <u>Martha</u> (his secretary, Martha

22

Dahlund) <u>notify</u> <u>us</u> when he will not come home at nite (sic), instead of staying away without any word to us."

Lil was also concerned that Ann's relationship with her boyfriend, Harold Shackelford, was becoming too serious, too quickly. She was sensitive to her oldest daughter's unhappiness in her new setting and understood how Harold, who was becoming known by his preferred name of "Harry," supplied affection that Ann needed so badly. Ann hardly knew her father, Bob O'Hara, who died when she was only three. Her first stepfather, Roy Chalman, was never the loving father Ann would have preferred. And now there was Howard and the problems he presented. Thus she had turned to Harry for her emotional needs. Lil understood that. But when Ann expressed an interest in dropping out of high school, her mother's understanding was greatly diminished. The adjustment to a new school, something that Ann had not wanted to do in the first place, had been awkward. Her mother understood that, and was particularly sensitive because she had instigated the move. But the thought of her daughter dropping out of school, as with most parents, was an unhappy prospect. Lillian highly valued her education and experience as a teacher. Howard had promised to send Ann to college. And although his earlier promises were turning to naught, Lillian still hoped that her children would have an opportunity for a college education.

The existence of the Shackelford family had been marked by tragedy and difficulty in making ends meet. Marvin, the oldest son, was stricken by a crippling attack of polio at the age of ten. Two years later, Wayne Shackelford, the father of four, was killed when a smoke stack that he was helping to demolish in Guthrie Center fell and crushed him. Harry, then "Harold," was a small boy at those times. His mother, Mildred, was left to raise her four children—Marvin, Dennis, Harold, and Marie—on her own. She passed the hat at the local sale barn when auctions were held to help pay for Marvin's medical bills. Later she worked for many years as a janitor at the local high school.

While the people of Guthrie Center saw Mildred Shackelford as a courageous and gritty woman, Howard's view of the Shackelford family was that it did not measure up to his standard of social status. He was displeased that Ann was dating Harry and told her so. When she continued to see him, Howard told her that if she did not break off the relationship he would disinherit her. Ann responded by telling Howard that he could do as he liked, and continued her relationship with Harry.

Howard was widely regarded as a coward. When people "stood up" to him he had a pattern of either backing down or going to other measures to get his way. Indeed, he seemed to show respect for those who resisted his pressures. For those who did give in to him, he pressured them even more, and took advantage of them.

When Ann refused to quit seeing Harry, Howard switched his wrath to Lillian, who was in a more vulnerable position because of her family responsibilities. Howard was learning that if he bullied her, she usually backed down. Lillian had concerns over Ann becoming too involved with Harry, but chose to offer her counsel rather than threats. Howard, in contrast, was intent upon immediate and total control over his new family, as though it was part of his business operations. If he had any warm and loving intentions, they were hard to see under his often unfeeling and insensitive actions. He was seen increasingly by his new family as more of a dictator than a husband or father. Ironically, when Lil made one of her infrequent attempts in the early years of their marriage to stand her ground, Howard accused her of "trying to be the boss." Even Howard's own birth family knew him as a man who "had to have it his way or no way." Lillian and her children were learning exactly that, often in a very harsh way.

On the Saturday before Mother's Day in 1959, Lillian heard Wendy crying in the attached garage of the Randolph home. Wendy was three years older than Vicki and more defiant in her nature, but only ten-years-old at that time. She had taken to challenging Howard on occasion, including this unhappy Saturday morning. The worried Lillian ran into the garage and asked Wendy, "What happened?" Howard then struck Lillian in the side of the head and knocked her to the concrete floor of the garage, yelling at her, "Don't interfere with my discussion with Wendy!" Howard then demanded that Wendy and Vicki get into his car "to go for a ride." During the next two hours, while Howard was absent with Lil's two youngest daughters, she was sick with worry.

The next day was Mother's Day. The Reverend William Lubkeman, the pastor of the Guthrie Center Lutheran Church at that time, made a courtesy call at the Randolph home. Howard unashamedly told the pastor that he had "belted" Lillian the day before for interfering with his punishment of Wendy, as though that was appropriate behavior for the circumstances. Reverend Lubkeman was speechless.

*****

Lillian's father, Gustaf Hedman, was celebrating his eighty-fifth birthday in May of 1959, an event that Lillian and the rest of the Hedman family planned to combine into a family reunion. When it came time to make the trip to Gustaf's home in West Duluth, however, Howard informed Lillian that she and Ann would not be going to the celebration. Instead, he took only Wendy and Vicki. The Hedman family was unhappy that Lillian did not attend her father's birthday at an age when it was uncertain as to how many more there would be. There was the appearance that Howard cared more about her father than did Lillian. Howard looked for ways to have "his little princesses' to himself. Gustaf's birthday presented such an opportunity.

Lillian was in a dilemma. If she revealed that Howard forbade her from going to the reunion, her family would know that the marriage was not going well, a marriage that Lil still hoped could be repaired. If she did not tell her family the reason for her absence, it looked as though she had intentionally missed the family gathering. Lorraine knew that her sister was "disappointed" in the marriage, and Helen, her oldest sister, knew that she was "unhappy," but neither knew that she had already suffered physical and other forms of abuse from Howard. Indeed, Lil's family and children never knew the full level of torment she suffered in her relationship with Howard. For a variety of reasons she kept many of her problems in the marriage to herself, including a continuing effort to make the marriage work, not wanting to worry her children and to provide them with as normal a childhood as possible, and not wanting her father and siblings to know that she was in another marriage involving physical abuse and other forms of torment. Her children and her birth family knew that she had money problems and was unhappy, but they never knew the full depth of her difficulties. Apparently she felt that there was little others could do to help her in that respect, and there was no reason to worry them over something that they could not help.

On one occasion when Howard was supposedly out of town, Ann and Lillian switched beds. Howard later arrived unannounced at a late hour and crawled into bed with the sleeping Ann. When she discovered what had happened she leaped from the bed and ran from the room. Howard said afterwards that it had been a mistake, and that he had thought it was Lil in the bed. Ann accepted his explanation, but still she wondered.

Ann, at age seventeen, was old enough to understand appropriate and acceptable behavior. Vicki, who had just turned seven years old when the family moved to Guthrie Center, did not understand. Thus she took Howard's habit of stroking her leg as a sign of affection and individual importance. Wendy, only two years older, did not place any great significance in such behavior either, but did note that her mother was uncomfortable and watched Howard closely. He seemed to be taunting Lillian. Later Howard insisted on kissing Vicki on the lips and sometimes thrust his tongue into her mouth. Wendy witnessed those acts as well and discussed such with Vicki, but neither understood how inappropriate Howard's behavior was until some years later.

The first time that Lillian angrily moved out of Howard's bedroom, he insisted that Vicki take her place in his bed. That occurred on a number of occasions. Vicki remembers that when she tried to exit the bed that Howard would restrain her, but she does not recall that he ever made an overt attempt to molest her.

Vicki, no doubt because of her younger age and more compliant personality, was Howard's only apparent target for physical involvement among Lil's three daughters. He was apparently not willing to test the reactions of the mature Ann or the independent Wendy, if he had such in mind. In both his business and personal existence he preyed upon those that he perceived to be especially vulnerable. Vicki was that.

While the resources for running the household were meager for Lillian, Howard was having a new office constructed for his business operations. To celebrate the "grand opening" of his new office, Howard hosted a dinner for friends and business associates at the Midway Restaurant on the eastern edge of Guthrie Center. He did not include Lillian. She had prepared meals for many of the same people when Howard chose to entertain them at home, occasions in which she typically referred to Howard as "Mr. Randolph." In the beginning that appellation reflected a lack of intimacy and, perhaps, pride in being "Mrs. Randolph." Later she apparently used the term to convey a sense of distance from Howard.

From the Randolph home on a slight hill to the southeast of the Midway Restaurant, Lillian could see people gathering for the festivities organized and hosted by Howard. She was disappointed, hurt, angry, and confused. She had endured Howard's physical abuse to herself and had witnessed the same to Wendy. She had observed his inappropriate physical attention to Vicki. She had struggled to meet the expectations of Ann for the spring formal. The penury of Howard made maintaining a household a major challenge. Participation in church activities and the enjoyment of her family, the two most important things in her life, were made awkward and difficult because of the lack of support from Howard. Lillian's expectations of a good family life in the new marriage had moved beyond disappointment and into despair.

When Howard returned from his party later that night he told Lil to be ready the next morning to go to Minnesota to clean his fishing cabin on Lake Winniebigoshish. Lil's considerable patience had now reached the breaking point. She had not been included in the grand opening dinner, but was now expected to clean Howard's cabin, no doubt while he was fishing.

At a moment when Howard was away from the phone, Lillian called her son, Hank, and asked him to come and get her and the girls the next day. She wanted him to take them to the bus depot in Des Moines so they could take a bus to escape to Duluth. There she would have the comforts and support of her family, and be far away from Howard. Lil and her daughters would be going to Minnesota all right, but not to clean Howard's, in her words, "dirty fishing shack." Instead, they would be enjoying the hospitality of her family.

Lillian was uncertain about continuing an existence with Howard that was driving her to desperation. Her uncertainty centered more on the lack of options than any personal preference. She had had enough of Howard Randolph, but her family responsibilities continued. She no longer had the house on 59th Street in West Duluth to return to. When she and Howard had been married he had paid off the mortgage, making them "joint owners" of the house. Since then the rental checks, at his insistence, had gone directly to him.

When Hank arrived at the Randolph house the next morning Howard was, fortunately for Lillian, in town at his new office. She left a note for him saying that she and the girls had gone to Duluth. At the bus depot in Des Moines, Lillian used the money from Ann's social security check for the bus fare and Hank gave her five dollars for food.

Lil and her children always received a warm welcome in Duluth where her father still lived in the family home and her sisters Amy and Helen were nearby, as was her brother Cliff. Lil was closest to Helen and had written to her about problems with Howard. Helen, in turn, had written to Howard and Ann, trying to smooth matters in the Randolph household. Lil, in an effort not to trouble her sister and to hold her marriage together, had never mentioned the depths of her difficulties with Howard. To Helen the problems of Lil were superficial matters of "finding happiness." Helen had written to Ann and asked that she give her mother "comfort" and to allow her to "get things off her chest." She went on to tell Ann, naively, that "your love and understanding is all the comfort and assurance she (Lillian) needs for future happiness." Earlier Helen had written to Howard: "Lillian's greatest desire in life is kindness and thoughtfulness."

Unfortunately, Lil's closest sister and the larger family did not know the depths of her agony. When Lil hinted to her family of leaving Howard and perhaps needing some assistance, she did not receive a ready response. They knew that she had allowed her second husband, Roy, to squander her assets before they finally divorced. She never told them of the physical abuse she had suffered in that relationship. Her father was eighty-five. Her brother, Buck, to whom she was also close, thought that "she was bailing out of another marriage and didn't want to contribute to that." Lillian concluded that she had no option but to return to Guthrie Center and try again to make the most of her existence there for her children and herself.

*****

27

On September 24, 1959, Ann Elizabeth Randolph and Harold Roland Shackelford became man and wife. Because Ann was still a minor at the age of seventeen, Howard and Lillian, as father and mother, had to give their written consent for the marriage. Harold, also seventeen, received the same required consent from his mother, Mildred. The wedding was held at the Randolph home, with the Reverend William H. Lubkeman of the Immanuel Lutheran Church in Guthrie Center conducting the ceremony.

Howard, faced with the fact that Harry was now his son-in-law, took the newly-weds to Chicago on a honeymoon. He also took Wendy and Vicki, but left Lillian behind. When they returned to Guthrie Center, Howard offered Harry a job as the manager of one of his farms, located a mile southwest of the Randolph home. The position included use of the house located on the farm. Harry would be paid a salary and a percentage of the profits from the farm. Harry accepted Howard's proposal. He and Ann moved into their new home and Harry, who had no farm experience, began to learn his new occupation. He would soon learn that working for Howard Randolph meant hard labor. Harry's oldest brother, Marvin, recalls that Howard "used" Harry and "worked his ass off." But Harry did not have any other immediate options, and a home for his wife and approaching family was better than unknown alternatives.

The young Shackelford couple faced a daunting future. They were no longer carefree high school students, as were most of their friends. Parenthood was approaching. Harry had to learn to be a farmer and Ann a homemaker. They knew of Howard's reputation for working his employees hard and paying them little. But Ann had the benefit of no longer living with Howard and having the freedom of her own home. Even more importantly she was with a man she knew she could depend upon for love and support.

Howard was miffed that Lil had gone to Duluth in the summer of 1959 without his permission and blamed her for the circumstances that led to Ann's marriage and departure from his house. He did, however, give Lil money just before Christmas for a coat, but it was not nearly enough for the expensive fur coat he had promised. By that time the earlier promise of a luxurious fur coat was of little importance, since she had to use the money, not for a coat, but "to buy necessary items for my girls and me," as she later wrote.

Howard's business practice had been, like the words of Bobby Kennedy, "Don't get mad; get even." When he did not receive the attention he wanted from Vicki and Wendy he cut off their allowances. That made Lillian even angrier. She left a hand-written, underlined message for Howard—she had apparently given up trying to talk directly with him—which demanded bluntly, "What manner of man <u>are</u> you? Referring to Wendy and Vicki, she continued, "You want <u>their</u> love, you want me to <u>urge</u> them to love you. But what do <u>you</u> do to deserve and foster their love and respect for you?"

Lillian had become increasingly exasperated over the lack of money to run the household. Howard's approach to grocery shopping was to bring home those items he thought were necessary, or in Lillian's words, "I have to fix only what you choose to bring home." She continued in her message: "Have you ever tried to wash dishes without soap? Or get kettles clean without scouring pads? Or make salad without salad dressing? Not to mention being out of potatoes, vegetables, etc."

What seemed to trigger the neatly folded, two-page message that was addressed simply "Howard" and left on his desk was his failure to return home the previous Saturday night. Howard had told Lillian that he had "paid a visit" to a woman, but that it was of such a "very strictly personal nature," that he could not tell her any of the details. Lillian, as would be expected of a wife, wrote in her message: "Anything <u>that</u> personal between you two should have ended the day you and I married." Referring to Howard's proposal of marriage, she reminded him that he had made "so many false promises and pretty speeches of a happy life to-gether (sic)." Lillian concluded her message to Howard with unusually harsh words for a woman who was known as a gracious and soft-spoken lady, writing, "I am filled with nothing but contempt for you. I never care to have you touch me again."

Lillian's complaints to Howard about his relationships with other women did not alter his behavior in that respect. But in response to her complaint about not having enough food, Howard took an inventory of the food in the house. He even kept a written inventory of his own, listing items in three neat rows, starting with "potatoes" at the top of the first and ending with "Cream of Wheat" at the bottom of the third. He then added "and many small items."

When the summer of 1960 approached, and looking for ways to avoid again asking to borrow money from her family in Minnesota, Lil hit upon the idea of raising strawberries in the substantial garden plot south of the house and selling them. She told Howard nothing of her marketing plans. He had always been keen on gardening and was supportive of Lil's efforts to become a strawberry farmer, remaining ignorant of her real intentions.

With the assistance of Wendy and Vicki, Lil's strawberry patch produced sixty quarts of produce. She quickly reaped a profit of twelve dollars by selling the strawberries for twenty-five cents a quart. She had in mind that she would buy each of her co-workers a badly needed pair of shoes. She did purchase shoes for Wendy at John Miller's shoe store in Guthrie Center, but had not yet found a pair for Vicki when Howard learned

29

of the strawberry sales. He was furious, apparently embarrassed that people would think that he, the richest man in town, could not or would not support his family. He also questioned the need for new shoes for the girls. Finally, he decided that Vicki would not get new shoes and that the remainder of the twelve dollars would "go into the bank." The nine-year-old Vicki began to cry. When Lillian tried to console her daughter Howard struck Lil on the side of the head, knocking her down. She later wrote: "He grabbed my wrist and pulled me to the davenport and while still holding me by the wrist, he ordered Vicki to come sit on his lap and said to her, "Kiss me! Hug me!"

After the strawberry fiasco in the early summer of 1960 Lillian again retreated to Minnesota for refuge with her family and to care for her elderly father. Howard was willing to purchase a one-way airplane ticket for Lillian from Des Moines to Duluth, and promised to come to Minnesota and drive her home. Indeed, he was quite willing to pay for her transportation whenever she traveled from Guthrie Center and left Wendy and Vicki in his care.

From the relative comfort of Duluth, Lil had apparently been able to put the strawberry patch fiasco behind her. In a letter to Howard postmarked June 24, 1960, and sent from Duluth, she addressed him as "Honey," underlined words for emphasis, and told him how she "flew over a rainbow" before landing in Minneapolis. She asked him to "write me a nice letter" and said that she was "looking forward to spending the week-end at Winnie (at Howard's cabin at Lake Winniebigoshish) with you, dear." She signed off by writing, "I love you and miss you," and "Lovingly, Lil." Lillian was once again trying to put the pieces together of a shaky marriage. She knew that Howard liked indications of love and affection for him, and was apparently attempting to comply with his needs.

Only three days later Lil was beginning to wonder if Howard was coming to Minnesota to spend time with her at "Winnie" and to take her home. In her earlier letter, lathered with indications of affection, she had asked: "What day do you plan to come to Duluth to get me?" By June 27 she was writing, this time by postcard: "If you get this card it means you are late in coming up with my little ones." Howard, enjoying the company of Wendy and Vicki, was in no apparent hurry to keep his promise of driving to Minnesota to bring Lillian home. Eventually she returned to Guthrie Center alone on a bus.

That was a familiar pattern in their marriage. Lil had few resources and many unknowns in her life. She tried to feed Howard the affection he demanded, but he seemed more interested in the love of Wendy and Vicki. Her exasperation would show when there was ill treatment of her children, particularly physical violence. She tried to conceal from everyone physical and other forms of abuse she had suffered. When Howard shot the children's six pet kittens Lil kept the truth from them, telling them only that "they must have wandered off."

When Lil revealed the full story to her daughters a few years later they were not surprised. They had witnessed Howard's violence towards animals. A year after their arrival in Guthrie Center the girls acquired pet dogs, "Tip" for Wendy and "Spot" for Vicki. When Tip and Spot got into the hen house of a neighbor, Jim Finnegan, and killed a number of chickens, Howard called the Sheriff, Bennie Sheeder, and had him destroy the dogs. Wendy later replaced Tip with a new dog, "Baby Doll," and Vicki did likewise with a dog she named, "Eva." When the dog tag tax came due Howard shot the two dogs. On another occasion, an unusually balmy Thanksgiving Day, a stray dog wandered onto the Randolph property. As Vicki recalls: "He told me to come with him. He put bread on a plate for the dog to eat, and when he did he shot the dog. He wanted me to watch that." On yet another occasion involving animals, Wendy and Vicki decided to "free" a couple of chickens from their portable wire coop. When Howard saw them open the coop door and allow the chickens to escape he was furious. He ran down the chickens and chopped off their heads with a hatchet. He then cut open the chickens, extracted their eggs, boiled them, and made the girls eat them.

In the late summer of 1960 Lillian's life insurance premium became due on a policy that she had had for thirty years. Howard refused to pay the ten-dollar premium. Lil then borrowed the ten dollars from her sister, Helen, and asked for her advice. Helen loaned Lil the money for her immediate need, but advised her to cash the policy because she needed money so badly. Lil did so; repaid Helen the ten dollars she had advanced, bought Wendy a winter coat, and hid the small remaining amount for future needs. Those needs would occur very soon.

Howard decided to "skip" Christmas in 1960 and told Lil that there would be no Christmas tree or gifts. Wendy and Vicki were crestfallen over the prospect of a Christmas without decorations or presents. The increasingly resourceful Lil attempted to solve the problem by replacing the normal Christmas tree with a large tumbleweed that she found behind the house. Wendy and Vicki recall fondly the colorfully decorated "tree." Lillian used the remainder of the cashed life insurance policy to buy Christmas gifts. Howard was unhappy with Lil's "extravagance," but she did manage to salvage a Christmas for her family.

The following summer Lil again went to Minnesota to spend time with her family. To Howard's delight Wendy and Vicki remained in Guthrie Center. He relished the times he had alone with the girls. They posed no threat to him, and although they were leery of him and concerned for their mother, they were young and dependent. Wendy recalls that although

Howard never bought them the horses that he had promised when they first moved into his house, he did later buy them saddles so they could ride his horses. She also remembers Howard helping her with multiplication table drills. She now better understands the pressures and unhappiness that her mother was suffering, but concedes that "there were good times too." Apparently Howard was at his best when Lillian was absent. Wendy recalls that those times "were not awful."

Lil wrote home almost daily from Minnesota. A June 2, 1961, postcard addressed to "Dear Girls and Daddy" said that she had plans to go shopping with her sisters and is signed "Love-Mother." The next day Lil sent another card, also addressed to "Dear Girls and Daddy," in which she described her shopping trip and the nice lunch to which Helen had treated her. She also expressed concern over not receiving any letters, saying, "You promised to write." (Wendy and Vicki were indeed writing to their mother and giving the letters to Howard to mail. They discovered later that he never sent them.) She also indicated her usual concern for how she would get home: "You have to let me know who is coming up for me and when." She closes with "I'm getting lonesome for you dear people," and signed the card, "Love, Mother."

On June 4 Lil again wrote to "Girls and Daddy." She apparently understood Howard's parental interests and attempted to appease him by calling him "Daddy." In this letter she showed concern over not hearing from "one of you people," and again asked, "Who is coming up for me and when." Lil signed that card, "Love, Mom." Later that evening she received a call from Howard in which he told her to take a bus home.

Lil wrote a card the next day to Howard saying that if she were to take a bus the next Sunday that she would not get to Des Moines until Monday morning and added plaintively, "The trip takes so long." No doubt Lil could remember that a year before she had flown over a rainbow on her way to Minnesota, an experience, as she wrote, "thrilled (me) down to my toes." Now she was facing the unhappy prospect of another long bus trip.

Lil wrote two more cards hinting that it would be nice if someone would come and get her. No one did. She finally took the bus, arriving in Des Moines early on a Monday morning. Her baggage had been stolen along the way. It was not a happy trip. Although she was puzzled as to why Wendy and Vicki had not written to her, she was glad to be back with her daughters. Together, they would once again attempt to maintain an existence with Howard Randolph.

Chapter III

No Escape

"His face was twisted into a horrible distortion, it was like his mouth was a grin but yet his eyes made him look as if he was a maniac ready to kill."

Lillian Randolph

Lillian fled to Minnesota when she could to escape her problems in Guthrie Center. While in Duluth and enjoying the company of her birth family, she reflected on her existence with Howard Randolph. Her thoughts, as expressed in letters to Howard and her children, followed two avenues. One was a desire to make the marriage work. Those messages included sentimental and semi-romantic comments. A sense of hope pervaded those communications. The other avenue indicated that Lillian was thinking of leaving Howard. That correspondence was filled with disdain and threats. But in either case she always returned to Guthrie Center and resumed her existence with Howard Randolph. It seemed that Lil had no escape.

When Lillian and Howard married he proposed that he pay off the remaining mortgage on her modest house on Fifty-Ninth Street in West Duluth. That would make them joint owners, as he explained his plan to her, in profiting from the house as a rental property. Lil liked the idea of retaining a personal connection with Duluth and no longer worrying about monthly mortgage payments. She was especially fond of the city where she had been born and spent most of her life. She loved to visit there and spend time with her birth family. She enjoyed going downtown for lunch and shopping with her sisters. She was fond of staying with family members at her father's log cabin on Caribou Lake, a structure he and his eldest son, Buck, had built during the 1930s. And she liked visiting the Duluth harbor where ships of many nations docked after crossing Lake Superior.

And thus Lil became a business partner of Howard. Being in business with Howard Randolph, as a long history of disputes and legal battles indicated, had a great potential for disappointment or worse. More often than not Howard ended up reaping more of the benefits than his partner. Lillian's house in Duluth was no exception.

33

The rental payments of Lillian and Howard's tenants, the Pedersons, were sent directly to Howard, who claimed the status of senior partner with controlling interest. Lil assumed that the rental money would be apportioned according to their respective investments. She had paid $1,000 down on the house with money borrowed from her father and had been making monthly payments. But with the prospect of being married to a man who had been generous to her and her children during their abbreviated courtship, was a wealthy businessman, and had promised her expensive purchases, the details of the ownership of the house and the disposition of the rental payments were initially of little concern to Lillian. After all, Howard had promised to send her children to college, take them all on luxurious vacations, and buy them "nice things." The rental payments on the house in West Duluth seemed small in comparison. When Howard's wedding promises went unfulfilled and the financial difficulties and other problems of life with Howard began to set in, it was too late to reverse the *de facto* control of her former house. That was a pattern all too familiar to those who had done business with Howard. Lillian, like many others, had learned the hard way.

In the spring of 1962 Howard convinced Lil that it would be wise to sell the house in Duluth. By then Lil was desperate for money and had not been receiving any revenue from the house in any case. She assumed that she would receive the $1,000 from the original down payment, plus her share of the appreciated value of the house. Howard handled the transaction. When he did not give Lillian a check for her interest in the house, she asked him for it. Howard told her that her share had already been spent when he paid Dr. Todd for removing Wendy and Vicki's tonsils at the Guthrie County Hospital. Lillian received nothing. That was bad enough, but even more troubling was her inability to repay her father. Later Howard sold the house on contract with monthly payments of $65. He continued to receive those payments for many years thereafter.

*****

Ann and Harry's family continued to grow. Their daughter, Dana, was two in the summer of 1962 and she had a baby sister, Julie. Howard, who was especially fond of little girls, shifted more of his attention to Dana and Julie. Wendy and Vicki were adolescents by then and had become increasingly defiant toward Howard and his erratic and abusive ways.

The difficulties that Ann and her mother had experienced in their relationship during the last months they lived together in the Randolph home subsided as Lil took an interest in being a grandmother and watched her oldest daughter and son-in-law raise their family. She shared her experiences and points of view on motherhood with her oldest daughter. Ann had a measure of freedom that Lillian did not enjoy. She no longer lived under the same roof as Howard, and she and Harry had a car for transportation. But she also had two small children, and another was soon to follow.

Ann and Lillian did share, however, one common factor: both were under the substantial control of Howard Randolph. In the case of Lillian the control was pervasive and a factor in her life twenty-four hours a day. Ann recognized that her house and her husband's job belonged to Howard. Ann and Harry were still only twenty, had two small children, and were dependent upon Howard for their housing and income. They had each other and their children, a factor that would prove to be their salvation, but they were vulnerable to the controlling nature of Howard.

Lillian and Ann began to pool their energies and resources, as best they could, in order to mutually improve their lives. Lillian helped with Ann and Harry's children, and Ann would, as circumstances permitted, help supply transportation for her mother and sisters. Howard, who knew of some of the previous differences between Ann and her mother, made an effort to play one off against the other. The collaborative efforts of Ann and Lil were a threat to Howard's interest in controlling both of them. In particular, Ann's willingness to provide transportation for her mother undermined Howard's efforts to keep Lil isolated and dependent upon him.

Howard soon ordered Ann to quit supplying transportation for her mother and sisters, with the threat of firing Harry if she did not comply. Ann was in a terrible dilemma. What would she and her family do if Howard fired Harry? Where would they live? How could they feed and care for their children? Harry had now been working for Howard for nearly three years. He knew of Howard's business practices and how quickly he fired people who defied his wishes. Ann tearfully told her mother that Howard would no longer allow her to provide transportation for her and Wendy and Vicki.

Lil understood the circumstances all too well. Ann, although now living under another roof, had not totally escaped the clutches of Howard. She, like her mother and many others, was more controlled by Howard than she wanted, but had no immediately plausible way to avoid it. Howard knew when he had people trapped in his web and enjoyed it. Lil had come to understand that. She did not blame Ann for the circumstances imposed by Howard. But Ann suffered at the thought of not being able to be more helpful to her mother and sisters. Lil, Wendy, and Vicki had done a lot of walking before. They would return to that familiar routine.

Lillian now turned to her professional background, elementary teaching, in an effort to earn some money. She approached Harley "Hap" Merritt, the

Superintendent of the Guthrie Center Schools, about working as a substitute teacher in the local elementary school and succeeded in finding occasional work. She received $30.00 per day, and netted $23.42 after state and federal taxes were deducted. She had the occasional checks sent to Ann, in order to keep them out of the hands of Howard. Lil would then pick up the envelopes, marked "Att. L.R." in the lower left-hand corner, from Ann. She then found a way to cash the checks through friends, thereby avoiding the Guthrie Center bank that she regarded as "owned by Howard". Later she opened an account at the Iowa-Des Moines National Bank in Des Moines and did her banking by mail, since she did not drive. She also rented a safety deposit box at the bank in nearby Panora.

The 1962 Christmas in the Randolph home was luxurious compared to previous ones. There was a Christmas tree and Howard gave Lil $100 for gift shopping. Most of the money went for desperately needed groceries, but she did manage to buy twelve small gifts for family members.

The better circumstances of the 1962 Christmas were reflected in the card that Lil sent to Howard on the occasion of their Fifth Anniversary, January 30, 1963. Her continuing hopes were revealed in a "Happy Anniversary to My Husband" card that included the inscription: "Let's have a whole lot more, And make each one more wonderful than those we've had before!" She signed the card, "Love, Lil."

A few weeks later Lil's forced optimism changed when Howard asked her to accompany him, an infrequent occurrence in their marriage, to a convention in Kansas City. Lil thought the circumstances so unusual that she might be in physical danger and that the trip to Kansas City might a setup. She expressed her concerns to Ann in writing and to Wendy verbally. But she went along. She did not know how to do otherwise.

Lillian felt isolated, lonely, abused, and under-supported. She had taken to hiding food in Wendy's closet to escape Howard's inventory. Howard forbade her to buy coffee, so she traded butter and eggs from Howard's business for coffee from neighbors. When Howard discovered Lil's stash of coffee in the pantry he poured gravel into it. To the sugar that he suspected Lil was using for her coffee he added white sand.

Wendy and Vicki had no transportation to town for school events and other activities. Lil's sister, Lorraine, and her family had moved to Boone, a city several times larger than Guthrie Center and located seventy miles to the northeast, where Jim had been hired by Howard to manage an egg and poultry station. Lil saw the conveniences the Bellucis had living in a city and approached Howard about moving to the Boone/Ames area. She felt that they needed a fresh start in a new setting.

Lil took Howard's response as affirmative, something that no one who knew him well would ever believe. Guthrie Center was the seat of

Howard's business empire. He lived for his business above all else. The likelihood of him leaving was nil.

But Lil clung to her hope of a move. She wanted to live in town where she would not have to depend upon others for transportation. In Boone she would be near her sister, Lorraine. Wendy and Vicki could walk to school events, and Iowa State University was nearby for the girls when they reached college age.

Lillian's exasperation and frustration with Howard had again reached the breaking point. The two of them had discussed their marital problems from time to time. In such discussions, as she wrote later, she felt overwhelmed and berated: "You do all the talking and all the criticizing. You never stop your tirades to ask me what I thought you might do to correct a very shaky marriage." Money problems and differences of opinion on family life were common topics. "Even most of your Sundays are taken up with business," she wrote. She then penned with emphasis that his priorities had resulted in her placing "the girls FIRST in my life and you SECOND." She continued, "They need the feeling of love and self-sacrifice from at least ONE PARENT!"

Howard had told Lillian that he wanted a "close knit" family. Seemingly that type of family for him consisted of a loyal and non-complaining wife who managed the household on whatever resources he chose to provide, a wife who did not complain about his relationships with other women, a wife who was happy with whatever scrap of time he had for a home life, and a wife who would encourage her daughters to show affection for him.

Lil spelled out a quite different view of how a family should operate. She wrote: "The mother is head of the house" and "the father is head of the business." And then her thoughts become very pointed: "You get paid for your share of the work. I want to be paid for mine. And that does not mean merely grocery money. I want a weekly allowance, and I want it EVERY WEEK, whether you are in the mood to give it to me or not." Lil then compared how lavishly Howard treated those in his business world where she said he tried to produce an image as a "big-spender." She added: "If only your business associates knew you as I do!"

While Lil was passing along written thoughts to Howard, he chose to write notes to himself. In his notes he referred to himself as "HR" and Lillian as "Lill," adding an extra "l" to her nickname. One such note, dated "5-6-63," describes how he had returned from a trip to Des Moines that evening. Ann Shackelford and Iris Webber, the wife of a long-time employee and friend of Howard, Wayne Webber, were at the Randolph home. Howard gave Lil a letter from her sister, Helen, which had arrived at his business, where all household and business mail was delivered. After

Lil read the letter she gave it to Ann to read. Apparently Howard expected that he would be the next in line to read the letter. But when Ann handed it back to her mother, Howard recorded with a hint of paranoia: "She then hid the letter so I could not read it."

Iris had come to the Randolph home to persuade Lil to accompany Howard, herself, and husband Wayne on a business trip to Cincinnati. Lil believed that Howard took her on out-of-town business meetings for purposes of appearance only, and not because he enjoyed her company. She was often left alone on such trips. She was also growing apprehensive of Howard's new interest in getting her away from Guthrie Center. This was the second time in recent months that Howard had expressed an interest in taking Lillian on business trips, first to Kansas City and now to Chicago and Cincinnati. In the past he seldom took her on business trips, but now he was eager and coaxing in his invitation. She had to wonder why.

Later that evening, Dick Loftus, a close business associate and friend of Howard's, called Lil and asked her if she would at least come as far as Chicago on Howard's trip to Cincinnati. Dick Loftus and Wayne Webber were regarded as flunkies of Howard who would do his bidding under any circumstances. Lil was wary. She told Loftus that she would not make the trip, and finally told him she was going to "hang up on him," as Howard wrote in his diary.

For Mothers' Day of 1963, but two days late, Howard purchased two gifts for Lil, a set of "Melmac" plastic dishes, which he recorded in his notes as "MarMot," and a $100 gift certificate at Younkers Department Store. While Lil was at church at an evening meeting Howard showed the plastic dishes and gift certificate to Wendy and Vicki. As he recorded it: "HR told them he had present(s) for Mom." He then asked them to sign the belated Mother's Day card beside his name. He was upset when they refused. "They said they didn't want any part of it," Howard wrote.

Wendy, a plucky fourteen-year-old who was obviously not afraid to voice her feelings to Howard, told him, according to his notes, "It (is) to (sic) late to make up this time." Howard then asked her "what they were going to do." Wendy responded, "Just wait and find out." Wendy then told Howard, "Mother won't accept the present nor the $100," apparently now fully aware of just how desperate her mother was.

Vicki, according to Howard's notes, "just set (sic) silent and would not talk." She did tell him, however, that "she didn't want to sign the gift card." Now in her twelfth year, Vicki was showing more independence in her behavior. She remembered that Howard had whipped her with a willow branch for not handling one of his horses correctly. She also recalled that when he discovered her wasting pea seeds she was planting in the garden he slapped her so hard that her nose bled. Howard passed that incident off when he wrote in his diary: "She didn't cry or show any signs of hurt but laughed about it." Lillian had another view and left a note on Howard's bed, which she was not sharing with him at the time. Howard recorded the incident: "Lill did not talk to HR but put a letter on bed listing her complaints."

Howard questioned the girls about their feelings. He apparently could not understand why they would not want to participate in giving a gift to their mother.

Wendy's response, according to Howard's notes, was that "they had been abused and was (sic) not going to take any more from me." Howard concluded his notes: "Wendy said she was not going to like me as it was to (sic) late to start now."

Wendy had her reasons for not liking Howard. Lillian used the word "attack" in describing in writing an altercation between Howard and Wendy. Wendy had fled the house with Howard in pursuit, and then huddled on the ground to protect herself. Howard "boxed her ears," and then dragged her by the hair to his car and drove her to his office. Wendy was trembling and began to pray. "We won't have any of that," Howard said. Martha Dahlund, Howard's secretary, then opened the door and his demeanor changed. When Howard returned Wendy to their home Lillian ran to hug her. Howard told her to "leave her alone," but in a rare act of direct defiance Lil told him to "shut up."

Wendy and Vicki were also angry after discovering Howard's theft of gift money. Their biological father, Roy Chalman, had attempted to send them money for birthdays and Christmas. Because all mail was sent to Howard's office, he opened the cards, kept the money, and said nothing to Wendy and Vicki. When Roy failed to receive "thank you" notes, he began to wonder if his gifts were reaching the girls. Thus he placed a note in a finger of a pair of gloves he sent to Wendy. Howard gave the gloves to Wendy as though they were from him. When she tried them on she discovered Roy's note. In the note he asked if the money he had sent had been received.

Howard gave Lil the dishes and gift certificate, accompanied by a Mother's Day card that did not include Wendy and Vicki's signatures. He told Lil of the confrontation with the girls and again berated her for not convincing the girls to care for him. Lillian shared the discussion and her unhappiness with her sister, Helen, writing, "Howard tells me constantly that I won't let the girls love him." Helen then wrote to Wendy, telling her in the early part of the letter about details of her personal life, the weather, and asking about Wendy and Vicki's pet bird, Opie, so named for Ron Howard's role in the "Andy Griffith" television show. And then Helen went to the heart of her message: "I pray every nite (sic) that you will get hate out of your heart and try to be nice to a certain person," obviously referring to Howard. "I know if you would change your ways and be nice to him when he talks to you things will be much more pleasant around the house." Helen continues, "You can't hold hate in your heart for anyone." And then in a clear reference to Lil she added, "It makes you unhappy and other people who love you are unhappy too."

After Wendy and Vicki were out of school in the spring of 1963 Lil took them to her family refuge in Duluth. She needed some quiet moments to contemplate her uncertain future. She had understood Howard to promise that they would move to Boone or Ames, but she was painfully aware of how often he broke his commitments. She also understood that she was counting on a change of scenery to alter Howard's behavior, an even less likely occurrence than the desired move. She was playing lottery-like odds, but had no easy alternatives.

Once again Lil considered not returning to Guthrie Center. Wendy and Vicki were not happy with their school and home lives in that setting, where other adolescents often ridiculed them about Howard Randolph being their father. They would be happy to stay in Duluth. Indeed, some of the happiest moments in their young lives had occurred when Lillian and her children moved into their new home in West Duluth after the ill-fated business venture in Bennett, Wisconsin, and her divorce from Roy Chalman.

During her yearly trips to Duluth Lillian had felt the importance of her birth family and the comforts of being with her father and siblings. If she were to stay in Duluth, she would have to have some support until she could once again get a new life underway. Her father, Gustaf, was now eighty-nine. Because of his age and the fact that the earlier $1,000 he had loaned her to buy a house ended up in Howard's pocket, she did not feel comfortable asking for Gustaf's support again. She also felt uncomfortable asking help from her siblings who had loaned her money and treated her during her visits to Duluth. She had no savings. Indeed, she was struggling to feed and clothe Wendy and Vicki.

If she returned to Guthrie Center she knew she had housing. She received comfort from her association with the local Lutheran Church. She had several good friends at the Church and in Guthrie Center. Ann and Hank had grandchildren that she enjoyed. And yet she thought, perhaps dreamed, of remaining in Duluth—and far from Howard Randolph.

The temptations of staying in Duluth were so strong that Lil felt she could negotiate the conditions for a return to Guthrie Center and the resumption of her marriage. On June 20, 1963, Lil sent Howard a packet of letters, one each from her, Wendy, and Vicki. Lil's letter started with small talk about Wendy going to a dermatologist and other family news, and then went to the larger intent of the letter: "We (Lil, Wendy, Vicki) have been giving our situation at home in G.C. a great deal of thought and discussion and all of us dread going back to the conditions that existed prior to our leaving there." (One can only speculate as to why Lil would include her adolescent daughters as part of the message to Howard. Perhaps she realized that he had a special need for Wendy and Vicki that surpassed any feelings he had for her. In that respect perhaps mentioning them was a way of buttressing her case.) Referring once again to Wendy and Vicki, Lil continued: "We have decided we cannot be happy living with these same conditions any longer." Lil had concluded that "the only solution" was to find a "completely new way of life in new surroundings." She again expressed an interest in moving to Boone or Ames. "We," she wrote, "want to buy or rent a home there close to school, church, and shopping district." She then suggested that Howard's house could easily be rented to "new teachers moving to G.C."

The notion that Howard would ever leave the center of his business operations and his cherished house was a fantasy. The possibility that he would buckle under pressure from Lillian was even more absurd. She had to know that. Perhaps she had in mind separate residences, with Howard remaining in Guthrie Center and she, Wendy, and Vicki moving to Boone or Ames, seventy or eighty miles away. She was certainly intent on making that move, as later events would reveal.

Lillian continued her June 20 letter by writing about the transportation problems associated with living outside of town: "Wendy and Vicki have missed too many school functions by living in the country without transportation." Lil had precise thoughts about a new home, which she described as "a nice little home with a moderate sized yard," an obvious contrast to the large Randolph house with its massive yard and garden.

She called the suggested move "the only solution to our domestic problems." Apparently she thought Howard would be encouraged to make the move if he got to choose the house when she wrote: "Try to find something suitable for us." And then she added, "But of course we want to pass judgement (sic) on it, too."

Lillian began the conclusion of her letter with expressed hope: "I'm sure that by doing this we can pick up the pieces of our badly-damaged family life and try to put them to-gether (sic) again." However, the preceding sentence of hope is followed by an ultimatum: "If you care to do this and care to come up for us, let us know." She did not close the letter with her customary "Love" or "Lovingly." Instead she simply signed "Lil, Wendy, and Vicki."

To reinforce her ultimatum to Howard, Lil asked Wendy and Vicki to also write letters. Vicki, in the scrawl and prose of a twelve-year-old, addressed her letter to "Dear Dad." She asked, "Is Opie all right?" and expressed her worry about weighing ninety pounds. She wrote: "I am on a diet but I keep eating and eating so it isn't very easy." She concluded her letter with: "I think mom is right about going to another town." There is no closing, just her printed signature, "Vicki."

When Wendy wrote to Howard she did not heed the advice of her Aunt Helen to take a softer tone in her communications with him. Whereas Lil used the address, "Dear Howard," and Vicki, "Dear Dad," the fourteen-year-old Wendy used none at all. She omitted any small talk and got to her point: "You are always saying how much you love us. Well I don't think you do. If only you would do the simple things we ask. You have so much—can't you share it with us." Wendy continued her harsh tone: "You say we don't cooperate. Well have you ever tried to help any? No. Everything is business, how you can make more money. But what's the use trying to say that to you when you already know it." Wendy continued by telling Howard that she had "cried" over the thought of returning and would "rather die than live in that house." Wendy concluded her letter by repeating the wishes of her mother and sister: "If you have any love you would take us some place out of Guthrie to live. Where we could have friends, a family, and pretty clothes like the other girls have. You can do those things." She then added an ultimatum of her own: "And if you don't we'll leave and we don't want to do that." Wendy wrote no closing and did not bother to sign her name.

The packet of three letters, which Howard received from Lil, Wendy, and Vicki, had the immediate intended effect. He called Lil and told her that he did want the marriage to continue and said he would drive to Duluth as soon as he could get away. He also promised they would take a family vacation before returning to Guthrie Center. The possibility of moving to Boone or Ames was not mentioned. Lil clung to that hope but did not press the issue at that time.

Lillian, Wendy, and Vicki awaited Howard's later arrival while staying with Lil's sister, Helen, who had recently moved into a smaller home following the death of her husband. Lil enjoyed helping her sister get settled in her new house, writing in a letter to "Ann, Harry, and Girls" that she had been "fixing (Helen's) drapes, unpacking boxes, (and) painting some out-door furniture." There was a hint of envy in the letter—perhaps Helen was living in a small house like Lil dreamed of for herself in Ames or Boone—when she wrote of Helen's "real pretty little home."

During their extended stay in Duluth in the summer of 1963 Lil and the girls were enjoying the social and sightseeing advantages of being with Lil's father and siblings. Duluth and family were a sanctuary of love, enjoyable activities, and contentment far removed from the stressful and often bitter existence in Guthre Center. Lil savored every moment. During this visit she took her girls downtown by bus for shopping, mostly of the window variety. Lil's daughter-in-law, Peg, was in Duluth visiting her family also. Lil and the girls, as she wrote to Ann and Harry, "saw Peg a couple of times" during their shopping trip in downtown Duluth. Lil reported that "Amy (her sister) is coming out to-morrow" (sic) and that later in the week "Peg is taking us to the zoo."

Howard was constantly critical of Lil for "interfering" with his relationship with Wendy and Vicki. He seemingly had a craving for their love and affection, something that indeed Lil did encourage of her daughters. It was the best method, in her view, to maintain some semblance of peace in the family. But the two girls, Wendy in particular, were growing more resentful. They resented Howard's physical abuse of their mother and them. Lillian tried to hide her own physical mistreatment from the two girls, but they saw the marks and other indications. They knew.

Wendy and Vicki resented the totally unnecessary privation forced upon them by the niggardliness of their "father," the wealthiest man in town. They resented his continuing efforts to dominate their existence in erratic, incomprehensible, and often cruel ways. They saw elements of sadism in Howard. And although they did not know that term or its meaning at the time, they felt it. They knew what it meant from the harsh realities of their existence.

As part of the settlement that Lillian had negotiated with Howard for their return to Guthrie Center, the girls were supposed to show more affection for him, and to begin by writing him letters. Lil did indeed encourage Wendy and Vicki to write to Howard in her unceasing efforts to find peace in the family. They were not enthusiastic about writing to Howard, a man they saw as bringing more grief than happiness into their lives. Lil tried to cover for them by writing to Ann and Harry and asking them "to tell Howard 'hello' from us and that we will drop him a line to-morrow (sic)." Lil held hope that Vicki would write to Howard according to the negotiated agreement, but she knew it was unlikely that the older and more independent Wendy would do so.

When Howard arrived in Duluth a few weeks later in his latest Buick he made sufficient amends with Lil that they decided to spend some time alone. They left Wendy and Vicki with their Aunt Helen and checked into the Edgewater Motel in North Duluth. The letterhead of the Edgewater Motel proudly described its location as "overlooking beautiful Lake Superior." It seemed like a perfect place for a romantic reconciliation.

After their sojourn at the Edgewater, Howard and Lil picked up Wendy and Vicki at Helen's home and made a trip of several days along the shores of Lake Superior. Wendy recalls the excursion as a "fun trip." She even thought at the time that perhaps "Howard had changed." They all returned to Guthrie Center in his large and comfortable Buick Roadmaster.

43

The euphoria of the time spent with Howard in Minnesota was not to last. After their mid-July return to Guthrie Center the "family" life quickly returned to the unhappy, bitter patterns of the past. Three weeks after their return Lillian wrote a message to Howard: "Things are pretty much the same as they were before we went to Duluth." Apparently Howard and Lil had once again discussed their problems, but as Lillian saw it, she was only the listener. "You sat and pointed out my mistakes and what I should do to correct them," she wrote to him. "You did all the talking and all the criticizing and I did all the listening." She also wrote that she still felt "bitter" towards him and mentioned his "promise" to move to Ames in a threatening manner. "If you go back on your word on moving to Ames none of us will ever have faith in you or trust you again." Her message did not include her usual closing of "Love" or "Lovingly" and was not signed. She simply typed "Lil."

To make matters worse, if that was possible, Lillian had learned that Howard had another girl friend, "Peg." She told her son, Hank, about Peg and that she worked at a Holiday Inn near the airport. Lillian did not know the name, "Veronica," of Howard's girl friend in Algona, Iowa, but knew of her existence. She apparently did not know of "Marion" in California, or the several others in Des Moines, Chicago, and elsewhere.

The torment of the Randolph household had returned. On an envelope that Lil had retained from the Edgewater Motel in Duluth she was again keeping track of her pennies. Her notation of the time indicated she had "$32.79 cash left out of Xmas and clothes money."

The sleeping arrangements of the Randolph household reflected the divisions and tensions that had developed. Lillian had not shared a bed with Howard for some time before their reconciliation at the Edgewater Motel. When the new attempt at harmony did not endure, Lil returned to sharing Wendy's double bed with Vicki, while Wendy slept in a makeshift bed on the floor of her closet. The fact that the three of them were in the same bedroom and at the farthest possible point in the house from Howard's bedroom provided a measure of security and comfort to them. Wendy recalls feelings of "protecting" her mother and sister.

*****

The mid-summer reconciliation with Howard had not lasted. It would be Lillian's last effort to make the marriage endure. As with several previous times, she pondered ways of gaining more control over her existence and providing a more satisfactory home life for her children. Options for providing her own financial support seemed exhausted. She had cashed the insurance policies of herself and her children. Ann's Social

Security check, which had come in handy on a number of occasions, was no longer available. Her efforts to raise and sell strawberries had only drawn Howard's wrath and violence inflicted on Wendy. The small stipends she received from substitute teaching were infrequent and undependable. She was uncomfortable about asking her father or sisters for another loan.

Lillian decided to turn to her oldest brother, Leonard "Buck" Hedman. The two of them had always been close and Buck had prospered as a resort owner near Grand Rapids, Minnesota. She wrote to him and asked if he could help her break from Howard and return to Minnesota. Lillian also wrote to a friend, Mary Bennecasse, who lived in Zanesville, Ohio. Lillian had come to know Mary after marrying Howard. Mary's husband, Jimmy, was a business associate and friend of Howard. Mary had told Lil that if she ever needed help to get in touch with her.

The responses to Lil's pleas to Buck and Mary arrived by letter on the same day. Mary explained that because her husband was such a good friend of Howard's she did not want to get involved. Mary's careful choice of words and message between the lines, indicated that Mary was fearful of Howard. Mary's earlier "promise" of help had turned to a "sorry."

Buck's letter was no more promising than Mary's. Buck had known Howard for many years. He had seen the flashy side of Howard with the treats and gifts that accompanied it. He did not know the dark side of Howard that Lil had experienced. Buck saw his younger sister as "bailing out of another marriage" and did not want to contribute to that outcome. He saw Lil as more "foolish" than threatened. He did not know of the physical and mental abuse that his younger sister had suffered. Lorraine, Lil's youngest sister, knew that she was "disappointed" in the marriage, and all of her sisters knew that there had been "money problems." But none of them knew the full extent of the abuse that Lil had suffered.

Lillian, her head bowed in disappointment, handed the two letters to Wendy. Her nearly fifteen-year-old daughter read the letters. She could feel the chagrin of her mother. She knew that the latest failure of reconciliation had left her mother feeling increasingly disconsolate. The discouraging letters had added one more measure of finality to Lillian's desperation.

*****

A new school year was approaching. Wendy would be a sophomore and Vicki was entering junior high. The younger and more subservient Vicki had a better relationship with Howard than Wendy. Lil and Aunt Helen had urged Wendy to be more responsive to Howard's declared need for affection from the girls, but with decreasing success. Helen had written

45

to Wendy and told her that "Vicki gets everything (an obvious exaggeration for rhetorical purposes) because she plays up to him."

Wendy's hopes during the "fun trip" on Lake Superior that "Howard had changed" had been dashed. She was not as resilient in that respect as her mother, and not as naive as the twelve-year-old Vicki. Howard, not receiving what he wanted from the relationship with Wendy, did what was normal for him—he counter-attacked with a money issue. He refused to pay the $3.75 for Wendy's schoolbook rental. Lil found the money for the books, probably out of the Edgewater Motel envelope with the stashed "Xmas and coat money."

Wendy's birthday was a short time later, Saturday, September 20. For the occasion Lil had given Wendy permission to have her best friend, Trudy Garrett, stay overnight. Trudy had initially been impressed with the charm of Howard when she first befriended Wendy. But as time passed and Wendy confided in her more and more, Trudy developed a different view of Howard, both out of support for her friend and as a rational conclusion to what she observed.

Howard had decided that Wendy's birthday would be a suitable occasion for him to exact another measure of revenge for her unwillingness to show more affection for him. He presented her with a "gift," a large box elaborately wrapped with metallic paper and ribbons and bows. Wendy knew her mother did not have money for an elaborate birthday party and was doing the best she could to make her daughter happy. Both Lil and Wendy knew it was out of the question to ask Howard to provide for the birthday party, given the friction between him and Wendy and his previous refusals to pay for such festivities. And now here was the large, beautiful package before her.

Wendy noticed that the package was very light when she lifted it. But nice things, like clothes, do not weigh much, she thought. When she opened the box it was empty. Howard laughed and told her it was "a good joke."

The crestfallen Wendy did not see the humor in Howard's antics, nor did the others present. An argument ensued, and Trudy entered into the fray. Howard, already incensed by the "sass" of Lillian and Wendy, had even harsher views of Trudy's involvement in his notion of family business. He ordered her to leave the house, presenting a difficult situation since it was night time, Trudy was too young to drive, and lived more than a mile away on a gravel road.

Lillian called Mabel Garrett, the mother of Trudy and a good friend of hers, and explained that "someone should come and pick up Trudy." John Garrett went immediately to the Randolph house to get his daughter. Trudy returned home quiet and morose.

At the Randolph house Wendy went to bed with feelings of grave disappointment over the destruction of her birthday party. She was angry and humiliated that Trudy, who she saw as courageous in defending her, had been forced to leave the house. As her resentment of Howard Randolph reached new depths, her fears for her mother and family reached new heights.

After Trudy had departed with her father and Wendy and Vicki had gone to bed, Lillian and Howard continued their heated argument. Twice he threatened her in ways that made her fearful that he would physically attack her, telling her that he was "going to knock her down." She had had that experience before. This time he did not strike her, but she was deeply frightened. She wrote later: "His face was twisted into a horrible distortion, it was like his mouth was a grin but yet his eyes made him look as if he was a maniac ready to kill."

When Lillian went to bed that night in the room she shared with the girls, her last hope for another reconciliation had disappeared. Her concerns over the marriage had given way to fears for her life. This was not a new fear. She had previously written a letter to Ann with instructions "To be opened in the event of my death." It read:

> Dearest Ann,
> You know better than anyone else what kind
> of life the girls and I have lived in G.C. I can't bear
> to think what a future faces Wendy and Vicki in the
> event of my death and they are left alone with Howard.
> So I want you to consider this my last request:
> Get word to Roy. Explain how things have
> been and how unhappy the girls have been. Ask him
> to do everything in his power to get the girls back.
> He can make a better home for them than they have
> had here, because material things are not important
> when real love, understanding, and compassion are
> missing.
>
> /s/ Mother

Lillian had been terrified by Howard's rage. She used the rest of the weekend to determine her next move. On Monday, September 22, 1963, she sought counsel from Bob Taylor, a local attorney.

Bob Taylor had done battle with Howard Randolph in the courtroom before. He had beaten him in the "McLaughlin Case," one of the few legal defeats Howard had suffered. Howard hated Bob Taylor. Bob knew that and had reciprocal feelings.

47

Howard had an attorney in Guthrie Center, Frank Thompson, and several others in surrounding communities. Bob knew that Howard's local influence was high. He thought that Lillian's interests would be better served by a Des Moines lawyer he knew and respected, Paul Steward, the senior partner of the law firm of Steward, Crouch, and Hopkins. He recommended Steward to her. Lillian agreed, and Bob made an appointment for her to see Paul Steward.

The next day Lillian took the bus to Des Moines for a meeting with Paul Steward, whose office was conveniently located in the Des Moines Building on Sixth Avenue, only a block from the bus terminal. Lillian's relationship with Howard was about to enter a new phase.

Chapter IV

Premonitions

"In the event of my death. Wendy—Very Important.
Consult my checkbook."
Mother

Lillian described to her new attorney, Paul Steward, how she and her children had experienced various forms of physical and mental abuse at the hands of Howard Randolph, as well as meager and erratic financial support. Steward needed specifics. Lillian related a lengthy list: Howard was physically violent with Wendy, Vicki and her, actions which resulted in being knocked down, having ears boxed and noses bloodied; he was seeing other women and buying them expensive gifts; he had deposited Social Security checks in the name of her oldest daughter into his personal bank account; he had banished friends of hers and of her children from their home; he had taken all the proceeds from the sale of her house in Duluth; he had destroyed family pets; he refused to supply dependable transportation to church; he had refused to pay for school clothing and supplies for the girls; he had supplied such meager financial support that she and her daughters had raised and sold strawberries to buy shoes; and he had shown inappropriate physical attention to Vicki and had forced her to sleep with him.

Steward heard enough. He explained that Iowa law provided for divorce under circumstances of adultery, desertion, conviction of a felony, chronic alcoholism, or cruel and inhuman treatment. There were certainly indications of adultery on the part of Howard, but that would be hard to prove. However, there was abundant evidence to support a charge of cruel and inhuman treatment.

The thought of another divorce was distasteful to Lillian. She had been through one divorce and knew of the stigma and hardships of being a divorcee. To be a double divorcee was both unthinkable and unnecessary. Lillian had no intentions of remarrying. She and Howard did not truly live as husband and wife. They no longer shared a bed, there was no affection between them, and they did not socialize as a couple. Lil's daughters thought that Howard had become oblivious to their mother's existence— "like she was dead." Lillian no doubt shared that view. Thus her objectives were clear and simple: She wanted lodging and the financial means for a normal life for herself and her two minor daughters. The satisfactions of sharing romance, love, and affection with a husband had never materialized with Howard. Her objectives had been reduced to the basics of supporting her family.

Steward explained to Lillian another option called "separate maintenance," something of an anachronism which dates back to times when divorce was a socially unacceptable means of separating and, indeed, was specifically forbidden by a number of religions. The grounds for divorce and separate maintenance were identical under Iowa law. In effect, separate maintenance was alimony without divorce. A wife could thus force a husband to supply support that he was otherwise unwilling to provide. The major drawback to a decree of separate maintenance, Steward advised, was that neither party could re-marry. The two parties would remain husband and wife.

The illegality of remarriage did not concern Lillian. Her priority was clear: a home and the means for a normal existence for herself, Wendy, and Vicki. The separate maintenance solution seemed ideal. Howard would be required by legal order to provide money for food, clothing, school supplies, transportation, health care, and other normal items of a household budget that he had refused to supply in a normal and dependable way.

Steward explained additional details of a decree of separate maintenance as applied to the specific circumstances of Lillian, such as housing, child custody, child visitation, and financial support. The Randolph house was under title to Howard, but Lillian would have a claim to housing for herself and her minor children. Likewise, because Howard had officially adopted Lillian's children, he would have a claim to the legal custody of Wendy and Vicki. Thus her petition for separate maintenance included a request for sole custody of Wendy and Vicki.

Seward advised Lillian that she would certainly win legal custody of her minor children, but Howard would be entitled, as their legal father, to visitation with them. There would be no probable way to get around that outcome. There were times when Howard had been good to Wendy and Vicki, and they would be going on his visitations together. Wendy was now fifteen and growing increasingly protective of her mother and sister. She had already exhibited a willingness to express her defiance, if need be, to Howard. Lillian concluded that Howard's rights of visitation would not present an insurmountable problem.

Lillian's entitlement to financial support under a decree of separate maintenance would be based on the income and wealth of Howard. Given the enormity of his wealth, the requested figure could be sizeable. Steward suggested that she petition for $1,000 per month.

Lillian could only wonder at such a figure. It far surpassed the support she had received during the nearly six years of marriage to Howard. It was twice the sum Lillian could earn by teaching full-time as a substitute teacher, an opportunity that was highly unlikely in any case. It was nearly three times the average earnings of a woman in the United States at that time. Steward knew that a judge would probably reduce the petitioned amount in a final decree. Starting on the high side was a standard strategy among lawyers.

Lillian gave Steward her consent to file the petition for separate maintenance as they had discussed it. He would petition the court to allow Lillian and her two minor children to live in the Randolph residence, for her to have sole custody of Wendy and Vicki, and for Howard to be required to provide Lillian with $1,000 per month in financial support. The basis for the petition would be "cruel and inhuman" treatment.

Steward recommended that Lillian also file simultaneously for a restraining order requiring Howard to vacate the Randolph house. He held title to the house and could otherwise continue his normal property rights. A decree of separate maintenance, because a couple remains legally husband and wife, leaves property rights in limbo. A restraining order would presumably allow Lillian to run the household as she chose, and give her protection from any potential harassment from Howard. Lillian agreed that Steward should also file for the restraining order.

The combined legal force of the petition for separate maintenance and the restraining order would require Howard to pay $1,000 per month to Lillian, exchange his daily parental rights with Wendy and Vicki for occasional visitation, and to vacate the house to which he held title. The petition was filed at the Guthrie County courthouse on September 27, 1963. The accompanying restraining order was filed in the County Clerk of Court's office on the same day, and the necessary documentation was sent to the Sheriff's office for service. The petition for separate maintenance allowed for a response, but the restraining order would require Howard Randolph to vacate his house as soon as it was served.

The best part of being a sheriff for Lester Peterson was "working with people and settling problems." Serving legal papers was not that, and not something that Lester relished. But he had not had any difficulty when serving legal notices on Howard in the past, something he had done a number of times. Lester recalled that the receipt of legal papers by Howard "didn't seem to bother him much," and that "he would just turn them over to his attorneys." Lester recalled no memorable reaction by Howard when served with the restraining order that forced him from his house.

Lillian was frightened by the prospect of a personal confrontation with Howard over the restraining order. Wendy recognized her mother's dread and suggested that they hide behind bushes across the road from the house. From there, Lillian, Wendy, and Vicki watched apprehensively as Howard drove into the driveway. He entered the house and, not finding anyone inside, exited and circled the dwelling, apparently searching for them. When he found no one outside he re-entered the house, placed several arm loads of clothing and personal items in his automobile, and drove away.

After Howard's departure Lillian, Wendy, and Vicki entered the house and re-arranged their bedrooms. Vicki had been sharing Wendy's bed with her mother while Wendy slept nearby on a makeshift bed of comforters and blankets on the floor of a narrow, sliding-door closet. There had been a sense of security among the three in being together and at the opposite end of the house from Howard's master bedroom. Now that Howard was gone Wendy could move back into her double bed with the bookcase headboard, and Lillian and Vicki could return to the twin beds in Vicki's room where they had slept before moving to the greater security of Wendy's room. None of them ever again slept in Howard's master bedroom, the largest and most luxurious bedroom in the house.

*****

Howard's several attorneys advised him that his extensive property holdings were at stake because of the legal proceedings initiated by Lillian. A careful and reasoned response was in order. It was filed on October 17 by Frank Thompson, Howard's Guthrie Center attorney. In the document Howard denied being guilty of "cruel and inhuman" treatment and indicated he planned to resist his wife's petition for separate maintenance. He further responded that he had no desire to separate from Mrs. Randolph and wanted the marital relationship to continue.

The *status quo ante* was certainly preferable to Howard. If he could resume the marriage, his right of possession to his house would no longer be in question. He could resume a daily parental relationship with Wendy and Vicki. He would not face a required and expensive monthly payment to Lillian. He had no marital relationship with her in any case, and could continue to see his several lady friends. And, perhaps most importantly, he could protect his business empire while regaining control over a family he had thoroughly dominated for nearly six years.

Lillian never intended to retain possession of the Randolph house. She simply needed housing for her family and some distance from Howard until she could sort out her life. She still hoped to move to the Boone/Ames area and live in more modest accommodations, perhaps even a trailer house. Howard's promise to move the family to Boone or Ames disappeared, as did the reconciliation orchestrated at the Edgewater Motel, soon after they returned to Guthrie Center. Howard and Lillian only spent a few nights together in the master bedroom of the Randolph house before another eruption occurred and Lillian, Wendy, and Vicki resumed their defensive arrangement in Wendy's room.

Lillian understood that forcing Howard from his house would make him angry and potentially dangerous. Mabel Garrett and Ruby Krakau, two of her closest friends, felt that she was "playing with fire," and advised her to move out of the house. Local public opinion, seldom favorable to Howard Randolph, was more divided on this issue. In a rural area where property ownership has a special significance, there were those who believed that Lil had no right to occupy a house that Howard had built and owned before her arrival. Some believed that "she was trying to get his house away from him."

Lillian had at last made the big decision. She had decided there would be no further reconciliation with Howard. Now her efforts would be directed at running the family household in her own way, supporting Wendy and Vicki in their education and personal lives, and eventually making plans of her own to move to Boone or Ames. Occupation of Howard's house would be an interim measure until she could make the move. That interim arrangement endured longer than Howard's patience.

Howard's initial plans of building a house and becoming a family man had flip-flopped and gone awry. The impressive house he had built to entice a woman with children to marry him was now occupied by a wife and children all right, but he was excluded from it by a restraining order. The relationship with the children that he had legally adopted, his apparent major goal in the marriage, was now reduced to visitation rights. He was faced with paying for the support of a family over which he was losing his command, and his business empire faced a potential threat. Howard was losing control of his existence to a woman that he had successfully intimidated since their marriage in 1958. Howard had had years of experience in manipulating others with his financial, business, and legal powers. Being on the losing end was a new and bitter experience for him.

Restraining orders are difficult to enforce. They are designed to protect an individual or individuals from the potentially harmful incursions of someone else, a former husband being a very common "someone else." There is seldom a law enforcement officer present to enforce a restraining order. The *de facto* enforcement is left to the person or persons to be protected. If they feel threatened in ways that violate the order, they can call the police. The problem is, as one experienced lawyer put it, "one day there is a complaint and the next she is sleeping with the guy."

Lillian never again shared a bed with Howard after she filed for the restraining order, but she was conscious that she was living in his house and

53

knew she had to accommodate his visitation rights with Wendy and Vicki. That necessitated visits to the Randolph house. Lillian also agreed to Howard's request to maintain a garden in its usual location near the dwelling. That supplied yet another reason for him to come to the house. And thus Howard retained some involvement with Lillian's household.

Two months after the restraining order went into effect Howard was present as Lillian and her extended family watched television reports on the assassination of President Kennedy. They were glued to the television set, like the rest of the nation, and deeply disturbed—except for Howard. He obviously did not like President Kennedy and told the assembled group that he was "glad another Democrat was gone." Lillian was so miffed at Howard's untimely and insensitive comment that she re-registered as a Democrat to nullify his Republican ballot.

Lillian was granted a decree of separate maintenance by the District Court that went into effect on January 1, 1964. She received all that she had asked, except the requested monthly stipend of $1,000 was reduced to $800, still a princely sum compared to the scant support she had previously received. Howard had moved out of the house. Wendy was now fifteen and a freshman in high school. Vicki, a junior high student, was about to celebrate her thirteenth birthday. And thus Lillian was starting a new life. She had a comfortable home to share with her two youngest daughters, her other children and grandchildren were not far away, she could look forward to a substantial monthly income, and she would not have to endure the daily face-to-face conflict with Howard.

Lillian began to make plans for a move to Boone or Ames. Her life was seemingly on the upswing. And yet there was a dread, a foreboding in her manner that Wendy and Vicki remember vividly. Lillian was obviously fearful for her future and that of her children.

Lil had remained on speaking terms with Roy Chalman, her second husband and the father of Wendy and Vicki. She had seen him briefly in December, just before the final decree of separate maintenance went into effect, and told him that she had separated from Howard. They had then discussed the future of their two daughters.

Lillian related to Roy that Howard had told her shortly after their marriage that he had legally adopted all of her children. They had then assumed the name "Randolph." She had bitterly learned, however, that Howard was weak at keeping promises and that his word was not good. Roy had not signed away his parental rights as the father of Wendy and Vicki, adding to the confusion that Lillian felt about the legal status of her two youngest daughters.

In her new and uncertain circumstances Lillian was increasingly worried about the future of Wendy and Vicki. She had previously given Ann a sealed letter with the exterior notation: "To Be Opened in the Event of My Death," which expressed her concerns.

Lillian told Roy that she would write to him after she had an opportunity to check on the legal parental status of Wendy and Vicki. A year passed, however, before Roy received a letter from her in January of 1965. In the meantime, she had requested proof from the Iowa Department of Archives that Howard had in fact legally adopted her children. She explained in her message to Roy that it would be to their daughters' financial benefit to have Howard as their legal father.

Lillian feared that Howard might one day gain custody of Wendy and Vicki, as expressed in her earlier message to Ann, but wanted her two youngest daughters to benefit from Howard's fortune. Roy Chalman had remarried and was living in Sacramento, California. His new wife, Vivian, and he agreed that having Wendy and Vicki as Howard's legal children was, in his words, "a practical solution."

Lillian wrote to Roy again a few months later. Apparently she was concerned that Roy, in the event of her death, might do something that would interfere with the inheritance her children might receive from Howard. She informed Roy of the contents of her message to Ann and her intention that he be granted legal custody of Wendy and Vicki if she did not survive their minority. Lillian and Roy were in apparent agreement on that approach.

Lillian's communications with Ann and Roy, as well as her efforts to secure the future of Wendy and Vicki in the event of her death, are obvious indications of the uncertainty she felt over her future. Although she had been legally successful in her petitions against Howard, she had an obvious premonition of death. A message to Wendy, written a few months later, added further evidence of Lillian's fears.

Howard had been through several informal separations and reconciliations with Lillian during their marriage. In each instance he convinced her to return. Their vacation along the shores of Lake Superior in the summer of 1963, after she threatened not to return to Guthrie Center, was a case in point. Howard had reason to believe, based on previous experience, that he could once again woo Lillian into returning to him.

After being served with the restraining order, Howard moved back into the boxy gray stucco house on the corner of Third and Prairie that had served as his office and home prior to the construction of his new house. He found reasons and pretexts to make the five-minute drive from his dated and modest stucco dwelling to the modern home where Lillian now lived without him. Apparently he thought that he was in the midst of yet another episode of separation and reconciliation and that Lil would eventually return to him. When that did not develop, he turned to other methods of persuasion.

On previous occasions of separation from Lil, Howard had asked Ann to intercede to help effect a reconciliation. She was willing to make the effort, but could not succeed if her mother did not respond. This time Lillian seemed more adamant than in the past. Moreover, Ann was in a very delicate position. She and her husband depended upon Howard for their housing and income, and they had three small children. Howard complained to Ann, "in a disgusted manner," about the $800 he was paying each month to Lillian. Howard suggested to Ann, in an apparent effort to drive a wedge between her and her mother, that the money he was now providing each month to Lillian could be better spent on Ann's family. Ann told Howard that her mother was not interested in his house on a long-term basis, but that she did need housing for the moment. There was little that Ann could do to resolve the dispute. She was not anxious to become more involved.

Howard also made a trip to Des Moines to talk with Peg, Hank's wife whom he knew to be very close to Lillian, about convincing Lillian to return to him. He described the problems between him and Lillian as "silly." He then told Peg that if she would help get him and Lil back together, then he would have the money to take the entire family to New York to the World's Fair when it opened that summer (1964).

Peg and Hank were also in a delicate position. Hank worked for Howard and they had two small children. Peg and Hank had witnessed Howard's avarice and coercive methods on many occasions. In fact, they had become disgusted with his tactics. Peg told Howard that she thought he was only interested in money. He left abruptly and angrily.

Soon thereafter Howard fired Hank. He had no great interest in working for Howard, whose unethical business practices worried him. Indeed, he had been searching for employment elsewhere for some time. The abruptness of immediately losing his paycheck, however, with a wife and children to support, stunned Hank. That evening he and Peggy took their children and went to Lillian's home in Guthrie Center to give her the bad news. The family sat on blankets on the front lawn while Beth and Robert, Hank and Peg's children, ran and played. It was a beautiful summer evening; the kind that Iowa families enjoy after the heat of the day has subsided. However, there was no joy for the family that evening. They were shaken by the uncertainty that faced them.

Howard was also pressuring Jim Belluci, Lillian's brother-in-law who ran Howard's produce plant in Boone. While the two of them were returning from a Chicago business trip Howard told Jim, "You testify in my behalf or you don't work for me," referring to potential legal moves Howard might make against Lillian. Jim responded by telling Howard to "take a fat jump." A month later Howard was in Boone on business. Jim had invited him to come by the Belluci home for a noon-hour barbeque. That morning the Bellucis had learned that Lorraine and Lillian's father had passed away at his residence in West Duluth. Lorraine and Jim explained to Howard that they would have to "move the barbecue along" so they could depart for Duluth, a seven-hour auto trip from Boone.

While Lorraine was preparing the meat on the barbecue grill, Howard took Jim aside and told him that he was closing the Boone plant. Jim knew what that meant. His family of five, with three teenage children, would be without an income. He had, in effect, been fired. To the sorrow of the loss of a father was now added the worry over the loss of their livelihood.

The Bellucis drove that afternoon to Duluth while the Hedman family attempted to locate Lillian who, accompanied by her youngest two children, was on a camping trip with John and Mabel Garrett and their daughter, Trudy. The funeral for Gustaf was delayed until Lillian could be located and arrive in Duluth.

The funeral of her father provided Lillian with an opportunity to again assess her circumstances and discuss them with her family. She learned that her brother-in-law, Jim Belluci, had lost his job. That made two members of her family, Jim and Hank, who had been fired by Howard. Her son-in-law, Harry, who also worked for Howard, was also vulnerable. Lillian sensed that her problems with Howard and its impact on her extended family caused an uneasy element in the family atmosphere. That added to her worries.

Lillian wrote to her sister, Helen, about the possibility of moving back to Duluth, but despaired over "how she could possibly make a living." Moreover, she knew that Howard's visitation rights established by an Iowa court would make it difficult, if not impossible, to move Vicki and Wendy to Minnesota. With all the uncertainties ahead of her, Lillian saw no alternative to returning once again to Guthre Center

One of Lil's first acquisitions after Howard's separate maintenance checks began to arrive was an older, tan Ford Fairlane that she purchased at Logsdon's Ford dealership in Guthrie Center. Howard was not happy to see his money converted to transportation for Lil, something he had kept from her throughout their marriage. Lil, however, was determined to learn to drive and earn her license. Wendy, who was approaching her sixteenth birthday and the opportunity to gain her license, had already taken driver's education at school and had a learner's permit. Wendy and her mother practiced driving in the fields and on country roads. Wendy recalls that her mother was "wonderfully patient and didn't seem too scared." The time was approaching when Lillian, after seven years of living outside of town and needing transportation for church, school, and shopping, would at last have transportation of her own. It was a happy prospect. By the fall of 1964 both Lillian and Wendy were proud possessors of Iowa drivers licenses. Henceforth, they would be able to get back and forth to town without depending upon others.

Although Lillian was developing new satisfactions in her existence, Howard's visitations with Wendy and Vicki were not going smoothly. Wendy recalls: "We NEVER wanted to go with him, and he was supposed to have limits where he took us, and if we said we didn't want to go, we weren't to be forced. Mom held him to it and it made him crazy and desperate."

Howard's diary notes of the time support Wendy's recollections. One of his notations states: "Lillian said I could not see them Sunday." Another diary item of Howard's, dated "7-27-64," states: "HR (Howard always used his initials when referring to himself in his notes.) called at 7 p.m. (and) talked to Vicki first." After Vicki balked at going on his proposed trip to Boone and Ames and Des Moines, Lillian came on the line. His notes of that date conclude: "Lil (said) 'not going to say anything to them,' " an apparent reference to the girls not being forced to accompany Howard. Lillian then told Howard that "Vicki did not want to go" and "Wendy said she would not go unless forced to." Wendy then apparently came on the line. Howard noted: "Wendy said she didn't want to go," and then Howard overheard Wendy talking to her mother while still on the line and asking, as he noted, "Wendy asked Lill if she had to go."

A week later Howard tried again to arrange visitation with Wendy and Vicki. Howard's notes of that date indicate that Lillian answered the phone when he called. His diary reports the following conversation:

Howard: "Are the girls ready?"

Lillian: "Where are you taking them?"

Howard: "I was going to take them to church."

When Lillian indicated that she planned to take the girls to church, Howard asked her, "Are you turning me down?" Lil told him, "Yes," and according to Howard's notes, "hung up" on him.

Howard's diary indicates that he was persistent in his efforts to spend time with Wendy and Vicki. Howard called Lillian two days later, August 4, 1964, and told her that "he wanted to plan to have the children tomorrow." Lillian responded that she "wanted to know where we would go."

Howard told her, "Maybe Carroll or Denison."

Lillian, who knew that Howard had businesses in those two locations, responded, "That would be a business trip and the paper (an apparent reference to the governing legal document) said I (Howard) was to be free of business" (during visitation). Howard then responded that they could go to "the lake or some place." Lillian told Howard that "Wendy came home with (a) headache last time and the children didn't want to go." Howard's notes of that date conclude with Lillian's final comment: "Said she would not require them to go until she gets (an) order that she has to let them go and the children do not want to go on their own."

For legal and/or personal reasons Howard was keeping a diary of his difficulties with visitation and related matters. Eventually he wrote a synopsis of his view of the marriage and the connected problems. Using roman numerals to outline his thoughts, Howard first wrote of his interpretation of why Lillian married him: "I. Never any love but an arrangement to raise the family." In a confession of his physical abuse of Lillian, but minimizing its significance, he wrote: "II: Lillian never complained to them (presumably her children) about HR being abusive or hitting her." He was partially correct in that statement. Wendy and Vicki observed some, but not all, of the physical abuse their mother received at the hands of Howard. Like many other problems and forms of abuse in the marriage, Lillian spared her daughters much of what she had suffered. In "III." Howard listed "the many trips together" and specifies "Miami, Yellowstone, Niagara, Duluth, and Winnie (Lake Winnibigoshish in Minnesota)." Apparently this list of trips suggested to him good times together provided at his expense. Under "IV." Howard referred to instances when Lillian had left Wendy and Vicki under his care, perhaps insinuating that it should not be a problem under the terms of visitation if it was not a problem in the past. He noted: "Lil left children with HR while she, A- took care of her (sister), B- took care of Peg, C- went to Duluth, D- Let children go to Chicago with HR." Howard concluded his summary with "V.," and wrote: "Bought children clothes & presents, tried to gain their love by this."

While Howard was lamenting the lack of "love" from Wendy and Vicki he was chafing over being forced out of his house. He told Winston Everson, the operator of Everson Produce in Manson, Iowa, that he was "going to get the house back or else." To accomplish that end, as well as his other objectives of gaining custody of Wendy and Vicki and terminating the obligation of paying $800 per month for separate maintenance, Howard was looking for legal leverage against Lillian. Knowing of the power of adultery in divorce proceedings, Howard made an effort to fabricate such charges against Lillian by enlisting fraudulent affidavits from cronies and business associates.

Howard approached Jerry Sheridan, who managed Howard's Iowa Produce Company in Lenox, Iowa, and showed him a statement signed by Dick Loftus, a crony of Howard's from Tama, Iowa. In the statement Loftus claimed that he had had sexual relations with Lillian. Howard suggested that Sheridan should also sign the statement, but he refused.

Howard also spoke with Raymond Curtis, who managed Howard's produce business in Russell, Iowa. It was November of 1964 and Howard had been making payments to Lillian for eleven months, a total of $8,800 to that point. Howard told Curtis that Lillian was "bleeding him" with the monthly support payments. He also told Curtis that he wanted to get back into his house, and that he was "looking for a way to force a divorce." Howard referred to Lillian as "a damned whore" and showed Curtis statements of several men who claimed that they had had sexual relations with Lillian, but with the bottom portion, presumably showing signatures, folded under and out of sight. Howard claimed he had the signatures of Richard Loftus, John Snowgren, and LeRoy Cold, all business associates or employees of his. Howard also wanted to implicate another business associate, Iver Mendenhall, and asked Curtis to sign a statement saying that he knew that Mendenhall and Lillian had spent time together in a motel. Howard told Curtis: "She won't want to walk into court with all the evidence I have against her."

Curtis sensed that "Howard had a vicious hate for Lillian," and that Howard was suggesting that Curtis' job depended upon his signing the affidavit. Curtis refused to sign the document. He was fired shortly thereafter.

*****

Lillian took Wendy and Vicki to Duluth to spend the Christmas of 1964 with her family. Wendy did most of the driving of her mother's Ford Fairlane. Lillian preferred to visit her Minnesota relatives in the summer to avoid the snowy and cold Minnesota winters. But in 1964 there were urgent details to conclude on her father's estate.

Gustaf Hedman's estate was not large. He owned a small log cabin on Lake Caribou, not far from Duluth, that was willed to his youngest daughter, Lorraine. He also owned a modest house in West Duluth and had a small sum of money in the bank. When the net proceeds of Gustaf's estate were distributed among his children, Lillian discovered that she had inherited enough money to buy a new car. The old Ford Fairlane that she and Wendy had used to practice their driving skills was marginally functional. Its days seemed numbered. When Lillian returned to Guthrie Center she purchased a medium-blue 1965 Dodge "Coronet," paying cash, and registered it at the temporary courthouse in the upper level of the two-story city hall. Iowa's ninety-nine counties were numerically identified at that time by alphabetical order. Guthrie County was number "39" in that order. Lillian was issued license plate 39-2449.

Wendy, more confident in her driving skills than her mother, became the family's principal chauffeur. She was excited about driving the new Dodge and supplying transportation for her mother and sister. Lillian drove short distances to have coffee with Mabel Garrett or Ruby Krakau, to buy groceries at the United or Super Valu grocery stores, or to participate in activities at the Lutheran Church. She was timid about driving longer distances or at night.

The satisfaction of having the new Dodge and, finally, reliable transportation was accompanied by a continuing sense of fear and dread. Mabel Garrett, a 1936 graduate of the local high school who had known Howard nearly all her life, continued to advise her friend Lil to "get out of that house." Lillian was making plans to do so and to move to Ames or Boone when Wendy and Vicki finished the school year in the spring of 1965. In the meantime, Lillian thought she should add some measure of personal protection and sought the advice of her son, Hank.

Hank was now twenty-six, married, and the father of two children. Lillian did not attempt to shield her son from her difficulties as much as she did her daughters, especially Wendy and Vicki. Hank and his mother enjoyed an adult-to-adult relationship. He was the one that she depended upon for an adult male perspective. Lillian told Hank that she had purchased a pistol and kept it loaded in her nightstand.

Hank had worked for Howard for a number of years and knew of his ruthless business nature. Hank also knew of strange happenings at Lillian's home, such as knocks on the door when Lillian was alone and calls from strangers. Hank did not dissuade his mother from keeping the loaded revolver.

Lillian also told her sister, Lorraine, of the strange occurrences at the house and the loaded revolver. Lorraine was skeptical that Lillian would "know how to use it," an opinion contrary to that of Hank. Vicki, who shared a room with her mother, had discovered the revolver, but thinking that she had discovered something she was not to know about, never told anyone. Wendy, who sensed her mother's fear and felt within herself an "impending something," never knew that her mother possessed a handgun.

The strange phone calls to Lillian arrived with increasing frequency. A pattern had developed. The calls came when Lillian was alone, and the caller seemed to know that. The voice was always that of a man, a stranger. Often the calls began by asking for Howard. When Lillian replied that he was not there, the caller would then ask, "Are you alone?"

When the calls persisted Lillian told a number of people: Peggy (Hank's wife), Ann, Wendy, Vicki, Mabel Garrett, Ruth Flanery, and Ruby Krakau. Some thought that the calls were the work of Howard, who was using someone to frighten Lillian and make her so uncomfortable in the house that she would leave. Howard's anger over Lillian's continued presence in his house was no secret.

On an evening when Lillian was alone someone came to the front door and knocked. She knew it was a stranger because friends and family usually entered via the garage and kitchen door. Lillian chose not to answer the door and retreated into the security of the bedroom she shared with Vicki and where her loaded pistol was located. The knocking stopped and the stranger departed.

Wendy sensed the eerie atmosphere of their home. She felt protective of her mother and had repeatedly cautioned her to be very careful. Thus she was upset to return home on a Saturday evening and discover her mother asleep on the sofa in the living room. The front door was unlocked and the drapes were open. Lillian had fallen asleep while reading a murder mystery, one of her favorite forms of entertainment. Wendy scolded her mother for her lack of caution, and Lillian acknowledged that she had behaved unwisely.

Ruby Krakau, also advised Lil to be wary. Lillian told Ruby of strange happenings and fears for her life, and then pleaded, "Please don't tell, Ruby, please don't tell." Lil also related to Pauline Sheley, with whom she had re-established a friendship, of fears for her life, saying, "Howard is going to kill me."

In March of 1965 the water at the Randolph house, supplied by a well, suddenly developed a terrible odor and a brownish-green discoloration. During the seven-plus years that Lillian had lived in the house there had never been a problem with the water. Now she had what amounted to sewer water in her home.

Lillian called for a well specialist to examine the problem. He concluded that the well had been contaminated by steer manure drainage. He said it would cost $2,000 to resolve the problem. Lillian had no choice. She told him to do the necessary to provide the house with safe water. After the technician departed Lillian wondered to herself how the well could be contaminated by stockyard manure when the house and well were situated on a rise, and the closest livestock operation was at least one-half mile away. Was it possible, she wondered, that Howard had sabotaged the well?

A few days later while talking with Ann Shackelford, Howard mentioned that he had heard Lillian's well had "gone bad." Ann confirmed that information, and said her mother faced a $2,000 repair bill. Howard then told Ann to "pass along" the word to her mother that if she would vacate the house, he would pay for the well repairs.

*****

Howard expressed an interest in taking Wendy and Vicki to Chicago over a long weekend in early April of 1965. They had accompanied Howard to Chicago before and stayed in a luxurious penthouse of one of Howard's business associates. Howard and his friends, the Cuneos, had been generous and kind to the girls. It had been one of their better times with him. With all the difficulties over visitation it seemed like an opportunity for Lillian to appease Howard without upsetting Wendy and Vicki. But given the distance and time involved, Lillian thought it preferable to accompany the girls. Howard consented, and the four of them traveled to the Chicago area, arriving late on a Friday evening at the Hillside Manor Motel in the Chicago suburb of Hillside, fifteen miles straight west of the Loop. Lillian and the girls stayed in one room and Howard in another.

Howard went to the city on business the following morning. There was something about remaining at the motel that made Lillian uneasy, some intuitive feeling of danger that the girls perceived in their mother. Lillian took her daughters by foot into the business district of Hillside, where they spent the entire day aimlessly walking about. Wendy sensed her mother's apprehension and felt that she was purposely staying away from the motel, like a mother fox leading her offspring away from danger.

When they returned to the motel Lillian wrote a note to Wendy on the letterhead stationery of the Hillside Manor Motel. She addressed the note to "Wendy—Very Important." Lillian's message was brief and to the point: "Consult my check book. Balance and cash check immediately." She then wrote a blank check to Wendy on her Iowa-Des Moines National Bank account, signed it, placed it in a "Hillside Manor Motel" envelope, and sealed it. On the outside of the envelope Lillian wrote: "In the Event of My Death."

Lillian gave the envelope to Wendy and told her to "keep it in a safe place." Wendy was shaken by the words, "In the Event of My Death." At sixteen she had a long-term view of human longevity. But it was not the first time she had thought of her mother's mortality. A few weeks before, Lillian had purchased an artificial diamond ring, much like her wedding ring, and gave the real one to Wendy, telling her, "I want you to have this." Wendy had understood what her mother meant. Indeed, she and Vicki had understood for some time that their mother had a sense of doom. Many of her comments had a sense of finality. She occasionally drank too much, something they had not witnessed in the past. Wendy sensed a "feeling of dread" on the part of her mother.

Howard and his passengers left Sunday morning from Hillside to return to Guthrie Center. As they drove away from the Chicago metropolitan area, the girls, seated in the back of Howard's Buick, noticed that the car behind them also had Iowa "39" license plates, signifying that it was also from Guthrie County. They found that both interesting and odd. When they had cleared the suburbs of Chicago and could see the rural countryside along Highway 30, they noticed that the car with the "39" plates was still following them. Howard pulled off on the shoulder of the highway. The car behind them did likewise, stopping immediately behind them. It seemed strange to Vicki and Wendy to stop along the highway "in the middle of nowhere." Howard exited the car and went to the car behind. There he leaned into the open driver's window and began talking with the driver. Wendy recognized the driver of the other car as a young man, in his early twenties, whom she had seen in Guthrie Center. She did not know his name, but was sure that she had seen him before with Howard.

Howard returned to his Buick after a few minutes discussion with the young man, and then continued the journey to Guthrie Center. The other car was no longer following them. Wendy thought it peculiar that Howard would have a roadside meeting with someone from Guthrie Center, 300 miles from home. But nothing memorable had occurred, and the incident slipped from Wendy's mind. It only surfaced years later while recollecting the fateful events that were to follow.

As tax-filing time neared in mid-April of 1965 Howard approached Lillian about filing a joint return for 1964. Howard could save a large sum in taxes by the income-splitting provisions of a joint return. Because the separate maintenance decree left them legally man and wife, Walter Brown, Howard's tax attorney in Des Moines, advised him that a joint return would be fully legitimate and financially advantageous. There was no equivalent advantage to Lillian. Her independence from Howard was a high priority. She refused to sign. Howard was furious over her defiance.

A short time later, on Tuesday, April 27, Lillian soloed as a distance driver by making the 100-mile round trip to Des Moines in her new Dodge Coronet. It was a confidence-building experience for Lillian that she described with enthusiasm to her sister, Helen, a few days later in a letter. The trip to Des Moines had two purposes: She wanted to deliver a birthday gift to Hank and she needed to talk with her new attorney, A.B. Crouch, who had assumed her case from his law partner, Paul Steward, when Steward became ill and died. That was another shock to Lillian, who was fond of Steward and described him as a "dear friend" in a letter to her sister, Amy. Hank's birthday was the following Sunday, May 2. Lil would be busy on that day as co-chair for the Mother-Daughter Banquet at the Lutheran Church, and wanted to be certain that her son received his birthday gift on time.

Lillian discussed with Crouch her interest in vacating the Randolph house in Guthrie Center and moving to Boone or Ames. She had saved a little money from her support checks from Howard, but not enough to pay for a move and the purchase of a home. Lil told Crouch that she only wanted a modest home. They decided that $20,000 would be a sufficient amount for Lil to move to Boone or Ames and get settled into a new home. Thus, Crouch would demand that sum from Howard as, in effect, the price for regaining possession of his house.

The $20,000 sum to be demanded from Howard was not an insignificant amount. A comfortable home could be purchased at that price. Crouch told Lillian that he would talk with Clyde Putnam, Howard's attorney in Des Moines, and propose a possible settlement. Crouch would propose to Putnam that Howard could repossess his house in return for $20,000 to re-settle Lillian, Wendy, and Vicki in appropriate housing in Ames or Boone. The $800 per month support payments would continue. Crouch said he would bring up the issue with Putnam when they next met, sometime during the week commencing Sunday, May 2.

The same day that Lillian was in Des Moines conferring with A. B. Crouch, Howard was in the office of Fred Gardiner, the Guthrie County Clerk of Court. Howard was interested in the details of the decree that had granted Lillian separate maintenance. Howard studied the document carefully for nearly an hour, taking copious notes in the process. He was deadly serious in his demeanor. When he concluded his study of the document, Howard asked Fred a number of questions. It was clear Howard was reviewing the legal circumstances of his situation and contemplating his legal options.

The day after Lillian was reviewing her legal circumstances in Des Moines with A.B. Crouch and Howard was in Fred Gardiner's office studying his, the Guthrie Center *Times* published its usual movie advertisements for the area. Guthrie Center no longer had a movie theater, the Garden Theater having closed several years earlier. The closest movies available were at the Rose Theater in Audubon and Panora's Star Vu Drive-in. Playing the following weekend at the Star Vu was "The Killers" with Lee Marvin. At the Rose Theater, Jack Lemmon was starring in "How to Murder Your Wife."

Chapter V

Vanished

"Everyone was wondering, 'where is Lillian?' "

Joni Short

Lillian awoke early on Sunday, May 2. It was not quite 6:00 a.m. It was Mother's Day. She had a big day ahead of her. She was planning to take her grand-daughter, Dana Shackelford, to Sunday School; teach a Sunday School class; attend church with Wendy and Vicki; return home to see her two youngest daughters off on a trip to Des Moines with Howard Randolph to attend the Shipstad and Johnson Ice Follies; return to the Lutheran Church in the afternoon to set up tables and make other preparations for the annual Mother-Daughter Banquet; return home to dress for the banquet and await the return of Wendy and Vicki, who were to accompany her; attend the banquet; and then possibly drive to Boone, energy and time permitting, to participate in the grand opening of Jim and Lorraine Belluci's new pizza parlor and celebrate with her son his twenty-seventh birthday.

It was a daunting, but pleasant, prospect that so many of Lil's activities and pleasures would occur on the same day. She knew of the unhappy circumstances that had led to the new business of the Bellucis. Indeed, she was mindful that her own problems had spilled over into their lives.

Two years after Lillian and Howard were married he made an offer to Jim and Lorraine Belluci, then living in Minnesota, that they "could not refuse," as Lorraine recalls. Howard proposed that the Bellucis move to Guthrie Center where Jim would undergo a year of on-the-job training in the egg and poultry business. Howard would then employ Jim as the manager of one of his business operations. As it later turned out, the location would be Boone, Iowa.

Lorraine thought that part of Howard's motivation in hiring her husband was to bring her closer to Lillian, who was lonely in her new setting. Others, more cynically inclined towards Howard, believed his true motivation was to bring Lorraine, for whom he was forever fond, closer to himself. In any case, the Bellucis lived in Guthrie Center for more than a year before moving on to Boone to run Howard's business operation in that city. The two couples socialized together, and the Belluci family visited from time to time in the Randolph house. Howard showed a fondness for the three Belluci children, Jimmy, Kristine, and Lynn, buying them gifts and entertaining them in his home. But when Lillian filed for separate maintenance and had Howard removed from his home by court order, he took a different view of the Bellucis. When Jim refused to support Howard in his legal problems with Lorraine, he soon found himself unemployed. Jim viewed Howard Randolph as "a sissy (who) liked to see people suffer." He recalled, "I have seen a lot of cases where he got a lot of enjoyment out of it." The Bellucis, a family of five, learned how such treatment felt when they went without a steady income for over a year.

Lorraine remembers how she and Jim tried to keep the family going with periodic jobs "here and there" before finally deciding to go into the pizza business. Lillian was happy for them and excited that they would have their own business. She traveled to Boone on several occasions to help decorate and prepare "Belluci's Pizza" for its grand opening on May 2. She even placed a personal imprint on the restaurant by selecting a little black table to be placed near the entry for the placement of knickknacks, and gave the Bellucis an artificial fireplace to provide an element of warmth to the decor. If the Mother-Daughter Banquet ended in time, Lil hoped to drive with Wendy to Boone and join in the Bellucis' celebration.

Lillian, always busy with church affairs, had undertaken the co-responsibility for the Lutheran Church's annual Mother-Daughter Banquet, always held on Mother's Day. The other co-chair was Ruby Krakau, a close friend of Lillian who had moved to Guthrie Center six years before. Ruby knew of the problems in Lillian's private life. She had great respect for Lil's attention to motherhood and the church. It bothered Ruby that on this particular day her own family responsibilities would take her out of town. Ruby and Lil had worked together to arrange the Mother-Daughter Banquet, but it so happened that May 2 was also the birthday of Ruby's elderly father who lived in Jefferson, thirty miles north of Guthrie Center. Her father had not been in good health and Ruby wanted to spend time with him on his birthday. She asked Lillian if she could handle the banquet on her own that Sunday, explaining she needed to be with her father on his birthday. Lil smiled and told Ruby "not to worry." And thus Lillian assumed full responsibility for the evening of the banquet.

Since the festivities were on a Sunday, Lil would be mixing her usual Sunday School class responsibilities and church attendance into the demands of the day. Howard was taking Wendy and Vicki to the Shipstad and Johnson Ice Follies' matinee performance at the Veteran's Auditorium in Des Moines. Vicki was attending a Saturday night slumber party at Sherrie Bailey's home on a farm southeast of the Randolph house. Wendy was to take Lil's new Dodge and fetch Vicki so they could attend church services with their mother. Then they needed to return home right away from church so Howard could pick up the girls for the trip to Des Moines. He also planned to take them to lunch at the "Silhouette," a nice restaurant on Douglas Avenue on the way into Des Moines. Time would be tight if they were to arrive by the 2:00 p.m. beginning of the show.

At the end of the day, after the conclusion of the Mother-Daughter Banquet, Lillian hoped to go to Boone and attend the grand opening of "Belluci's Pizza," to meet her son there, and help celebrate his birthday. Lil was concerned about having enough remaining energy to make the trip to Boone. Earlier in the week she had driven to Des Moines to deliver Hank's birthday gift, just in case she did not get to Boone.

Despite her busy schedule on May 2, Lil still found time to write letters to her sisters, Helen and Amy. Her favorite place to write, especially on a sunny morning, was in the "sunroom," a room of many windows behind the attached garage and to the north of the kitchen. Lil redecorated the sunroom and added a day bed for summer naps after Howard's departure. It was now her favorite location in the house. The morning sun from the east supplied cheerful and plentiful light for writing. She began with a letter to Helen. Lil wrote of the beauty of her flowers as they blossomed in the unusually warm Iowa spring. She told Helen of her latest sewing projects, her church activities, and then described how heart-broken she was over the death of "a dear friend," Paul Steward, the attorney from Des Moines who had originally filed her separate maintenance petition. She mentioned driving to Des Moines by herself the previous week and wrote that she "enjoyed it." Howard, who was under a restraining order to keep clear of the house, was nonetheless, as Lil wrote, "putting in a garden by the barn." Apparently she had come to accept his gardening near the house.

Lil wrote also that she had requested A.B. Crouch, her new attorney, to ask Howard's attorney for $20,000 in cash to buy a home "near Des Moines or Boone." Lil, as she had told Ann, Lorraine, and others, had no interest in remaining in the Randolph house, but needed a place to which she and her minor children could move. Lil concluded her letter by telling Helen of the plans for the church banquet: "We are having a Mother-Daughter Banquet to-nite (sic) so we are setting up tables this afternoon. The girls have to go with Howard—But I hope they are back by six."

After concluding her letter to Helen, Lil wrote another to "Amy and Art," her sister and brother-in-law who also lived in Duluth. She told them of looking forward to teaching Sunday School at 9:15 and repeated the information she had earlier sent to Helen about her indoor plants and gardening projects. She mentioned that it was supposed to reach ninety degrees that day and that she was worried about the flooding of the

Mississippi River on the eastern border of Iowa that had caused so much devastation. She also told Amy and Art of her home-hunting plans, saying she was interested in purchasing a mobile home. She wrote: "I would like to have one providing I can make a deal with Howard." She continued, "Lorraine says there are nice trailer courts near Ames."

Apparently Lillian was not fully settled in her plans to move. She had added Des Moines to the list of possible locations, and was once again considering a mobile home. The $20,000 that she was planning to ask of Howard for relocation expenses was a plentiful amount for that purpose. She had written earlier that she planned to make the move when Wendy and Vicki were out of school for the summer. That date was rapidly approaching, and yet Lil's moving plans were still uncertain.

With her letters completed and the coffeepot on, Lil awakened Wendy and told her it was time to pick up Vicki at the slumber party so they would not be late for church. The sixteen-year-old Wendy, who enjoyed her role as the family chauffeur, dressed in her Sunday School clothes and went to the Bailey farm to get the red-eyed Vicki who, as is usually the case at teenage slumber parties, had been awake most of the night.

While Lillian was arising, thinking of a hot cup of coffee, and writing to her sisters, Howard Randolph was already up, dressed, and outside his house approaching two men in a white car parked on the west side of Third Street between the Cozy Cafe and the United Food Market. Roger Anderson, an eighteen-year-old employee of the A & G Farm Service, was on his way to work. Roger had graduated from the local high school the year before and then married Jean Wilson, his high school sweetheart. Roger and Jean established their home on Grand Street, two blocks to the north of where he now saw Howard Randolph in the street.

Roger was going south on the one-way street at about fifteen miles per hour. It was approximately 6:00 a.m. when Roger noticed Howard, the two men, and the white car. As would be typical at an early hour on a Sunday morning in Guthrie Center there was very little activity. There were no other cars, no other people, or any other distractions to Roger's vision or attention. The setting was motionless and quiet, except for the gentle chugging of Roger's GMC truck as he moved slowly southward. He was focused on the strange sight of the locally prominent Howard Randolph crossing the street before him in the early hours of that Sunday morning.

Roger took the same route to work every Sunday morning. He hated getting up and going to work on Sundays. He knew the route and the usual calm in downtown Guthrie Center at that time. It was unusual to see any activity, making more evident the sight of Howard Randolph walking across the street from his stucco house on the east toward a white car with two passengers on the opposite side.

Roger waved at Howard. Caught off guard, he hesitated but did not return the greeting. Howard continued towards the white car. Roger slowed his truck even more to avoid interfering with Howard's movement towards the white car. When Howard was approximately six feet from the car with the two male passengers, Roger saw the driver, a man with a swarthy complexion, exit and extend his hand toward Howard in a gesture of introduction. Roger had the impression from the formal manner of Howard and the stranger that they were meeting for the first time.

Roger saw the man to whom Howard was introducing himself as swarthy in complexion, dark-haired, forty years of age or more, approximately 5'8" tall, and wearing a suit or sport coat. Roger's attention was directed towards Howard and the stranger. He only saw the white car from the back. He recalled several days later: "I did not look too close at the car, but it was a quite long car. I thought it was one of the better Chevies, but I do not know."

Roger did not see the face of the second stranger who remained seated in the white car. He was looking in the same direction that Roger was facing and moving, and Roger was watching Howard and the other stranger, the driver, shaking hands. Roger proceeded to the A&G office at Second and Prairie, still puzzled by the sight of Howard Randolph greeting two strangers at such an early hour on a Sunday morning.

The next time Howard's whereabouts was noticed was a little after 7:00 a.m. He entered the Daree Den, a small café one block north of where Roger Anderson had seen him. Howard purchased a newspaper, the Des Moines *Register,* from Marie Davis and immediately departed.

Howard then went to Ann and Harry Shackelford's home where he was a frequent visitor. He enjoyed in particular spending time with their two oldest daughters, Dana and Julie, and occasionally took them to breakfast and other activities. Howard had been at the Shackelford home twice the day before. He had stopped by that Saturday morning and mentioned going to the Ice Follies. He said he had planned to go that evening and take Wendy and Vicki, but Vicki was going to a slumber party and Wendy had a headache. Ann suggested that maybe she could use the tickets, but Howard said that they were "in his name," and could only be used by him. Ann invited him to return that evening for dinner.

Before returning to the Shackelford house for dinner Saturday evening Howard called Lil's son, Hank, in Des Moines. The next day was both Hank's birthday and Mothers' Day. Howard made small talk about the pending trip to the Ice Follies, and then asked Hank if he or his wife, Peg, was planning to come to Guthrie Center the next day to see Lillian. Hank told Howard he had no such plans. Instead, he planned to go to Boone Sunday for the grand opening of the new pizza parlor of his aunt and uncle.

Lillian went by Ann's house early in the evening that Saturday to borrow the blue suit with a straight skirt that she planned to wear to church the next day. Howard arrived after Lil's departure, around 8:00 p.m. He had dinner with Ann and the children, and then left an hour or so later. Harry was working in the fields and did not arrive back at the house until after Howard had departed to close his office.

Earlier on that Saturday, around 8:00 a.m., Howard paid a visit to a work site of Gary Hopkins, one of his farm employees. In preparation for the spring planting, Gary was plowing a field directly across the road from the Randolph house. From his position atop his red Farmall tractor Gary had a clear view of the Randolph house. He had just completed one round in the field when Howard pulled up in his Buick on the gravel road adjacent to the field.

Gary was surprised to see Howard. He had never come by before when Gary was working a field. Howard approached Gary and told him that he wanted him to "stay out of here" and move to another field that was nearly a mile away. Gary was even more puzzled. It made no sense to move to another field when he had just started on the one at hand. Gary followed Howard's instructions, however, and moved to the other field, far from a view of the Randolph house. Several days later Howard told Gary to return to the original field he had been plowing when Howard interrupted his work the previous Saturday morning.

When Howard arrived at the Shackelford farm home on Sunday morning, May 2, the clock was approaching 8:30 a.m. Howard had not told Ann he would be coming by, but he dropped in so frequently that she was not surprised. He asked if the two oldest Shackelford children, Dana and Julie, would like to go fishing with him and a "Mr. Tipton" at a pond on the Randolph farm.

Ann had called her mother minutes before and asked Lil to take Julie to Sunday School. Lil was always delighted to involve her children and grandchildren in church activities. She had readily assented. A short time later, Ann called her mother again and told her there was a change in plans. Julie preferred to go fishing over going to Sunday School and was making demands on her mother accordingly. Ann had relented. Lillian was disappointed but voiced no objection.

Howard later stated that "Mr. Tipton," a business associate of his, did not show up at the pond. Discovering he had no bait, he then took the Shackelford girls to Panora, purchased some night crawlers, and began fishing on the Middle Raccoon River behind the Hide-A-Way Cafe. By then it was about 9:00 a.m.

In the meantime, Wendy had arisen, dressed, and picked up Vicki from the slumber party. Vicki spent a wonderful time at Sherrie Bailey's party.

She was thrilled to be invited along with Barbara Benton, Cindy McCarty, Debbie Merritt, Kristi Purdy, and Connie Schwab. Those were the "popular girls," in Vicki's words. She liked the social connection with them.

After fetching Vicki, Wendy drove back to her home to pick up her mother, who had dressed in Ann's two-piece blue suit. Wendy then drove the three of them to church, with Lillian seated in the front passenger seat with her white purse between her and Wendy. Vicki sat in back behind her mother. When they reached the church, Wendy parked the Dodge Coronet in the Guthrie County Hospital parking lot across the street to the east.

While Lillian, Wendy, and Vicki were at church and Howard was fishing with the Shackelford children, John Novy, the local highway patrolman, was on duty. Trooper Novy lived just east of the crest of Tank Hill on Twelfth Street Court. His home was a short distance, about 100 feet, to the south of Highway 64. He made a practice of keeping his black and tan patrol car, with "Iowa Highway Patrol" on the door, parked in plain sight from the highway. It slowed people down.

John Novy began his career, one that would last for thirty years, in Guthrie Center eight years before. By May of 1965 he was an experienced law enforcement officer, and one who was well-liked and respected in Guthrie Center. On the Sunday morning of May 2, between nine and ten o'clock, Trooper Novy was ascending Tank Hill on State Street in his patrol car, driving into the morning sun. A white Cadillac passed him going downhill in the opposite direction. The Cadillac caught his attention. He was sure it was from out of town. By local standards a Cadillac was a luxurious and rare automobile.

With the sun in his face and the white Cadillac passing quickly, Officer Novy was not able to get a good look at the license plate, but thought it might have been an Iowa "77," indicating Polk County where Des Moines is located. Novy did get a good look at the driver who was at his eye-level and momentarily out of the sun when Novy turned his head to the north to view him. Novy identified the driver of the Cadillac as a "Fernando Lamas" type with a dark complexion, black wavy hair, and sunglasses.

It is quite likely that the white Cadillac had just left Don Bates' Midway Service Station, one-quarter mile to the east of the crest of Tank Hill, when Officer Novy spotted it descending on the west side of the hill. It was the second time the white Cadillac had stopped at Bates' station, which was operated by Don and his sons, Bill and Don Jr. The day before, May 1, the white Cadillac with the mysterious, swarthy strangers had stopped around 10:00 a.m. for gas. Don always made sure his boys washed the windshields of customers. Don Jr. had done just that and got a good look at the two passengers in the process. Both had dark complexions and black wavy hair, combed straight back. The driver was wearing sunglasses.

Bill and Don Sr. also observed the car and its passengers, as did Bill Slater, a local man who was at the station at the time. From his office at the Midway Restaurant next door, Horace "Budge" Parrott, was leaning back in his office chair and looking towards the service station. He also noticed the white Cadillac and its swarthy passengers. Across the street from Budge's restaurant at Leonard Logsden's Ford dealership, Glen Kunkle, a salesman, had observed the white Cadillac going back and forth on several occasions that weekend. Lew Messner, a long-time resident of Guthrie Center, had sat on a bar stool at "Rosies," a local tavern on State Street, that Saturday and witnessed two men with dark complexions and black wavy hair enter the tavern and then leave again.

That same Saturday, twenty miles to the south of Guthrie Center, several people in the town of Stuart had seen the two swarthy men in the white Cadillac. Kenneth Van Landingham, the town marshal, saw the Caddy with the two men with dark wavy hair and briefly followed their car, but did not record the license number. It was between 4:00 and 5:00 p.m. "Knobbs" Couch, a non-practicing Stuart attorney who earned a living primarily by repairing electrical appliances, saw the two men at about the same time in his wife's bar, "Farmers' Tavern." Nita Couch had served the two swarthy men mixed drinks. Knobbs and Nita noted a white Cadillac outside and assumed that it belonged to the two men.

The two strangers made no apparent effort to conceal their presence. A Cadillac was an unusual and admired automobile in the area, and sure to draw attention. Swarthy, Latino-looking men were even more rare in the lily-white, northern European population of Guthrie County. By the time the weekend was over at least twenty witnesses in Guthrie Center and Stuart had observed and noted the presence of the two "Fernando Lamas" types. They disappeared just as quickly and mysteriously as they had arrived.

The descriptions of the two men supplied by witnesses to law enforcement officials were remarkably uniform in several respects. All but one witness identified their automobile as a Cadillac. All but two witnesses saw a white car. The other two, who had been looking into the sun, thought it was beige. All of the witnesses described the men as swarthy with dark hair. Several described their hair as "wavy" and several noted it was combed "straight back." Several noted that one of the men wore sunglasses, and a few noticed that when he removed the glasses he had a habit of dangling them from his lower lip.

The witnesses' description of the height, weight, age, and other facial features of the two men varied. Of those witnesses who saw the license plates of the car, four thought they were from Illinois, one thought they were "probably" Polk County (Iowa) plates, another said the plates were from "out of state, maybe Colorado," and another said it was not a Guthrie County car.

The times and places where witnesses observed the two men were consistent. There were no contradictions in placing them in two locations at the same time or in time patterns that could not be possible. There was simply no question that there were two swarthy, dark-haired strangers driving a white Cadillac with non-local license plates in the Guthrie Center - Stuart area over the weekend of May 1-2.

*****

Howard returned Dana and Julie from the fishing trip to Panora to their home between 10:30 and 11:00 a.m. He then went to his stucco house in town to change from his fishing clothes into dress slacks and a shirt for the afternoon trip to the Ice Follies in Des Moines. While Howard was returning Ann and Harry's daughters, Lillian, Wendy, and Vicki had concluded the Sunday School portion of their Lutheran Church activities and moved to the main church services conducted by Reverend Donald Lutz.

The local golf course to the north of the Randolph house, which shares a common boundary with the Randolph property, was busy that Sunday morning as golfers took advantage of the unusually sunshiny and warm day. The two strangers in the white Caddy were also present at the golf course. While Howard was changing clothes and Lillian and her daughters were attending church, the two strangers arrived at the golf course shortly before 11:00 a.m.

The clubhouse for the golf course was an old structure behind the Truman Nagle house to the east of the course. The white, clapboard Nagle house faced the north and Highway 64, set back a distance of fifty yards from the highway. Behind the house was a structure that had served as a utility building when the property was still a working farm, but was now a rudimentary clubhouse. Inside the building that Sunday morning were Nick Dowd and Mark Lykke, two local high school boys who worked occasionally at the clubhouse taking fees, selling snacks and beverages, and renting golf equipment.

To the south of the clubhouse is a gravel parking lot. It is the only parking lot available to players and is conveniently located near the first tee. Nick and Mark noticed a Cadillac with two male passengers slowly circling the parking lot shortly before 11:00 a.m. The Cadillac was interesting to the two teenagers, and they thought the slow movement of the vehicle strange. The parking area was not large, having space for perhaps two dozen cars. There were a number of cars in the lot. The driver of the Cadillac had to maneuver around the parked cars. Nick and Mark could not see the faces of the passengers from their vantage point inside the clubhouse, but they could easily tell that there were two of them. The Cadillac made two slow circles around the parking lot, and then exited to the north towards Highway 64 and out of the line of sight of Nick and Mark.

Among the golfers that morning were three twosomes. One duo consisted of two high school basketball coaches, Roger Underwood and Duane Stewart. Roger Wickland, a 1952 graduate of Guthrie Center High School, was playing in a twosome with Ron Wilson, a local sixth grade teacher and the reigning city golf champion. Another pair of golfers was Leland and Ron Purviance, a father and son from Panora.

While the golfers were enjoying a morning of sunshine and recreation, the slow-moving Cadillac left the clubhouse parking lot, went north to Highway 64, turned west on the highway, passed along the 400-yard northern perimeter of the golf course, and then turned south on the gravel road that passes the Randolph house approximately one-half mile further to the south. The two strangers parked their car on the side of the gravel road, about twenty yards west of the fourth tee. They then exited the car, walked eastward across the road, traversed a shallow ditch that was part of the rough, and climbed a slight hill to the fourth tee. There they seated themselves on a bench that provided a clear view of the Randolph house and its driveway, some 700 yards to the south.

Hole number four at the Guthrie Center golf course is a par four of 306 yards. As golfers walk from the tee towards the green, they walk downhill at first. The Randolph house is initially in view as the golfers descend the hill, but is hidden by the time a golfer reaches the bottom of the incline, about one-half way towards the green. The fairway then rises, and the Randolph house again comes into view as one walks in that direction. On the fourth green the view of the house is hindered by bushes and trees on the south edge of the course. The house is located another 400 yards beyond.

Leland and Ron Purviance were the first of the golfers to notice the two strangers seated on the bench near the fourth tee. They had never seen non-golfers seated on the bench and could only wonder who the two dusky-skinned strangers might be. A few words of small talk were exchanged with the unknown men staring to the south towards the Randolph house, and then Leland and Ron teed off and walked towards the fourth hole. It was approximately 11:00 a.m. When the Purviances left the golf course around noon they glanced at the bench near the fourth tee and noticed that the two strangers had departed.

Roger Wickland and Ron Wilson approached the fourth tee after the Purviances and saw the white Cadillac parked on the gravel road. Roger noticed the Caddy first and remarked to Ron, "You don't see many of those around here." They thought it odd that a car would be parked on the road, where they had never seen an auto parked before, when there was parking available at the clubhouse. It also occurred to them that there was a safety factor involved because the shoulder of the road was not wide enough to fully accommodate the large car that was positioned partially on the road surface. The Cadillac was not far from the intersection with Highway 64, perhaps 100 feet or so to the south. A car turning off the highway would have to maneuver around the Caddy. Roger, who is known locally for his fastidious care of automobiles, was also wondering why anyone would leave a luxurious, white car where it was certain to accumulate dust from the gravel road.

After admiring the Cadillac, Roger and Ron noticed the two swarthy men with dark wavy hair sitting on the bench. That was also unusual. The bench was designed for golfers waiting to tee off. Roger and Ron, like the Purviances, had never seen anyone sitting there who was not golfing. The two were obviously strangers. Roger assumed that the white car was theirs, but said nothing to them. Roger and Ron teed off and walked toward the fourth green in the straight-line direction of the Randolph house.

Roger Underwood and Duane Stewart were the last golfers to see the two mysterious figures seated at the fourth tee bench. They noticed the two men when they approached the third green, near the fourth tee, from the east. It was between 11:15 and 11:30 a.m. Their descriptions of the two men were similar to those of Roger Wickland, Ron Wilson, and the Purviances: two swarthy men, dark hair, combed straight back, wearing sunglasses, and about thirty years old. Duane addressed the men by saying, "Hi, how are you?" There was no response.

Duane's tee shot on number four sliced into the ditch along the side of the road. While looking for his ball he had to walk towards the white Cadillac. He noted that the license plates were similar to those of his sister who lived in Illinois.

*****

Wendy chauffeured her mother and sister home from church in Lil's blue Dodge Coronet, taking the route between the cemeteries as they had so many times before by foot. They enjoyed the comfort of having a car to drive to church and not having to ask others for rides. Wendy stopped at Highway 64, crossed the paved road, and proceeded towards their house on the gravel road that bordered the west side of the golf course. They paid no attention to the white Cadillac parked along the road and did not see the two men seated on the bench at the fourth tee.

The telephone rang at the Randolph house almost simultaneously with the arrival of Lil and the girls. Lillian placed her white purse on a TV tray in the kitchen and answered the telephone. It was Howard saying he would come by in a few minutes to take Wendy and Vicki to the Ice Follies. Howard had first invited them to go to the Follies by a call to Vicki at noon on the day before. Vicki planned to attend a slumber party that Saturday evening. She told him she needed to discuss the matter with her mother. When Howard called back at two o'clock, Vicki told him Wendy was sick in bed and Lillian had gone to the Garrett's home to have coffee with Mabel. Howard then suggested they attend the matinee on Sunday, and arrangements were made accordingly.

Howard pulled his Buick into the driveway in front of the double garage a few minutes after his call. Lillian's Dodge Coronet was parked on the north side of the garage with a vacant car space between it and the door to the kitchen on the south. The north garage door behind Lillian's car was open and the south door behind the empty car space was closed. Wendy and Vicki departed from the house via the kitchen door into the garage, crossed the vacant car space, and exited the house via the open garage door behind Lil's car.

As Howard backed his car out of the driveway Lillian put her coffeepot on the stove and went to her room to change clothes. She had a busy day ahead, starting with moving tables at the church in the afternoon for the banquet that evening. In preparation for that chore Lil changed from her church clothes to black Capri pants, a white blouse with squares of floral images, and black flats.

Vicki and Wendy did not enjoy the time they were forced to spend with Howard. Lil explained the legal necessity for their cooperation, and they made the most of it. It seemed to make life easier for their mother. For visitations with Howard, Wendy and Vicki had a working agreement whereby one would sit in the middle of the front seat on the outbound trip, and then they would change positions for the return home. They found sitting beside Howard to be particularly distasteful because of his well-known, pungent B.O. Vicki recalls that he smelled like "button weeds."

For the trip to Des Moines it was Vicki's turn to sit beside Howard. When he backed his Buick out of the driveway the girls had anticipated he would turn and go north along the west side of the golf course to Highway 64, and then turn right and go to Des Moines. That was the usual and most expeditious route. Instead, Howard went south and away from the golf course, explaining that he had to stop at Harry and Ann's "to look at some machinery." When they stopped at the Shackelford residence, one-half mile south and one-quarter mile west, Howard got out of the car and approached the house where Dana and Julie were playing in the yard. Howard greeted the two children and then talked briefly with Ann as she came out of the house.

Howard asked Ann if her family would like to go to the Ice Follies with them. She was surprised because Howard had been pushing Harry hard to take advantage of the weather to get the necessary fieldwork done for the spring planting. Howard said that Harry did not have to work on a Sunday afternoon, something that he had never said before, and which Harry was in the field doing at that very moment. Ann would have liked to go, but their baby, Laura, was ill. She had to decline.

Howard returned to the car where Wendy and Vicki were waiting. They wondered why he said that he "had to look at some machinery," but made no effort to do so.

When exiting the Shackelford's driveway Howard started to turn left, as if by habit, towards the Randolph house and the most expeditious route to Des Moines. And then, as though he remembered something, he jerked the car back to the right, and said he had forgotten the Follies tickets at his office. Howard then drove into Guthrie Center via the gravel road that passes John and Mabel Garrett's house and eventually leads to Highway 25 on the south edge of Guthrie Center. From that point it was only another minute to Howard's combination living quarters and office. Wendy and Vicki again waited in the car while Howard went into his office to get the tickets.

When Howard returned to the car he gave Vicki a stack of eight or nine tickets, and she passed them along to Wendy. Both wondered why he had so many tickets. They also wondered why the usually efficient and organized Howard was so befuddled. It seemed as though he was purposely killing time. They were an hour's drive from Des Moines and Howard had told them that "they would stop at a nice restaurant for lunch." It was obvious that their schedule was tight. And yet Howard seemed to be lingering.

Howard proceeded up Tank Hill very slowly. He accelerated as he got to the crest of the hill, and then slowed again, as they reached the point where John Novy's Iowa Highway Patrol vehicle was parked when he was not on duty. Trooper Novy was home for lunch, and the patrol car was indeed parked in plain sight. Howard took a hard look in the direction of the black and tan police vehicle. Vicki asked what he was looking at and he responded that he was viewing a birdhouse near the Novy residence. Both girls thought that Howard's comment, along with his general behavior, was strange and fabricated.

As they continued eastward and came within view of the Randolph house a few seconds later, Howard was only going fifteen to twenty miles per hour in a zone where the speed limit is forty-five. Wendy noticed two things. One was that Howard was watching the Randolph house out of the corner of his eye. The other was that a large white car was parked in the driveway. Wendy mentioned that there was a white car parked in their driveway. Vicki replied that it must be Sandy Greenlee's car, a white Chrysler. Wendy then told Vicki that it could not be the Greenlee's car—Sandy was one of Wendy's best friends—because they had traded their white Chrysler.

Howard had obviously seen the white car in the driveway, but when Wendy asked him if he knew whose car it was, he replied, "What white car?" Wendy still recalls that moment vividly: "I knew something was wrong. It was like it was all in slow motion."

Vicki, showing the effects of staying awake most of the night at the slumber party, soon fell asleep in her position between Howard and Wendy as they traveled towards Des Moines. The sight of the unknown white car in their driveway puzzled Wendy. She remained silent throughout the hour-long journey. Howard later recalled that "the girls had been moody" that day.

The three ate lunch at the "Silhouette" restaurant on Douglas Avenue in Des Moines, just east of the intersection with Merle Hay Road, on the northwest corner of the city. From there they proceeded to the Veteran's Auditorium on the north edge of the downtown business district. Howard parked the car on the street nearby. They arrived at the auditorium at 2:10, ten minutes after the show had begun.

At the intermission Wendy and Vicki went on their own to search for cotton candy. They found none, but during that time they saw Howard talking on a pay phone. They observed his manner as "serious." When they returned to their seats for the second half of the performance Howard was still on the phone. He rejoined them ten or fifteen minutes later.

*****

At the Lutheran Church in Guthrie Center the ladies who had gathered to set up tables, decorate, and prepare food for the Mother-Daughter Banquet began to wonder why Lillian was late. They knew that Ruby Krakau, the other co-chair, would not be present that day, but they expected Lil would be on time, as was her usual practice. They had seen her at church services that morning and she had told them she would see them again at the church that afternoon. They knew her as thoroughly devoted to the church and regarded her as "a really good, reliable person." They thought it unusual that she did not arrive at the appointed time, 1:30 p.m. She had told others to be there at that time, and they had assumed that Lil, in her normal efficient and responsible manner, would be there to greet them.

At two o'clock Joni Short called Ann Shackelford from the church and asked if she knew where her mother was. Ann knew that Lil was involved with the banquet but did not know the details of her schedule. She told Joni that she had talked with her mother by phone that morning, but had not seen her since the night before when she had stopped by to pick up a suit she planned to wear to church. Perhaps, Joni suggested, Lil had car trouble en route. Or maybe there had been a mix-up on times, although that seemed highly unlikely. But Lil was only thirty minutes late and some of the other committee members also had not arrived. Ann had her hands full with a sick baby and two other small children. Joni and Ann left the matter in the "surely she'll show up" mode.

Trudy Garrett, Wendy's high school classmate and best friend, did not know her chum was going to attend the Ice Follies with Howard. She called the Randolph house between 1:30 and 2:00, but received no response. Trudy knew that Lil was involved in the Mother-Daughter Banquet at the Lutheran Church. She assumed that Lillian had gone to the church, which indeed was the plan, to help with arrangements for the evening banquet. Trudy was disappointed that Wendy was not home and available to talk to her, but attached no significance to her absence.

When Lil still had not arrived at the church by 3:30 the women present had become quite concerned. This time Marilyn Hatch called Ann and asked if she had heard from her mother. Ann, now alarmed, said that she had not and was going immediately to the Randolph house.

When Ann pulled into the driveway of her mother's home she observed that both garage doors were open and her mother's car was gone. She walked into the open garage and saw that the screen door into the kitchen was closed, but the inner door was open. "Joey," Wendy and Vicki's pet Manchester dog, met Ann at the kitchen door. She called into the basement for her mother and looked out onto the sun porch. In the kitchen a coffeepot was on a burner set at "low."

Ann did not find the warm coffeepot particularly disturbing. Her mother liked coffee and might have decided to have warm coffee ready for her return. But finding Joey at the door did trouble Ann. He was always kept in the basement when no one was home. Lil was insistent upon that.

There was a cup of coffee on the kitchen table that had lipstick on the edge and was partially filled. There was a box of noodles sitting on the stove, which seemed strange to Ann because no one would be eating dinner there that evening. There were four dirty coffee cups in the sink. There was a pack of cigarettes on the TV tray where Lil had placed them beside her purse after returning home from church. The purse was missing, but Ann did not know that it had previously been placed there. Ann walked further into the house and found that the front door was slightly ajar. She found nothing else disturbed or out of the ordinary.

Ann drove around Guthrie Center and past the Lutheran Church looking for her mother's medium blue Dodge Coronet. She stopped at the Midway Service Station and asked Bill Bates if her mother had stopped to purchase gasoline. She had not. Not knowing what else she could do for the moment and thinking she should be near her telephone, Ann returned home.

*****

The Ice Follies show in Des Moines concluded at 4:00 p.m. Howard and the girls, this time with Wendy in the middle, drove back to Guthrie Center on the familiar Highway 64 route through Grimes, Dallas Center, and Panora.

Lillian had been slightly concerned that Howard might not have the girls back in time for the banquet. She knew the legal requirements of visitation and had encouraged the girls to go with Howard. She also knew he was not always prompt in returning them. Indeed, that morning she had expressed such a concern to her sister, Helen, when she had written, "I hope they are back by six."

Lillian told the girls before they left with Howard that if her car was not in the garage, that would mean she had gone on to the church and Howard should drop them off there. Thus they were not surprised when they pulled into the drive and saw Lil's Dodge missing. Both garage doors were now open, whereas only the north door had been open when they left. But they thought nothing of it and assumed their mother was at the Lutheran Church.

Vicki asked Howard to drop her off at the church, as her mother had instructed, and Wendy, saying she did not feel well, decided to stay at home rather than attend the banquet. She told Howard to go ahead without her. Howard seemed in a hurry and quickly backed his Buick out of the driveway for the short trip to the church. Wendy entered the house.

Ann had put Joey back into the basement. Wendy did not notice anything out of the ordinary, but she was not looking for unusual circumstances. She was primarily interested in calling her friend, Sandy Greenlee, and did so almost immediately.

When Howard dropped off Vicki at the Lutheran Church she fully expected to find her mother there. Instead Vicki Howland approached her, told her that Lil had never arrived at the church, and asked Vicki if she knew why. Vicki responded that she had no idea where her mother might be if she was not at the church.

Vicki then called Ann from the church and asked her of the whereabouts of their mother. Ann replied that she did not know and was worried. She told Vicki that she would drive into town and pick her up, a trip of five minutes or so from the Shackelford residence. When the two sisters returned to Ann's house they called their Aunt Lorraine in Boone, who was in the middle of the grand opening festivities of Belluci's Pizza, and asked if she knew where their mother might be. Lorraine said that she had "no idea." Indeed, she was anticipating the later arrival of Lillian for the grand opening of the new restaurant.

After Wendy had contacted Sandy Greenlee by telephone the two of them decided to go for a ride in the Greenlee's new car. When Ann called the Randolph house and could not reach Wendy, she became concerned about her as well. She was much relieved when Wendy and Sandy showed up at the Shackelford house a short time later.

Ann left Wendy and Vicki by the phone at her home and drove to the residence of family friends, John and Mabel Garrett, who lived just beyond the southeastern city limits of Guthrie Center and near the Shackelford farm. Mabel knew of Lil's fears for her life. Lillian had tried to keep the details of her deepest concerns, as best she could, from her daughters, but had revealed much to Mabel. The Garretts immediately counseled Ann to call the sheriff, Lester Peterson.

Lester Peterson was the primary law enforcement in town. Although his responsibilities were for the county rather than the city, people did not care much about jurisdictional lines, and they knew Lester. As he recalls, "If people called, I went."

When Ann called Lester at his home that evening he assured her that he would immediately try to locate Lillian. Ann and the Garretts then went to the Randolph house and looked for indications of misdoing. John thought the carpet in the front room had two long scuffs in the nap, like someone's heels had been dragged along, but he did not say anything to Ann about it. They discovered nothing else beyond what Ann had observed earlier. Ann then returned home and walked out into the fields where Harry was still working in the twilight to tell him of the disappearance of her mother.

Lester Peterson immediately began calling friends of Lillian to see if they might know of her whereabouts. He had seen the white Cadillac with the two strangers in Guthrie Center the day before and was sufficiently suspicious that he wrote the license number on the palm of his hand. Unfortunately, perspiration had erased the number, but that was of little significance for the moment. He had not yet connected the white Cadillac with the disappearance of Lillian. Lester had learned that in law enforcement the simplest explanation is usually the correct one. He had never had a missing person not show up. The possibility of a kidnapping did not enter his mind. To his knowledge there had never been a kidnapping in Guthrie County.

The phone was ringing when Ruby and Floyd Krakau walked in their front door after returning from the birthday party for her father in Jefferson. It was Lester. Floyd and Ruby were good friends of Lester and Beulah Peterson. Floyd had purchased a hog station from Lester and the two couples sometimes went dancing together. Lester knew that Lillian and Ruby were good friends. It was shortly after 8:00 p.m. when Lester called the Krakaus.

"Lillian seems to have disappeared. Do you have any idea where she is?" Lester asked Ruby.

Ruby spontaneously blurted, "She's probably dead." Then she paused to absorb the thought that had passed her lips so quickly. Ruby had such a high regard for Lil and her sense of responsibility that she thought that only death would keep her away from the Mother-Daughter Banquet. Ruby also was aware of Lil's problems with Howard. They had had many discussions on the subject. Ruby remembers well the plaintive voice of her friend pleading, "Please don't tell, Ruby, please don't tell."

Floyd and Ruby immediately left their home and went to search for Lil. They drove slowly along the shoulder of the road between the two local cemeteries, thinking that perhaps Lillian had walked to church and been struck by a hit and run driver. They got out of their car and walked along the side of the road searching with a flashlight through ditches and weeds. They were relieved that they did not find a body.

In the meantime, Ann had frantically tried to reach Howard by phone. She made her first call at 8:00 p.m. and received no response. She called repeatedly for several hours. Still there was no answer. Ann did not know that Howard had sped back to Des Moines after dropping off Vicki at the church. With little traffic during the early Sunday evening, Howard's powerful Roadmaster delivered him to the Des Moines airport around 6:30 p.m.

At the airport the hurried Howard crossed paths with Henry "Hank" Buche, a creamery operator from Slater, Iowa, who had known him for over a decade. Howard was walking south from the United Airlines counter when Hank made eye contact with him. Hank greeted Howard with a smile and a "hi," but noticing that Howard was in a hurry, said nothing further.

At 6:59 p.m. Howard checked into the Howard Johnson Motel on Grand Avenue, near the north end of Fleur Drive, the four-lane road that runs from the west edge of downtown Des Moines to the airport two miles to the south. Howard requested a room for one night and registered as a representative of Randolph Foods in order to qualify for the commercial rate of $9.25. He listed only himself on the registration form under "Number in Party," and gave his auto license number as Iowa 39-2824. He was assigned

Room 230 by the desk clerk. Later a maid at the motel said there might have been two people in the room that night, but was not sure.

Ann resumed her efforts to contact Howard early the next morning, Monday, May 3. She began calling him at 6:30 a.m. When she had not received a response by seven o'clock, she decided to go to his office, arriving there about thirty minutes later. Howard had arrived by that time.

Ann told Howard she had been trying to contact him since 8:00 p.m. the previous night and asked him where he had been. Howard replied he had spent the night in Des Moines. Ann then explained that her mother had been missing since the early afternoon of the previous day.

"You're kidding!" Howard exclaimed.

Ann began crying.

"Did she leave a note?" Howard asked.

"No," Ann responded.

Howard told Ann that he had spent the night in Des Moines "with a woman." He went on to explain that he had been seeing the woman "throughout the winter." "You'll find out sooner or later," Howard told Ann. He then explained that "the woman" had been "nursing him back to health." "The woman" was to have surgery the next day, as Howard explained, and he had wanted to spend some time comforting her.

Ann, with graver issues on her mind and wondering why Howard would even raise such matters, told him, "I don't care about that."

Ann then asked Howard if he knew anything about the whereabouts of her mother. He told her, "No," and indicated that he knew a lot about Lillian's personal life because he went through her garbage looking for notes and messages. He even told Ann he had read many of her communications with her mother. Howard's comments about spying on Lillian, particularly given the urgent circumstances, puzzled Ann.

Howard made a point of showing Ann his reservations for a United Airlines flight to Cincinnati on May 5. Until then she did not know that Howard had been to the Des Moines airport the previous night, only that he had been in Des Moines "with a woman." He seemed intent on telling her that he had also been to the airport, and the reason was to make plane reservations to Cincinnati, a trip he never took.

Howard asked Ann if Wendy and Vicki needed anything. She replied that she and Harry were looking after them. Ann departed from Howard's office. She was terribly distraught. It had been plausible that the absence of the evening before of both her mother and Howard had meant they were together somewhere. They had resumed their marriage several times before, and Howard had asked Ann to help with another reconciliation.

Now that Ann had found Howard and learned he was with another woman the night before, any hopes that he could explain her mother's disappearance had been shattered. Ann knew that Howard was a cool and collected sort, but was dismayed that he showed no visible indications of sharing her worry and concern for her mother. She recalled later that he had been "very calm," surprisingly so to her under the circumstances.

*****

The "woman" that Howard had seen in Des Moines the night of Lillian's disappearance was Amanda "Peggy" Alston, a long-time friend and periodic companion. They had become acquainted shortly after World War II when they accompanied mutual friends on a trip to the Badlands of South Dakota. Howard became a part of the group when a male friend of Peggy's backed out at the last minute.

When they returned to Iowa, Peggy told Howard, "You know you cost me a boyfriend."

"You didn't need him anyhow," Howard responded.

And thus the relationship between Howard and Peggy began, an association of many dimensions that would last until Howard died in 1994. During those many decades their relationship took many turns. Between them they married five times. They shared an interest in horses, travel, and farming. At one time or another Peggy fulfilled many roles in Howard's life: traveling companion, nurse, chauffeur, hostess, and fellow equestrian. She also shared his roof on occasion, sometimes for a number of months.

Howard admired Peggy's spirited independence. When her first husband, a glider pilot in World War II, came home drunk one summer evening, Peggy chased him from the house, clanging him on the head with a frying pan. On another occasion, many years later, a relative of Howard's witnessed an angry Peggy "smack him with a fist."

Peggy's infrequent outbursts of anger were defensive in nature. Most of the time she was a gentle, caring, and loyal companion to Howard. He liked that. They had common interests, and he liked that. She made a strict and written accounting of every penny of his that she spent. He especially liked that, and she did not mind, thinking it "quite appropriate."

People who traveled with Howard saw him at his best. He liked to travel, and it seemed to jar him from the restrictive, niggardly mode that characterized his business and personal lives in Guthrie Center. Those who recall Howard's infrequent generosity, almost always do so in recalling moments of vacationing or traveling with him. Peggy Alston was one of those people.

Peggy valued a relationship with Howard in which she could maintain an emotional distance, and get in and out of the relationship as she chose. Even when she shared a roof with Howard she maintained a separate residence. She cared for him, even though she knew of his character flaws, and responded loyally when asked.

Peggy recalls that the tickets Howard used to take Wendy and Vicki to the Ice Follies originated with her. She was working as a secretary to the manager, Willard Brittin, at the Holiday Inn-South in Des Moines, on Gray's Lake near the Des Moines airport. The Ice Follies personnel were staying at the motel and their manager had left a stack of complimentary tickets with Brittin. He, in turn, had told motel employees that they could "help themselves" to the tickets. Peggy remembers giving a number of them to Howard, who had renewed his relationship with Peggy a year before Lillian filed the restraining order against him.

Peggy recalls that she had coffee with Howard that Sunday evening at the Howard Johnson's Motel where he was staying, but did not spend the night with him. In his Monday morning conversation with Ann, Howard had made a point of telling her that he had been in Des Moines the previous night to purchase a plane ticket and to spend time with "a woman who was going to have surgery." Peggy did have a tumor removed from her shoulder, but that took place later in the year. She does not recall that Howard expressed concern over her health or visited her in the hospital at that time. Was it possible that Howard knew the details of Lillian's disappearance and was using Peggy as an alibi?

Chapter VI

The Search

"Do you have any enemies that would kidnap mom?"

Ann Shackelford

Ruby and Floyd Krakau did not sleep much the night of Lillian's disappearance. Ruby had a "gut feeling," as she recalls, that Lillian would never be found alive, perhaps never found at all. She knew Lillian would have made every effort to fulfill her responsibilities at the Mother-Daughter Banquet the day before. She had a key to the church for that purpose. Perhaps, Ruby thought, Lillian had gone to the church early, before anyone else arrived, and something had happened to her at that time. Ruby had to find out for herself.

The Krakaus drove to the Lutheran Church to see if Ruby's hunch might be true. They found the door to the church locked, an unusual circumstance during daylight hours. Was it possible, they wondered, that Lillian's body might be locked inside? They went to the residence of Reverend Lutz seeking a church key, but he was not home.

In the immediate aftermath of Lillian's disappearance there was concern for anyone linked to her who could not be located quickly. The evening before Ann had such concerns about Wendy when she could not immediately find her. Now the Krakaus had similar concerns about the Reverend Lutz. But their more immediate concern was the possibility that Lillian's body might be found in the church. Ruby called the sheriff's office.

Roger Brown, one of Sheriff Peterson's two deputies, took Ruby's call and went immediately to the Lutheran Church, a drive of only a few minutes from the sheriff's office. Roger was joined by the Krakaus. Roger and Floyd forced the locked church door open and the three of them thoroughly searched the building. They found nothing. Their only gratification was learning a few minutes later, when he arrived at the church, that Reverend Lutz had not also disappeared.

Lester Peterson would have gone to the church, but he could not get away from his office. There was much to be done and the phone was ringing, ringing, ringing. People who knew of Lillian's disappearance, and the number was growing rapidly, wanted to know if she had been found and, if not, what action Lester was taking. It was impossible for him to do much of anything with the phone constantly ringing. His normal manner was to try and ease the anxieties of people who called him with problems, and that would be the large majority of Lester's calls. He was used to telling people, "Don't worry, everything will be all right." Or perhaps, "Don't worry, I'll take care of everything." But in this situation Lester's normally soothing words did not work. They seemed hollow to him as well as to those on the telephone line. He needed to ease the growing tensions of the community. But what words could possible serve that purpose when the news was spreading quickly and anxieties were rising rapidly?

A formal missing person report, according to standard law enforcement regulations, could not be filed until an individual had been absent for at least twenty-four hours. The experience of law enforcement agencies indicates that more than ninety percent of supposedly missing persons are located within twenty-four hours. Typically the problem is not that a person has disappeared, but that the "missing" person simply forgot to inform someone of his or her plans. It is not cost efficient for law enforcement officers to spend valuable time searching bars and fishing holes for people who have not truly disappeared. That had been Lester's experience as well. There had been only a few missing person problems during his tenure as sheriff, and all had been resolved within a few hours. But, as Lester recalls, "This one felt different."

Lester Peterson managed to get along with Howard Randolph. Indeed, he and Beulah had just moved into a house built on south Twelfth Street on land that Lester had acquired in a deal with Howard at a land auction. Howard and Lester had been bidding on the same piece of land when Howard approached him and suggested that they "split the land and save some money," rather than continuing to bid against each other. Lester agreed, and eventually built a frame house on his portion of the land, which also included a pre-existing small barn.

But Lester also knew, in his words, that "Howard did not do right by Lillian" and had a reputation for "taking advantage of people." Long before the disappearance of Lillian, Lester had concluded that Howard was a "mean man" who was capable of doing cruel things. That Monday morning Sheriff Peterson believed that a crime "probably" had taken place, and he thought Howard Randolph was involved.

Lester had already informed other law enforcement officers of Lillian's disappearance by putting the information on the air with his police radio. The range of the sheriff's radio was about thirty miles. That would cover all of Guthrie County and into surrounding counties, but would not reach Des Moines, the largest city in the State, located fifty miles to the east. Within the local area he asked other law enforcement officers to be looking for a 1965 Dodge Coronet, medium blue in color, Iowa license number 39-2449, driven by a fifty-seven-year-old brunette female, who was 5'4" tall and weighed 125 pounds. Lester also asked that they spread the word so as to cover as large an area as possible.

When law enforcement personnel of the time received such information they made a note, typically on a tablet on a clipboard, and then were on the lookout for the individual or automobile. There was no specific form called a "Missing Person Report," or anything of the sort. It was also possible to give the search a greater range by putting the information out by teletype, which Lester did when the requisite twenty-four hours had passed in the early afternoon of May 3.

Sheriff Peterson was involved in a big case in a big way, and knew it. His interest in law enforcement began with service as an M. P. in the Marines during World War II, an experience that included witnessing from afar the atomic bombing of Hiroshima. Lester recalls that the blast "looked like giant sunflowers had melted and bent over."

After the war Lester resumed farming but never forgot his interest in police work. When J.C. McCool resigned as Guthrie County Sheriff in 1956, Lester expressed an interest in the position and was appointed sheriff by the County Board of Supervisors. His bid for re-election was unsuccessful when Bennie Sheeder was elected instead. When Bennie resigned in 1962 to become an inspector for the Iowa State Liquor Commission, Lester was again appointed sheriff. This time he was re-elected, and continued in office until he retired in 1980.

Lester held a low-key and pragmatic view of being sheriff, both of which were appropriate for a small town setting where violent crime was practically unknown. Soon after assuming his duties as sheriff, he discovered that the furnace boiler in the jail was in bad condition and dangerous. He was fearful it might explode and scald the two or three inmates typically detained in the small brick building adjacent to the courthouse. When the County Board of Supervisors denied Lester's request for a new furnace for the jail, he solved the problem by giving one of the "prisoners" a key. Word of Sheriff Peterson's solution, at a time when Sheriff Andy Taylor and his deputy Barney Fife were popular television personalities, found its way first to the Des Moines *Register and Tribune*, and later to the New York *Times*, appearing in both in brief articles.

Sheriff Peterson seldom wore a uniform and never carried a side arm in a holster, preferring instead to conceal a small Colt 32 in his jacket pocket. He felt the display of a weapon interfered with his responsibilities. Those responsibilities, as reported in a March 1965 issue of the Guthrie Center *Times*, only weeks before tragic events would consume the community, described a local increase in crime under the headline: "Much Activity at Sheriff's Office." The article listed a number of crimes that had been solved or were under investigation by the sheriff's office, including the apprehension of a fifteen-year-old window peeper, a traffic violation issued to a local man for reckless driving, a burglary at the local high school, and the rustling of cattle from the Laughery Brothers Sale Barn.

Cattle rustling and burglaries produced headlines in the local newspaper from time to time, but violent crimes were practically unknown. In 1950, however, there was a death that George Gibson, then-publisher of the Guthrie Center *Times*, called a murder. In a front-page editorial he referred to the case as "the dirtiest crime ever committed in Guthrie County." For many in the community, including Sheriff J.C. McCool and Coroner Harold Hill, there was doubt that Gibson had reached the correct conclusion.

The lifeless body of Alonzo "Lon" Beghtel, an elderly man who lived in a shanty near the railroad tracks, was found face down in a frozen pool of blood on a bitterly cold January morning. A broken whiskey bottle and the railroad track were nearby. It was possible to conclude that someone had struck Lon with the bottle, but it was also conceivable that, after a night of drinking, he had fallen and struck his head on the steel rail.

J.C. McCool, the sheriff at the time, had never investigated a murder. He was not certain it was a homicide, and Harold Hill, the County Coroner, could not provide much help. Harold was a mortician by profession and had no medical training. The death certificate signed and filed by Harold described the cause of death as "loss of blood,' but provided no explanation for the bleeding. The word "homicide" was not used.

Local opinion was divided on the cause of Lon's death between homicide and demon rum. For the former the case was concluded when their chief suspect was killed a few months later in an auto racing accident. Divine intervention and justice, in their opinion, resolved the case.

Eleven years after the death of Lon Beghtel a tragic murder/suicide shocked Guthrie Center. Merl "Sprout" Rutherford, the lessee of the local Conoco service station, was despondent over hostile divorce proceedings. He apparently believed that his daughter, Betty, was supplying undue support to his estranged wife. He ended Betty's life and his with two bullets from a revolver. It was a senseless and painful loss to family and community, but the case was quickly resolved and closed.

The crime that Sheriff Peterson now faced involved a likely kidnapping and possible murder at the hands of two hit men. The implausible had occurred—organized, big-time, Mafia-style crime had come to rural Iowa. Because kidnapping is a federal offense, it would have been appropriate for Lester to contact the Federal Bureau of Investigation. But he had never had a reason before to involve the FBI in local affairs. He felt more comfortable contacting the Iowa Bureau of Criminal Investigation in Des Moines. He had worked with BCI agents on a few cases before. He called BCI headquarters that Monday afternoon and told them what he knew of the situation, and asked for their assistance.

There is always potential for an uneasy working relationship between county sheriffs and the BCI. Sheriffs are elected officials with no legal requirement for formal training in law enforcement. Lester, who bears a resemblance to Smiley Burnette, the sidekick of Gene Autry in many western movies, dropped out of high school to work on the family farm. With the exception of his World War II service, Sheriff Peterson spent all his life in farming prior to becoming the Guthrie County Sheriff.

Most BCI agents had college degrees, causing Lester to refer to them with obvious disdain as "college boys." Many had attended the FBI School at Quantico, Virginia, as well as other advanced law enforcement training programs. In short, the BCI law enforcement operation was more professional than that of the typical Iowa sheriff.

But with all the differences in education, training, and perspective, BCI agents and Iowa county sheriffs needed each other. The sheriff knew the local people in ways a BCI agent did not. Who had a bad temper, who was highly regarded, who had marital problems, who went to church, who paid their bills, who was capable of committing a crime—that was the type of information a sheriff was more likely to know than a BCI agent. The sheriff had lived among the people who had elected him to office. His election was an indication of acceptance and standing among those people with whom he lived. He could pick up a telephone and call people, using their first names. In short, he had a form of personal access to people in his area that a state agent could not match.

On the other hand, the BCI had resources that the local sheriff did not, such as statewide records, expert technicians, and more advanced equipment. When Lester Peterson first became sheriff he had but one deputy, Bert Winn. He took his police radio home at night and Beulah, his wife, became the dispatcher. At a later date he gained a second deputy. At the time of Lillian's disappearance Lester's staff consisted of a secretary; two deputies, Roger Brown and Robert Shaeffer; and his wife filling in as necessary during evenings.

Thus there was a complementary connection between the BCI and county sheriffs. The sheriff needed the expertise and equipment of the BCI, and the BCI needed the access to local people and information that the sheriff could provide. Quite often the sheriff would accompany a visiting agent to introduce him to a local person. The endorsement thus provided by the sheriff typically eased the process of interviewing witnesses. People in small towns easily identify strangers and are wary of them, including state agents. Guthrie Center was no exception.

When Sheriff Peterson notified the BCI of Lillian's disappearance on Monday, he was told that an agent would be assigned to the case and come to Guthrie Center, probably the next day. If there were any changes in the case, and particularly if Lillian was located, Lester was asked to notify BCI immediately.

The friends and family of Lillian were demanding that Sheriff Peterson do more to locate her, such as putting her picture and news of her disappearance on television and radio. But Lester had no control over the media in that manner, a circumstance that was frustrating to him and not clearly understood by those asking him for more action. He did pass along what he knew to the editor of the local newspaper, Chick Gonzales, and the reporter who covered local events, Verle Lekwa. A brief article, entitled "Mrs. Randolph is Still Missing," appeared on the front page of the Wednesday issue of the *Times*. The article described a few details of the disappearance and mentioned that a statewide search was underway. The following Monday the companion newspaper to the *Times*, the *Guthrian,* reported that the search for Lillian Randolph was continuing under a brief front page item entitled, "Woman Still Missing."

As days passed without the discovery of Lillian, Sheriff Peterson remembers "working around the clock" and feeling the tension and fear that was building in the community. Ruby Krakau, who did not think the authorities "were doing enough," called Lester, and asked, "Why isn't more being done?" Lester, trying to comfort Ruby, told her "not to worry." And then added clumsily, "She probably just ran off with another guy. She's probably going through the change." However well intended Lester's comment, it did not soothe Ruby's feelings. She vividly recalls that she was "really ticked off."

Important news is circulated faster in a small town by word of mouth than by the local newspaper. By the time the Wednesday edition of the *Times* was delivered most everyone in town knew of the strange disappearance of Lillian Randolph. Many witnesses had seen the two swarthy men in the white car that had been in town the previous weekend. It was not difficult to connect her disappearance, which occurred simultaneously with their departure from town, with the two men. Local golfers were aware that the golf course, where several had seen the two men, was adjacent to the Randolph property.

Duane Stewart was the first of the golfers to contact Sheriff Peterson, doing so on Wednesday, May 5. Duane told Lester of seeing the white Cadillac and the two men at the golf course on Sunday morning. Duane said he had been playing golf that morning with Roger Underwood. Lester called Roger and asked him to come by and supply the details of what he had seen. Roger did so. Roger Wickland did likewise. One by one the golfers who had seen the two swarthy men told their stories. Some of them at first said that they had not seen anything, and then their recollections improved. Fear was beginning to grip some of the people who had seen the two men in the white Cadillac or who had anything to do with Lillian or Howard Randolph. But as word spread around town that people who had seen the two men were being summoned to the sheriff's office, more and more came forward, some more willingly than others. Some freely provided information about what they had seen, some initially said they could not remember seeing the two men and then changed their mind when other witnesses revealed their presence, some said they would talk but not be witnesses in a formal, public trial, and some came forward later—even years later. The law enforcement officers involved in the case believe some important witnesses forever remained silent.

Warren Stump, a Special Agent, was assigned by the BCI to head the investigation of the disappearance of Lillian. Lester had worked with Warren before and had a healthy regard for him. It helped in Lester's acceptance of him that Warren had started his law enforcement career as a deputy sheriff before moving on to the BCI. He was not a "college boy" in the eyes of Lester.

Lester recalls that Stump was "a good man," but "touchy." "I could work with him," Lester recollects, hinting that getting along with Warren took some effort. Some of Stump's fellow agents in the BCI thought of him as a handsome man who looked the part, but whose ambitions were greater than his abilities. Like Lester, they could get along with Stump with a little extra effort.

Verle Lekwa also attests to Agent Stump's touchy nature. Warren "chewed out" Verle, in his words, for reporting in the local newspaper that the two strangers were seen in a white Cadillac. He said the article "interfered with the investigation" and wanted to know who had leaked that information. During the heated discussion that followed Lekwa told Stump that he had overheard the information from Stump himself when the agent had not bothered to close a window near which Lekwa was standing outside.

Locals interviewed by Warren Stump remember him as "tall and slender," "professional," "nice looking," and "impressive." Stump even had something of a personal connection with the community. His mother was a traveling sales person, a rarity at a time when the occupation was known as "salesmen," who called on clothing stores, including that of Don and Delia Benton in Guthrie Center.

Lester and Warren had dozens of people to interview. There were those at the church, those at the golf course, family members, a few people in Stuart, several at Bates' Service Station, and Howard Randolph.

The interview of Howard was a good example of how a county sheriff can be helpful to a state agent. Lester had known Howard for a long time, had had some business dealings with him, was aware of his personal and business reputations, knew something of his personality, and, most importantly, that "he didn't do right by Lillian." There was no evidence yet of a crime, but the suspicions of Lester were high. He passed along to Agent Stump his suspicions that Howard was involved in the disappearance of Lillian.

If Lester and Warren now assumed that a crime had been committed, not a hard assumption to make, then the next question was simple: Who would have a motive to harm Lillian? Howard had been legally removed from his prized house by a restraining order requested by Lillian and served on him by Lester. Lillian had obtained an order of separate maintenance that required Howard to pay her $800 per month. Lester knew of the visitation problems with Wendy and Vicki that Howard had complained about, as well as his cruel treatment of Lillian. Warren and Lester went to see Howard.

Howard told Lester and Warren that he had no information on the whereabouts of Lillian and was as concerned as anyone about her personal safety. Lester noticed that while they talked to Howard a body odor, becoming increasingly powerful, was being emitted from Howard. Body odor and Howard were a well-known combination, but Lester found the B. O. to be even worse than Howard's norm. Lester took the sour aroma of Howard as an indication of his guilt. During the several interviews with Howard in weeks to come, Lester noticed that every time the subject of Lillian was raised Howard would perspire and project a "terrific odor."

Howard's description of his whereabouts on Sunday, May 2, matched what other witnesses had observed. He told Lester and Warren of purchasing a newspaper at the Daree Den around 7:30, taking Dana and Julie Shackelford to Panora fishing between 8:30 and 10:00, going home to change clothes to go to the Ice Follies in Des Moines, picking up Wendy and Vicki at noon to take them to the Follies, going to Ann and Harry's house, picking up the Follies tickets in his office, attending the Follies in the afternoon, and then returning to Guthrie Center around 5:30 p.m. to drop off the girls. Howard said that he had immediately returned to the Des Moines airport, purchased a plane ticket, spent the night at a nearby Howard Johnson's Motel, and returned to Guthrie Center the next morning. He related that he knew nothing of Lillian's disappearance until 7:30 the next morning when Ann came to his office. Howard told Lester and Warren that he had not seen a white Cadillac, or any car, parked in the driveway of the Randolph house when he passed by on Highway 64 on the way to Des Moines.

Howard did not mention talking to two swarthy men in a white car early Sunday morning, but Lester and Warren did not yet know of that important connection between Howard and the two strangers. Without evidence of a crime they had only their suspicions, and those pointed towards Howard Randolph.

Sheriff Peterson and Agent Stump turned their efforts towards locating Lillian's car. Parking lots, where a single car could be lost in a multitude of others, were good places to look for a missing auto. Lester concentrated his efforts in the Guthrie Center region, while Stump focused on the many parking lots in the Des Moines area where he lived.

******

Louis A. "Tony" Weibel, an Internal Revenue Agent stationed in Sioux City, Iowa, had been trying to arrange an appointment with Howard Randolph during the working week of May 3-7. Tony had had many years of contacts with Howard over tax matters. He knew him well enough to recognize his voice over the phone. Tony was working on a tax matter concerning Howard's business in Harlan, Iowa, a city forty miles west of Guthrie Center which was located within Tony's area of responsibility in western Iowa.

Tony Weibel was a highly respected IRS agent. Those who worked with him recall that he "tended to business" and was "extremely conscientious." They also recall that he was a "good man" who looked after two elderly aunts who lived in nursing homes in Sioux City.

Agent Weibel spent his entire IRS career in Sioux City, after his initial appointment in 1943 as a Deputy Collector. He eventually was promoted to the level of Senior Agent, with a Civil Service rating of GS-12.

IRS agents are trained to take thorough notes on every detail of their contacts with taxpayers. Indeed, the IRS has specific forms for agents to record the details of telephone conversations and meetings. The notes thus taken are invaluable to the IRS as a case may be passed from one agent to another, or a taxpayer may contest an IRS decision in court, or an agent may have need of information more precise and reliable than human memory. Tony Weibel was meticulous in taking notes when talking to taxpayers.

Agent Weibel's notes of May 3, 1965, the day after Lillian disappeared, records a conversation with Howard Randolph: "Called Howard Randolph. He said he was arranging an appointment with Walter Brown, his attorney, but he (Brown) had some conflict on that date; he is to call me back

95

sometime today." Howard, according to Weibel's notes, did not indicate that he would be absent on May 5 because of a plane trip to Cincinnati, an item of information he had seemed intent on passing along to Ann Shackelford earlier in the day. That was highly relevant if Howard and Weibel were to find a meeting time that week. Before leaving for home at the end of the day, Weibel recorded: "Randolph did not call me back today."

Weibel was out of town doing field audits on May 4, 5, and 6. When he returned to his office on the morning of Friday, May 7, he found a note from his secretary that indicated Howard Randolph had called during Weibel's absence and would call again on May 7. While Tony was talking on the phone to another party, Howard called as promised and was informed by the office secretary that Agent Weibel would have to call him back. She passed along to Weibel that Howard had called at 8:05 a.m.

Agent Weibel wrote in his notes: "Randolph called back today at 8:05 a.m." He then wrote: "I called Randolph back about 8:15 or 8:20." Howard apologized to Weibel for "not getting back to him earlier," explaining that he had had a "hectic week." Then, as Agent Weibel's notes continue, Howard made the following statement: "He informed me that his wife had died last Sunday and it appeared that murder might be involved. He said that he would not be available for awhile; I am to call him in about 3 weeks."

While Agent Weibel was recording the words of Howard, Special Agent Stump and Sheriff Peterson were looking for Lillian and her car in an effort to determine if a crime had been committed. In other words, Howard Randolph was reporting to IRS Agent Weibel that Lillian "had died" and "it appeared that murder might be involved" before there was any evidence that a crime had been committed or that she was deceased.

The same morning that Weibel was talking with Howard by telephone, Agent Stump was interviewing John and Mabel Garrett at their home. Mabel was a good friend of Lillian and her daughter, Trudy, was Wendy's best friend. Both John and Mabel had known Howard for many years. They had purchased from Howard the land upon which John, a professional carpenter, had built their house. John had also done some carpentry work for Howard from time to time.

The Garretts knew of Howard's abuse of Lillian and had had some legal problems getting clear title to the land he had sold them, because of "shenanigans," in their words, on the part of Howard. They did not trust him. Stump, providing locals for the first time an indication of what the BCI had in mind, asked them if Howard was capable of hiring someone to kidnap and murder Lillian. That was a stretch beyond what they knew of Howard. John told Stump that Howard was "cagey," but he did not think he would hire anyone to harm Lillian.

Mabel told Stump that indeed Lil, as she always called Lillian, had feared for her life. She had told Mabel of receiving calls asking for Howard, and when she responded that he was not there, was asked, "Are you alone?" Those calls seemed to occur only when Howard had taken Wendy and Vicki on a visitation excursion. Thus it was easy to surmise that Howard might be connected with those calls. Mabel had urged Lil to "get out of that house," thinking that her departure would reduce tensions with Howard, and whatever that might lead to.

Although the thought had already occurred to the Garretts that Howard might be involved in Lil's disappearance, they had not spoken of their suspicions to others. They did not think Howard capable of murder, at least at that time, and that was an outcome they did not even want to consider. When Stump raised the question of murder with them, John and Mabel knew the law enforcement officers investigating the case had such suspicions.

Later that day, May 7, Howard also paid a visit to the Garrett home, an unusual act for him. Small talk was exchanged, and then John, a man quick to the point and following up on Stump's earlier question to him, asked Howard, "Did you have Lillian killed?"

Howard responded, "Do you think I want to go to jail?"

Howard had not said "yes" or "no" to John's question. His manner was calm and, as John recalled, "Cold as ice." He showed no concern or anxiety over Lillian's disappearance. His cool manner and evasive answer gave the Garretts second thoughts about Howard's capabilities. They began to have some of the same suspicions voiced to them by Warren Stump. After Howard left, John loaded a gun and set it in the corner.

Agent Stump was suspicious of Howard Randolph. He had learned of Roger Anderson's statement to Sheriff Peterson that linked Howard with the two strangers seen in Guthrie Center the previous weekend. But he did not know of the telephone call between IRS Agent Tony Weibel and Howard, which was taking place almost simultaneously with his visit to the Garrett home. He would not learn of Weibel's telephone conversation with Howard until the following Wednesday, five days hence.

*****

Howard did not take the flight to Cincinnati on May 5 as he had told Ann Shackelford he intended to do, and for which he explained he had gone to the Des Moines airport on the evening of May 2 to purchase a ticket. He did call John Snowgren, a business associate in Marshalltown, Iowa, on May 4 and told him that "Lillian has disappeared." Howard told Snowgren that he had "no idea" of her whereabouts. He promised to keep Snowgren, who knew her well, informed on any further developments regarding Lillian. Four days later Howard again called Snowgren and told him that she was still missing.

Ann was growing increasingly suspicious of Howard. When she and Harry needed a home and employment, Howard provided both. He had even paid for the honeymoon on which he, Wendy, and Vicki had accompanied the newlyweds. He was good to their children. Howard worked Harry very hard, but Ann was grateful for the support they had received from him.

Ann was not afraid of Howard. He had never threatened or struck her. Lil had told her about some of the ill treatment she, Wendy, and Vicki had suffered at the hands of Howard, including Howard knocking Wendy down. Ann also could remember the problems of living under the same roof with Howard. But Lillian had spared Ann, as she had her other children, much of the agony she had experienced with Howard.

Howard had unleashed his considerable charm and means on Ann and her family, while also grumbling to her about the $800 separate maintenance he was forced to pay Lillian. Ann had been confused over the image her mother portrayed of Howard and what she saw for herself. Wendy and Vicki, who were now living with Ann and Harry, told Ann of their eerie perceptions of Howard the day they went to the Ice Follies. And Ann had observed that Howard did not share her alarm when she told him of the disappearance of her mother. He had seemed, in Ann's words, "very calm" at the time, much too calm Ann had thought for the circumstances. Ann felt she had to ask some direct questions of Howard.

On Sunday morning, May 9, one week after the disappearance of her mother, Ann was driving by the Randolph house. It was sad and strange that her mother was not there. She saw Howard working in his garden south of the house. It was a good opportunity to talk with him. She parked the car in the familiar driveway, exited the auto, and approached Howard.

Howard and Ann exchanged pained greetings, and then Ann went to the heart of her concerns. Referring to her mother's disappearance, she said to Howard, "I have to feel you had nothing to do with it." He looked at her with a blank face and said nothing.

Ann continued, "Do you have any enemies that would kidnap mom?"

"Yes," Howard replied, meaning he had enemies, "but none that would do anything like that." Then Howard offered, "Maybe a bum came across the fields and forced her into a car."

Howard, as was his practice, had not given his questioner a direct answer. He had not specifically denied any direct involvement. He responded only when she mentioned that perhaps a third party or parties had been involved. And then he suggested the improbable scenario of a bum wandering across the Iowa landscape, forcing Lillian into a car, and then driving away with her. That sounded totally implausible to Ann that Sunday. Two days later it would not seem so unlikely.

Of more concern to Ann than Howard's indirect responses and far-fetched scenarios was his general manner. He had been calm and composed during the seven days that Lillian had been missing. While others were in tears and a high state of anxiety, Howard had not shown any sorrow or sympathy, by word or deed. He seemed so removed, so mechanical about the tragedy that had absorbed the existence of Lillian's family and friends. Ann felt no better for what she had just heard from Howard. She left his garden more troubled than when she arrived.

Around 7:00 p.m. that evening Howard went to Ann and Harry's home. He handed Harry a twenty-dollar bill and said it was to help with the expenses for Wendy and Vicki. There were now seven people living in the Shackelford house: two adults, two teenagers, two small children, and a baby. Ann, her husband, and her two sisters did not feel comfortable with Howard's presence. He was not asked to stay for dinner.

Howard suggested that he take Dana and Julie, the Shackelford's two oldest daughters at five and three, for "a ride and supper," something that he had done on many occasions. Whatever uneasiness the Shackelfords felt about Howard, it did not extend to his relationship with their children. He had treated them on many occasions. Their parents relented, and Howard took Dana and Julie out to eat in Panora, returning them to their home about 9:30 p.m.

The day before Ann gingerly confronted Howard in his garden, he had telephoned the home of Hank and Peggy Randolph in Urbandale and talked with Peggy. Howard commenced the conversation by asking Peg if she had any news concerning Lillian's disappearance. It was an awkward and strange question. If anyone in the family had learned anything of the whereabouts of Lillian, there would have been instant communications and a collective sigh of relief. Howard was not good at small talk. Perhaps his awkward and bumbling way of commencing the conversation was unintentional. He then proceeded to the reason for his call. He told Peg that he was thinking about going to Des Moines and looking for Lillian's Dodge Coronet. He asked if perhaps the entire family— Hank, Peg, Ann, Wendy, and Vicki—would want to accompany him. Howard thought that they might locate Lillian's car in a public parking lot. He had in mind searching parking lots at grocery stores, schools, and specifically mentioned the Des Moines airport.

Peggy thought Howard's suggestion was strange. Sheriff Peterson and Agent Stump had notified all law enforcement agencies in the area to be on the lookout for the medium blue Dodge, and were looking themselves for the vehicle on a daily basis. They had kept the family apprised of the search efforts. One had to wonder what the family could accomplish that law enforcement personnel could not. Moreover, Peg and Hank were not eager to spend time with Howard. Peg declined Howard's invitation.

*****

Agent Stump's weeklong search in the Des Moines area for Lillian's car had been fruitless. Although Howard Randolph had suggested to his daughter-in-law, Peggy, that the Des Moines airport might be a good place to look, Stump did not begin a search of the airport parking lot until Tuesday morning, May 11. Stump did not have to look very long.

Lillian's 1965 medium-blue Dodge Coronet was parked in plain view, thirteen car spaces to the north of the main entrance to the terminal building. The car was unlocked and the keys were in the ignition. It was 9:30 a.m.

Special Agent Stump inspected the automobile, but did not touch it. There was an odor emanating from the trunk. A foul-smelling liquid was dripping from the trunk to the pavement. It was obvious to Stump that he had found a crime scene.

Agent Stump called T.A. "Tommy" Thompson, Director of the Iowa Bureau of Criminal Investigation, and told him of his discovery. He requested that Andrew Newquist, a BCI crime scene specialist, be sent immediately to the airport. Thompson dispatched Newquist to the scene. He also contacted the Des Moines Police Department, within whose jurisdiction the airport was located. The DMPD sent several policemen to the airport to search and secure the crime scene area. Three detectives were also sent to the scene to head the DMPD investigation. They were E. Dale Allen, Chief of Detectives, and two of his officers, Detectives Ray Steiner and Russell Lewis.

When the DMPD detectives arrived at the crime scene Stump told them, as Detective Steiner recalls, "This is the car. I think something is in it." Steiner thought that Stump was only pointing out the obvious. The odor was awful. Steiner knew from experience that it was the stench of death.

While BCI and Des Moines Police Department detectives were beginning their investigation of the 1965 Dodge, the Deputy Director of the BCI, Bob Blair, called Sheriff Peterson, told him that Lillian's car had been located, and to standby for further word. If a corpse were discovered in the trunk of the car, which every detective present was sure to be the case, an identification of the body would have to be made. If it was Lillian Randolph, the most likely possibility, then Howard Randolph, still her legal husband, would be an appropriate person to make the identification. It would be Lester Peterson's responsibility to see that Howard got to Des Moines for that purpose.

The matter of police jurisdiction would soon become important, but for the moment the assembled detectives were awaiting the opening of the trunk. That could be accomplished easily by using the trunk key, which was visible on the key ring dangling from the ignition switch. But the keys and the rest of the car could not be touched until Agent Newquist had finished dusting the car for fingerprints.

Newquist completed the task by 10:20 a.m. He had discovered a smudged finger print of little evidentiary value on the wing window on the driver's side of the car. No prints were found on the keys to the ignition or trunk. Small mounds of dirt and sand from the rear wheel wells had fallen to the pavement, indicating the car had been driven on dirt and/or gravel roads. The fact that the mounds had not been flattened indicated the car had not been moved after it was parked. There were dirt spatters on the tires that had been caused by rain splashing. The last time it had rained in Des Moines was May 3, the day after Lillian disappeared. Thus Newquist concluded the car had been parked in the same location at the Des Moines airport for at least eight days, or quite possibly the entire time Lillian had been missing. In all probability, he concluded, the car had been driven on dirt and/or gravel roads for at least a portion of the way to Des Moines and parked at the airport, probably on the day Lillian disappeared, May 2.

With the evidence search concluded, Stump took the key ring from the ignition, located the trunk key, and opened the trunk. Inside the six officers observed a bloated and badly decomposed body. It was located on the left side, with the head in the extreme left rear corner and the feet to the front. It was apparent to the experienced detectives that the individual had been deceased for a number of days. It was also apparent they were dealing with a homicide.

Agent Newquist took photographs of the body and the car. Dr. Leo Luka, Chief Medical Examiner for Polk County, was called to the scene. He arrived at 10:40 a.m. Dr. Luka made a quick visual review of the body, taking notes in the process. He then ordered a wrecker from the Owen Crist Body shop to tow the Dodge, with the body still in the trunk, to Dunn's Funeral Home on Grand Avenue, just a few blocks east of the Howard Johnson Motel where Howard had spent the night of May 2.

The next step in the police process was to have someone, normally the next of kin, identify the body. That would take place at Dunn's, as would the formal autopsy that Dr. Luka would perform later. In the meantime, Sheriff Peterson had been told of the discovery of the body, which officers assumed was Lillian Randolph because the clothing on the corpse matched what Wendy and Vicki had reported she was probably wearing after a search of her closet for missing clothes. The sheriff was asked to bring Howard to Dunn's for the official identification. Lester contacted Howard in Carroll, Iowa, fifty miles to the northwest of Guthrie Center and in the opposite direction of Des Moines, where he was on business. Lester told Howard of the discovery and that, as the legal husband, it would be his responsibility to make the formal identification.

The law enforcement officers particularly wanted Howard to make the identification because he was already a prime suspect. They realized that the traumatic experience of viewing a victim's body sometimes jars suspects into a confession or statements that implicate them in the crime. They were hoping a grief-stricken Howard Randolph might reveal his culpability.

Howard told Sheriff Peterson he would go to Dunn's Funeral Home directly, a two-hour drive from Carroll. Lester gave him the address, 2121 Grand Avenue, and told Howard he would be waiting for him there. The sheriff then went to Dunn's to confer with BCI agents and Des Moines detectives.

While awaiting Howard's arrival the assembled law officers were wondering aloud what his reaction might be and under whose jurisdiction the case would fall. The presumed kidnapping had taken place in Guthrie County, where the victim was a resident and the car was registered. That would be Sheriff Peterson's jurisdiction. But the automobile and body were found in Des Moines, and that would fall under the jurisdiction of the Des Moines Police Department. The DMPD was a large and well-trained force that typically handled all criminal matters within the city limits. The DMPD did not usually rely upon the Iowa Bureau of Criminal Investigation for assistance, as was common among county sheriffs and smaller police departments around the state.

Sheriff Peterson and BCI Agent Stump were already investigating the case because Lillian had disappeared from her home in Guthrie County, and Lester had asked for the assistance of the BCI. No one knew where the actual homicide had taken place. The DMPD was not looking for additional casework and as Detective Steiner, now retired, recollects, "We were tickled to death to give it (jurisdiction) to them." And thus the jurisdictional responsibility for the case fell to Sheriff Peterson.

Law enforcement agencies typically cooperate with each other. There was no exception in this case. The DMPD offered considerable investigative assistance, but not full responsibility. Sheriff Peterson, who had no previous experience with a homicide case, was happy to turn over the investigative leadership to the more experienced BCI staff. Thus a team of BCI agents was assembled for that purpose. It included: Warren Stump, Daniel L. Mayer, Wayne L. Sheston, Robert Voss, and Robert Blair.

Homicides in the lightly populated, rural, and generally law-abiding State of Iowa were not numerous. The BCI gave the matter its full attention.

Robert Blair joined Warren Stump, Ray Steiner, and Russell Lewis at Dunn's at 1:00 p.m. They discussed the case among themselves while awaiting the arrivals of Sheriff Peterson and Howard Randolph. Steiner recalls that Blair told him "his first thought was that Howard Randolph was responsible." Steiner agreed, saying he also thought Howard was "a good suspect." Lester Peterson joined the assembled officers at 2:00, and Howard Randolph arrived at Dunn's an hour later.

Howard was met by Sheriff Peterson and then accompanied by a number of officials to the rear garage of Dunn's, where the blue Dodge was parked with the body still in the trunk. Lester was at the side of Howard. He took him by the arm and said, "You will have to identify her." Warren Stump, who was on Howard's other side, tried to prepare him for what was about to take place by saying, "It will be an awful sight."

The trunk lid of Lillian's car was raised and Howard was asked if he could identify the body. At first he said he could not make an identification. Stump then asked if Howard could identify a ring worn by the victim.

"Yeah, I think that's the ring I bought her," Howard casually responded.

Howard's cavalier demeanor shocked the officers. They never forgot it. Lester Peterson recalls, "It was not normal at all. He was like a person looking at a dead animal. It didn't bother him a damned bit." Ray Steiner remembers: "He showed no emotion, no nothing." The notes of the now deceased Russell Lewis indicate much the same: "He did not show any emotion whatsoever in viewing it (the corpse)." Warren Stump later described Howard's behavior at the time as "not normal" and said he was "like stone."

After the identification process and a few minutes of informal discussion with Howard, he was taken to the BCI headquarters on the east side of the Des Moines River, near the state capitol building and a mile or so east of Dunn's. Present with Howard were Warren Stump from the BCI, and Detectives Steiner and Lewis from the DMPD. The intent of the officers was a general questioning of Howard.

Experienced police interrogators recognize that the initial opportunity to talk to a suspect is all-important. It sets the stage for all that follows and may determine the ultimate success of the investigation. It is not necessary to close the case immediately. But it is necessary that nothing take place that reduces the likelihood of a later successful conclusion.

The questions at a preliminary session are typically of a general nature. More specific questions can follow after the investigation has moved further along. The first interview is a good time to note responses to larger questions so that consistencies can be verified as the investigation progresses. In this instance, a seemingly innocuous question like, "Have you been to the Des Moines airport lately?" at a time when Howard had not been told where the body was found, might evoke an incriminating response or what later might be learned was a lie. That, in turn, would reduce the suspect's credibility, an important factor in establishing the tone of the investigation and accompanying interviews.

Stump took charge of the questioning. Howard was asked standard questions: "When was the last time you saw her?" Do you know anyone who might want to harm her?" "Do you know what was the cause of death?"

At first Howard was smoothly responsive. So much so that Detective Steiner, who did not participate in the questioning, thought that Howard acted as though he had already anticipated questions and practiced his responses and demeanor. Perhaps, Steiner thought, Howard had already received advice from an attorney.

After fifteen minutes Howard announced that "he had heard he had been implicated and felt that if he did any (more) talking he would take chances of himself being misinterpreted." He also said that he was "too traumatized" to continue. The officers understood the cagey nature of Howard's first comment—Steiner thought it was another indication that Howard had already been counseled by an attorney—but were totally disbelieving of the second. Howard had shown none of the grief-stricken emotions that were normal in such situations. Even if a suspect hated the victim, the sight and odor of a badly decomposed body would horrify most anyone. Apparently Howard was not most anyone. He had appeared emotionless.

Howard asked Stump if he could wait two or three days before continuing the questioning. Stump, believing nothing further could be gained at that time, granted Howard's request. Detective Steiner was of another opinion, but not in charge. He recalls, "I don't know why he let him get away with that. I would have been on him like a fly on crap."

The interview with Howard concluded at 3:35 p.m. Stump took Howard back to Dunn's Funeral Home where his car was parked. A plain-clothes detective in an unmarked car was waiting nearby. When Howard left Dunn's in his 1965 Buick, Iowa license number 39-2824, the detective followed him to see where he might go or if he might make a telephone call. Howard went west out of Des Moines on a normal route towards Guthrie Center. The detective quit tailing Howard when they reached the Des Moines city limits.

When Howard arrived in Panora he stopped at Beidelman's Funeral Home, adjacent to Highway 64 on the route that goes through Panora and leads to Guthrie Center. Howard inquired about caskets and said that there would soon be a funeral for his deceased wife. From there he went to his office in Guthrie Center.

While Howard was driving back to Guthrie Center via Beidelman's Funeral Home in Panora, two employees of Dunn's, Merlin Brubaker and Leslie Lee, were removing the remains of the victim from the trunk of her car. In the process Brubaker found a .25 caliber cartridge and gave it to Andrew Newquist, the BCI evidence expert who was observing the transfer.

The preliminary report made that afternoon at Dunn's by Dr. Luka indicated that the death of Lillian had resulted from "multiple knife wounds observed in the left breast area measuring approximately three-eighths of an inch in length." He also observed a superficial knife wound in the back. Dr. Luka returned to Dunn's in the evening to perform the formal autopsy. In the meantime, with the permission of Agent Newquist, Dr. Luka turned over several items of evidence to Sheriff Peterson: a watch, a ring, clothing, and the floor mat from the trunk. Because of the strong odor of the items, Lester placed them in a barrel for the return trip to Guthrie Center.

When Lester arrived home he immediately took the items of evidence to his barn, located to the east of his house. He recalls that he "did not dare take the barrel anywhere near the house because the odor was so strong it went right through the barrel." Lester chose the scoop board of a wagon to investigate the evidence at hand. In so doing he discovered a .25 caliber slug in the floor mat. The mat was saturated with body fluids. When Lester unrolled it to allow it to dry, the slug fell to the scoop board. Lester notified the BCI of his recovery of the slug and delivered the valuable piece of evidence to Agent Andrew Newquist at his office in Des Moines. Newquist then made the slug available for the official autopsy.

*****

It had been a long and painful wait for Lillian's family. Wendy and Vicki did not attend school during the first week of their mother's disappearance, but then resumed classes on May 10. Curious friends and classmates swamped them with questions. They did not know what to say. They did not have any answers. The next day there was conclusive and distressful news.

After Lillian's body had been formally identified, Sheriff Peterson called his office with the news. Ann Shackelford was notified immediately. Harry had been toiling in the field in his work overalls when he was called to the house by his wife and given the dreaded news. He then went to the home of his mother, Mildred Shackelford, informed her of the awful outcome and asked if she would accompany him to the high school to pick up Wendy and Vicki.

When Wendy saw Harry approaching in the school hallway in his work clothes, she knew he had bad news. He was so seething with anger that he was nearly speechless. Brusquely he blurted, "Get your things and come with me."

Harry said nothing further to Wendy and Vicki until they reached the driveway to the Shackelford house. Harry was still battling his anger. He pointedly told the girls of the death of their mother. Mildred leaned forward from the backseat and attempted to console the teenagers by grasping their shoulders. Wendy vividly recalls her feelings at that moment: "Now no one knows me anymore. I am alone—orphaned."

Howard Randolph arrived two hours later at the Shackelford residence and told Lillian's three daughters they should accompany him to Beidelman's Funeral Home in Panora to choose a casket for their mother. Howard was insistent that all three make the trip. The girls were numb with grief. They accompanied Howard to Panora and did the necessary.

On the return trip to Guthrie Center, Howard told the girls he wanted Lillian buried in Guthrie Center, and not Duluth. Lillian had told many people, including her daughters, that "if anything happens to me" she wanted to be buried in her native Duluth. Howard also knew of her wishes, but said it was his right to make the decision. Howard indicated, however, that he was willing to make a trade. The first condition of his proposed deal was that for the next three days Ann, Wendy, and Vicki were to live with him at the Randolph house and, in his words, "be a family." Howard's second condition was that if he allowed the burial to take place in Duluth, the girls would have to ride with him on the eight-hour trip from Guthrie Center.

Lillian's daughters were too stunned with grief and the experience of choosing a casket for their mother to respond to Howard's incredible proposition. It must have been an absolute fantasy on his part to think his proposal would be accepted. There was still a restraining order in effect against Howard entering his house. Ann had three small children to care for, including a baby. The discomfort of Wendy and Vicki in his presence during visitations must have been obvious, although he typically described such behavior as "moodiness." The timing and insensitivity of Howard's proposition added to the vacant feelings of his passengers. They said nothing.

That evening, at about seven o'clock, Howard went to Ann and Harry's house. He had called earlier and said he wanted to come by. They did not want to see him, but limp with sorrow, they did not actively resist his request.

Howard had a message for Harry, Ann, Wendy, and Vicki. He told them "to put all suspicions out of their minds." They did not react. They were too shocked to sort out much of anything, but they were insistent that their mother's request to be buried in Duluth be honored. Howard voiced no further objections. Later, however, he refused to pay for Lillian's burial plot, perhaps by way of retaliation. That was Howard's nature. If he did not get his way, he did not pay.

Howard's wish for living together for a few days "as a family" and riding together to Duluth did not materialize. The burial did take place in Duluth. Lillian's family would have that one small element of satisfaction in otherwise sorrowful circumstances.

At the time Howard was telling Lillian's assembled family members at the Shackelford house "to put all suspicions out of your minds," Dr. Leo Luka, the Chief Medical Examiner for Polk County, was performing a formal autopsy on Lillian's body at Dunn's Funeral Home in Des Moines. Upon completion of the autopsy, Dr. Luka noted his findings: "Death due to multiple stab wounds in the anterior chest wall which perforated the lung and caused exsanguination bilaterally. 12 stab wounds in the area of the left breast and one stab wound at the level of the 8th dorsal vertebra, ½ inch to the left of the midline. This latter was a superficial wound and the weapon struck the spine. There was no entrance into the body cavity from the wound to the back."

Dr. Luka determined Lillian had been deceased from seven to nine days, the latter number being precisely the period of time she had been missing. No undigested food was found in her stomach, indicating she had not eaten lunch at the time she was murdered. Because a .25 caliber cartridge had been found with the body, x-rays were taken of the skull, chest, and abdomen. No bone fractures or metal objects were found in those areas. Dr. Luka reported: "The possibility that the slug passed through the body without striking a bone was eliminated at the autopsy." The .25 caliber slug discovered by Sheriff Peterson had "no flattening," leading Dr. Luka to conclude that it had not struck a bone.

*****

On the eve of Lillian's funeral three local law enforcement officers spent the night in the Randolph house, thinking perhaps the villain(s) would return to the scene of the crime. John Novy of the Iowa Highway Patrol, Marlow Ray, the local game warden, and Ed Randall, a part-time local policeman, passed the night sitting in the dark of the sunken living room. They were armed but, as it turned out, for no good reason. It was a quiet and uneventful evening at the Randolph house.

An overflow crowd of 200 people attended the funeral for Lillian Randolph at the Immanuel Lutheran Church in Guthrie Center on Thursday,

May 13. The Reverend Donald Lutz, the pastor of the church and a friend of Lillian, officiated at the services and lauded her for being "a faithful contributor to her congregation." Howard Randolph entered the church a short time before the services began and took a seat at the back. A few minutes later he moved to the front pew reserved for family members and sat beside Ann.

The next day family members and friends made a long and sad trip to Duluth for the burial in Lillian's hometown. Howard drove to Duluth in his 1965 Buick, accompanied by two friends, Wayne and Iris Webber. Howard and the Webbers stood at the back of the crowd at the burial. A BCI agent, whose face was unknown to Howard, also attended the services. He was present to observe the behavior and emotions of the chief suspect. As others had observed in previous instances, Howard showed little emotion at the services.

There was a luncheon and gathering of family and friends afterwards at the home of Lillian's sister, Helen Erickson. Lillian's sister, Amy, had planned to invite Howard. But he told the Webbers that he "did not feel welcome," and had departed with them before Amy could extend an invitation.

In Des Moines agents of the Iowa Bureau of Investigation were continuing their investigation into the abduction and murder of Lillian Randolph. Howard Randolph was their primary suspect. They also had some ideas concerning the identity of the two hired killers.

Chapter VII

The Investigation

"Howard didn't care if he was seen with those killers."

John Quinn, Special Agent

The investigation into the disappearance of Lillian Randolph had been underway for over a week when her body was found in her Dodge Coronet at the Des Moines airport. Initially Sheriff Peterson stated to the press that he was "not unduly concerned" and "expected the case would resolve itself with her return." As a precautionary measure the sheriff had broadcast a lookout bulletin to police officers in the area on the Sunday evening of her disappearance to request that they look for Lillian and her medium blue Dodge Coronet. When she still did not return by the following day, May 3, Lester notified the Iowa Bureau of Criminal Investigation in Des Moines that Lillian was missing and had perhaps been kidnapped. The BCI sent a special agent, Warren Stump, to Guthrie Center the next day to head the investigation.

The first questions Agent Stump asked Sheriff Peterson when he arrived in Guthrie Center on May 4 were the standard: (1) What happened? (2) What evidence do you have? (3) Who would have reason to harm her?

Lester's response to Stump's first question was easy. Lillian had disappeared and no one had any idea where she was. That was why he asked for assistance from the BCI. Lester then gave further details to Stump that he had acquired from Lillian's family and friends. In answer to Stump's second question, Lester told the BCI agent that he had no evidence. In contrast to the lack of information for Stump's first two questions, however, Lester had an immediate response to the question concerning those with a motive for harming Lillian. Her estranged husband, Howard Randolph, had such motives and was, in Lester's view, "a mean man." What Lester related to Agent Stump at that time in general terms, and what further investigation revealed in depth, was that Howard had strong motives for wanting Lillian removed from his life. Stump then asked to see the house. He and Lester looked about the Randolph residence, but found nothing suspicious. Later, BCI technicians inspected the house more thoroughly for evidence. Little of value was found.

The discovery of Lillian's body and the accumulating information from witnesses about the two swarthy strangers who had been in Guthrie Center and Stuart over the weekend she disappeared made it possible to assemble a plausible scenario of what had occurred. The hit men had been in town to "case" the area and make plans to abduct and murder Lillian Randolph. They had been casual and brazen in their approach, making no effort to conceal their presence. They had spent time in Stuart apparently to check out the back road route from the Randolph house to the Des Moines airport. They had been informed obviously by someone knowledgeable of Lillian's Sunday routine that she would attend church in the morning and then return home shortly before noon. The bench on the fourth tee of the golf course provided a perfect observation post from which they could monitor activities at the Randolph house. Before seating themselves on the bench they had driven around the course and through the parking lot, apparently observing the layout and the people present. They then parked their car on the gravel road near the fourth tee, walked to the bench, and waited until they saw Lillian, Wendy, and Vicki return from church and enter the house. They waited a little longer until Howard had picked up the two girls in his car and driven south, away from them and towards Ann and Harry Shackelford's farm residence.

After Lillian was left alone, the two presumed killers left their seat on the bench, walked across the golf course rough to the gravel road where their car was parked, drove to the Randolph house, and parked the white Cadillac in the driveway. Because there was no evidence of a struggle at the house, it seemed apparent that Lillian was abducted by some kind of ruse. Perhaps the two men asked for directions, she stepped out of the house to point out a location, and was quickly overpowered. Or perhaps the two strangers told her they worked for Howard, there had been an accident at the Shackelford farm, and she should accompany them. It was impossible to tell how she was lured from the house, but it was clear she left without a struggle.

It was also obvious that Lillian had left in a hurry. A coffee pot was on the stove and the burner was on "low." A half-full coffee cup was left on the table. Lillian's white purse, with eleven dollars inside, was found under the driver's seat of her car. Was she so tricked by the two strangers that she took her purse and accompanied them voluntarily? Or had they taken her purse along with her auto to give the impression that she was voluntarily away from the house, giving them more time to escape? Or had she left her purse in the car after church services with the expectation that she would soon be returning? The latter seemed unlikely since Lillian had not driven home from church and Wendy remembered seeing her mother place the white purse on a TV tray in the kitchen.

Leaving the car with the doors unlocked, the keys in the ignition, and a purse under the front seat would serve several purposes for the hit men. They certainly did not want the keys in their possession because that would connect them with Lillian's auto. Leaving the car unlocked with the keys visible could be an enticement to a thief who would then alter the condition of the car with his own fingerprints and other contaminants, creating his own crime scene and tainting the original evidence.

After the abduction of Lillian, by whatever means, one of the hit men apparently drove her car and her toward the Des Moines airport by the back road route to Stuart, where they had been seen the previous day by several witnesses. A plausible explanation for their presence in Stuart, as reinforced by ensuing events, was to plot their escape route for the day of the crime. None of the witnesses at the golf course saw Lillian's car go north to Highway 64, suggesting that the car was driven in the opposite direction toward Stuart. Roger Wickland did see the white Cadillac go north past the golf course to the highway and turn east towards Panora. The two killers apparently rendezvoused somewhere between Stuart and the Des Moines airport and stabbed Lillian to death.

It was a tragic and sorrowful conclusion to what had been unknown to investigators during the nine days that Lillian was missing. They now knew for certain that a crime had been committed and had a general idea of what had occurred. Law enforcement officers knew they were looking for at least three suspects, quite possibly four. In that number was a person who had employed the two hit men, the two swarthy strangers who had most likely murdered Lillian, and possibly an intermediary between the hit men and their employer. There was also the white Cadillac to be located which might offer clues to the identity of its two passengers. There were numerous details to be checked out by the many law enforcement officials investigating the case.

Investigators were not surprised that there were two hit men. Contrary to Hollywood's portrayal of such depraved activities being the act of a single individual, it is a common practice. Two men can physically overpower a victim much more quickly than one. With two, one can act as a lookout if need be. Or one can engage the victim in a friendly and distracting manner while the other makes the initial attack. Or two can lift and manage a lifeless body quickly and easily. Or one can drive the victim's automobile away from the scene of the crime while the other drives the vehicle of the hit men. If both the victim and her car are missing, the logical explanation is that she went somewhere in her car. Indeed, that was precisely what occurred when Lillian disappeared. In the meantime the killers have time, in this instance days, to escape.

The disadvantage to hit men who work in pairs is that two rather than one know about the crime and the participants involved. For the purposes of the police, the more people who know about a crime the more likely someone will "talk." Talking leads to arrests and convictions. Criminals frequently "rat" or "snitch," they have their own vocabulary for such behavior, to gain an advantage for themselves, such as a lighter prison sentence or immunity from prosecution. In the instance of the murder of the Clutter family near Garden City, Kansas, a case that was the subject of Truman Capote's famous book, *In Cold Blood*, detectives were baffled until an inmate at the Kansas State Penitentiary provided a lead. The two suspects, Perry Smith and Richard Hickok, were apprehended and interrogated separately. Each blamed the other for the crime, providing important details in the process. Smith and Hickok were subsequently tried, convicted, and executed.

Leaving Lillian's car at the Des Moines airport was a common hit man strategy. It could mean the killers took a plane out of Des Moines. But it could also mean that they had intended to leave that impression and departed in the white Cadillac. An abandoned car in an airport parking lot, where large numbers of autos are left for long periods, is not likely to arouse suspicion, at least for some time. Leaving Lillian's car near the front entrance to the airport, however, was an obvious, easily located position. That suggested it was left where it could be quickly located by a third party, such as someone who wanted to verify its presence in a setting where a person walking among parked cars would not be out of the ordinary.

Detective Ray Steiner of the Des Moines Police Department undertook the long and arduous task of accounting for the hundreds of airline passengers who had flown out of Des Moines on the days following Lillian's disappearance by patiently examining dozens of airline passenger manifests. It turned out to be a fruitless search. Meanwhile, Warren Stump was checking information on the white Cadillac. The automobile had disappeared at the same time as Lillian. Stump searched the automobile registration records for Polk County and the surrounding area, but discovered nothing useful. He also went through the guest registrations of the Midway Motel in Guthrie Center and asked the desk clerks who had been on duty the weekend of May 1-2 if two swarthy men had spent the night there or if they had observed anything unusual. The Midway Motel is located on the eastern edge of Guthrie Center with the Randolph house within easy view. It would have made a good command post for the killers. Unfortunately, Stump discovered no good leads at the Midway. A visit to Stuart and similar discussions with desk clerks and employees of the Stuart Motel, the Maplecrest Motel, and Hotel Stuart also produced no useful information.

Information comes to investigators from two sources. Either they discover it by their own efforts, such as Steiner checking airport passenger manifests and Stump going through automobile registrations and motel records, or it is volunteered to them by private sources. The latter possibility gave officials an early boost in their investigation when Louis A. "Tony" Weibel and Henry L. "Hank" Buche came forth with valuable information.

*****

Louis A. Weibel drove the short distance from his Internal Revenue Service office to his comfortable home in the middle-class neighborhood on Idlewood Street in Sioux City. It was late afternoon, almost six o'clock, when Tony pulled into his driveway. The date was May 11, 1965.

Tony Weibel had received his appointment to the IRS when it was still called a "Bureau," rather than the more euphemistic "Service" of later years. World War II was on and the city where Tony would be working was given a measure of fame with the popular song of the time, "Sioux City Sue." Tony's initial title had been "Deputy Collector," and his primary responsibility was collecting taxes, the least glamorous work in the IRS. That function involves face-to-face contact with delinquent taxpayers. Such confrontations, seldom pleasant, run the full range of human relations, from grumbling acceptance to occasional physical violence. Tony, a mild-mannered individual of short stature and medium build, was never comfortable with the confrontational role of a Deputy Collector. Thus he was delighted when he was reassigned to the audit function and became an "agent" rather than a "collector." Henceforth, he would do the largely office function of assessing taxes, rather than having the more aggressive role of converting numbers on audit forms into greenbacks in the United States Treasury.

Tony had spent his entire IRS career in Sioux City. By 1965 he had advanced to the position of supervisor for the audit division for Western Iowa. He personally handled the most difficult audit cases, and that is how he became acquainted with Howard Randolph. Howard's produce empire included businesses in Guthrie Center, Carroll, Sac City, Boone, and Harlan that were within Tony's region of responsibility.

Because the primary function of the IRS is to produce revenue for the federal government, the agency pays special attention to those cases where tax liabilities are particularly high, i.e. wealthy taxpayers. Howard Randolph was a case in point. His annual income was in the highest category of taxpayers for whom Tony Weibel was responsible. Moreover, Howard's varied business of eggs, butter, poultry, cattle, and real estate made Howard's income tax return a volume of great complexity. Indeed, Howard's taxes were so complex that he retained a tax attorney in Des Moines, Walter Brown, for legal assistance. However, Howard did not fully entrust his tax matters to Brown. As with all his financial affairs, he did not delegate responsibility quickly or in depth. Howard saw Brown's job as advising him on minimizing his tax liabilities. Howard handled face-to-face negotiations himself, with Brown sometimes in attendance for advice. All lines on tax matters started with Howard. Tony Weibel and Howard Randolph had spent a lot of time together on tax audits. Tony knew Howard well.

A springtime tax session with Howard Randolph was an annual event for Tony Weibel. The spring of 1965 was no exception. Tony and Howard had played "phone tag" during the week of May 3-7 trying to find a mutually convenient time for the annual review of Howard's federal tax liabilities. The difference in the latest round was Howard's strange message on the previous Friday when he told Tony over the phone that his "wife had died last Sunday and it appears murder might be involved." Howard had asked Tony at that time to postpone their next meeting for three weeks.

Internal Revenue agents are accustomed to requests by taxpayers for delays in facing the moment of truth, but Howard's excuse was the most bizarre that Tony had ever heard. Indeed Howard's matter-of-fact tone had led Tony to believe that he was not really serious. A request for a delay in an audit session was not unusual and not that important to Tony, although taxpayers, not knowing that, invented all sorts of excuses to delay the inevitable. The requested delay did not trouble Tony. But Howard's strange explanation lodged in Tony's mind. He had carefully noted Howard's words on the IRS "Memorandum of Conversation" form, and inserted it into his "Randolph" file. It was Tony Weibel's habit to read the Des Moines *Tribune* before dinner. On this unusually warm day in Sioux City, Tony decided to combine reading the *Tribune* with the fresh air of spring. He settled into a lawn chair on his porch and unfolded the *Tribune*.

The headline of the *Tribune* was unusually large and read: "Find Woman's Body in Car." Beneath that startling announcement was the sub-headline: "Guthrie Center Farm Resident, Missing Since May 2." Below the headlines was a large photo showing several men viewing the open trunk of a car. An airport terminal and control tower were visible in the immediate background.

Tony read the caption under the photo: "Law enforcement officials examine body identified as that of Mrs. Lillian Elizabeth Randolph, 57, in trunk of car where it was found Tuesday at Des Moines Municipal Airport. Body was locked in trunk of auto, a 1965 Dodge registered to Mrs.

Randolph. She had been reported missing from home near Guthrie Center since May 2."

Could this be the wife of Howard? Could this be the murder that Howard had casually mentioned to Tony just four days before? Tony began to read the accompanying article.

He did not have to read far to find the answer to his questions. The third paragraph read: "Mrs. Randolph was legally separated from her husband, Howard Randolph, a wealthy Guthrie Center poultry firm operator, authorities said. Randolph came to Des Moines and identified the body a few hours after it was found."

Tony Weibel was stunned. Any previous thoughts that Howard had invented the story of the death of his wife evaporated from his mind. Tony read on.

The *Tribune's* article, written by Fred Pettid, reported Sheriff Peterson as saying that after Lillian's disappearance he had "feared she had been kidnapped and was being held somewhere," or "had been slain." Puzzlement was added to Tony's state of shock. Howard had told him that his wife had "died last Sunday," and that "it appeared that murder might be involved." But as Tony read the article it was clear that Sheriff Peterson and the BCI did not know of Lillian's whereabouts and physical state in the days that followed her disappearance, and only learned that she had been murdered on that Tuesday morning, May 11. How, Tony wondered, could Howard have known of his wife's death and murder before the police?

Auditing tax returns is a form of puzzle that Internal Revenue agents must resolve. And although IRS agents do not carry weapons, they are nonetheless law enforcement officers who frequently coordinate their efforts with those of the police. The answer to this particular puzzle and the question that was ravaging Tony's mind was horrifyingly simple. If Howard Randolph knew of his wife's death before the police and it was a homicide, then he must have been somehow involved in the murder!

Tony's job as an IRS agent was to assess taxes, and not to become involved in the business practices or personal behavior of taxpayers, unless there was a clear-cut case of fraud. In that infrequent event, he turned the case over to the "Special Investigations" section of the IRS District Office in Des Moines. Howard's business practices, even if not fraudulent according to the IRS Code, did indicate to Tony an aggressive and harsh nature. Businesses, which were partnerships one year, became the full property of Howard the next, and often with no payment to the former partner. Like a lawyer or accountant, a tax auditor learns much of a person's nature and character. Taxes tell stories. Howard's tax returns revealed the aggressive, perhaps ruthless, nature of his business operations. But murder?

Tony Weibel was a conscientious and careful man who was known among colleagues for his meticulous manner, including the maintenance of careful and detailed files. He was also a cautious, somewhat timid man, who did not easily jump to conclusions, and was not quick to involve himself in controversy. Tony knew it was his duty to report what he knew of the case to police, but first he wanted to be sure that his memory was absolutely accurate. He returned to his office to review his notes.

Tony opened the "Randolph" file and quickly turned to the "Memorandum of Conversation" for the preceding Friday, May 7. He noted that he had "called Randolph back about 8:15 or 8:20 a.m." His memo continued: "He informed me that his wife had died last Sunday (May 2) and it appeared that murder might be involved." Tony's memory was correct. He immediately called the Sioux City police and advised them of what he knew of the case. The Sioux City police passed the information along to the State Bureau of Investigation in Des Moines.

While Tony Weibel was contacting the police in Sioux City, 150 miles to the southeast in Slater, Iowa, Henry L. "Hank" Buche was also reading the Des Moines *Tribune*. He was equally shaken by the headlines and story about finding the body of Lillian at the Des Moines airport. He had known Howard Randolph for many years. And he had seen Howard at the Des Moines airport the day Lillian disappeared!

Hank had been associated with the Slater Creamery and Egg Processing Plant for twenty-nine years, the last twenty-three as the plant manager. He was in the same business as Howard Randolph and their paths had crossed many times. Although the Buche operation, a cooperative marketing business with stations in Slater, Glidden, Avoca, Logan, and Gowrie, was a competitor to Howard's business, there was a large market for their products. Howard and Hank, although only acquainted through their business operations, knew each other well and were on a first-name basis. Hank, a highly respected and popular man in his community, knew of Howard's questionable business reputation, but he had had only marginal business dealings with him.

Hank knew the site well that appeared in the photo on the front page of the *Tribune*. He had been a visitor to the Des Moines airport many times over the years. When his two sons, Henry Dean and Dale, were small boys, Hank and Hazel Buche often traveled the thirty-minute distance from Slater to the airport, where they watched airplanes land and take-off, and ate in the second-story restaurant which overlooked the runway.

Hank Buche loved airplanes and flying. One of the Buche family possessions was a picture of Hank proudly seated in a DC-3 during a 1948 business trip. The business operations of his creamery and egg processing plant were channeled through the Loblaw Stores in Buffalo, New York, necessitating occasional trips by Hank to that city. He also met business associates from Buffalo when they flew into Des Moines and treated them to dinner at the airport restaurant.

As the years passed and the Buche boys became men, Henry Dean, now also known as "Hank," became a pilot in the Iowa Air National Guard. From the airport restaurant where the Buche family had enjoyed many meals, Hank Sr. could watch his son fly F-86s from the Air National Guard base at the far end of the Des Moines runway that was shared with commercial airliners. Hank Sr. was very proud, perhaps envious, of his son's opportunity to be a jet pilot.

As Hank Buche Sr. looked at the headlines of the *Tribune,* the "Missing Since May 2" portion caught his attention. He and his wife, Hazel, had been at the airport late that afternoon. He read on. "Mrs. Randolph was legally separated from her husband, Howard Randolph," the article noted.

Hank had seen Howard at the Des Moines airport that Sunday afternoon. Indeed, they had exchanged salutations as Howard walked south of the United Airlines counter. An exchange of greetings, or any kind of verbal communication with Hank Buche was an experience. A basso profundo voice was his trademark and a source of amusement to his family and friends who compared him to Everett Dirksen, the Illinois Senator of the time who was also known for his deep voice and deliberate speech pattern. For as long as Hank had known Howard he had never seen him wearing anything but a suit. That fact lodged in Hank's memory.

Sunday night was not a popular time to fly out of Des Moines, a small airport by city standards with a limited number of airlines—principally United, Braniff, and Ozark—and a limited number of flights. It seemed to Hank Buche a strange time for Howard to be there, by himself, and not wearing a suit.

When Hank had completed the article in the *Tribune* he had learned that: (1) Lillian Randolph had been abducted from her home in Guthrie Center on May 2 in the early afternoon, (2) her car had been found at the Des Moines airport with her body in the trunk on May 11, and (3) that in all likelihood the car had been parked there throughout the time she had been missing. That would mean that at the very time Howard and Hank were exchanging greetings inside the airport terminal, Lillian's car with her body in it was parked only fifty yards north of the front door. Was it a mere coincidence that Howard was in the airport terminal within hours after his wife's car was parked there? Hank decided that that was not his decision to make. He called the Story County Sheriff's office in Nevada, Iowa, and passed along his information. A report was then relayed quickly to the Iowa Bureau of Criminal Investigation.

The new information received in BCI headquarters in Des Moines from Tony Weibel and Hank Buche reinforced the growing case against Howard Randolph as a prime suspect. Sheriff Peterson, because he considered Howard "a mean man" that "did not do right by Lillian," suspected from the beginning that he might be involved in the abduction and murder of his estranged wife. BCI investigators quickly reached the same conclusion. While BCI and Des Moines law enforcement officers awaited the arrival of Howard at Dunn's Funeral Home to identify Lillian's body on the afternoon of May 11, they were already discussing the likelihood that Howard was involved. Bob Blair, the Deputy Director of the BCI, told his subordinate, Warren Stump, and Ray Steiner and Russell Lewis, the two Des Moines detectives who were present, that he thought Howard was "responsible." All agreed that Howard was "a good suspect." Sheriff Peterson also shared that view. Nothing happened during the interview with Howard following the formal identification of Lillian's body to change any of the law enforcement officers' minds. They were convinced that they had been talking to a guilty man.

*****

Motives are not evidence. They simply point investigators in a murder case toward a person who may have a reason to harm another. Thus the determination of motives is a primary step in any criminal investigation, something that is deeply understood and taken for granted by detectives.

The only person known to have motives for murdering Lillian Randolph was her estranged husband, Howard. He had expressed to a number of people with revealing candor his unhappiness with Lillian and the circumstances in which she had placed him. When investigating officials delved into Howard's potential motives they discovered a lengthy list.

Howard had a special pride in the house that he had built and occupied prior to his marriage to Lillian Chalman. It was the nicest house in the area, and he took great satisfaction in the admiration that it brought. Lillian, with a restraining order, had forced Howard out of a house to which he held title, while simultaneously petitioning for an order of separate maintenance which gave her the right to live in the house with her minor children. The deed to the house was of little value to Howard when he could neither live in it nor sell it. Howard made no secret of his anger over being banished from his house. He had even told one business associate that he would "get the house back or else."

Being forced from his home had a heavy impact on one of Howard's greatest satisfactions, spending time with his stepdaughters, Wendy and Vicki. Lillian had gained full custody of her two youngest children.

Howard then had to negotiate with Lillian over visitation privileges with the girls. As they had grown older and more wary of his nature, and especially his treatment of their mother, they became more resistant to spending time with him. When there were difficulties over visitation he blamed Lillian rather than the girls. In short, Lil had become in his eyes, an impediment to one of his greatest joys, being the father of Wendy and Vicki.

Howard was also unhappy about being required to pay Lillian $800 per month as part of the decree for separate maintenance. He had groused to Ann Shackelford and others about having to pay the monthly stipend. He said that the money was going to Lillian's attorneys and her own excesses, and not truly to support Wendy and Vicki.

One of Lil's excesses, in Howard's view, was the purchase of a new Dodge Coronet. Although Lillian had used the inheritance she had received from her father's estate to purchase the modest vehicle, Howard was "outraged," as several people who were around him at the time put it. He had earlier told a business associate that he "wouldn't buy Lillian a damned car to run back and forth to town." By making her dependent upon him for transportation he had been able to hold her in isolation and domination. Her new car and her accompanying sense of freedom and independence aggravated Howard, a feeling that was exacerbated by the knowledge that his monthly check to her was contributing to her new persona.

Howard saw Lillian and her family as ungrateful. He had an expectation, based on considerable experience to be sure, of people fawning over him and his money. What he seemed to want in return was their gratitude, their admiration. When he did not receive that satisfaction, he had a history of retaliation. Over the years he had fired many people when they did not comply with his wishes, including his brother-in-law and his stepson. A number of people, including several who considered themselves friends of Howard, believed that he gained a special satisfaction in having power over others and seeing them suffer when they did not fulfill his expectations.

Howard Randolph liked to surround himself with people who praised him, fawned over him, expressed their gratitude to him, and never challenged or threatened him. Those with blind allegiance to Howard, who willingly submitted to his control, were rewarded with jobs and other forms of occasional gifts and financial assistance. Howard preyed upon those who were weak and vulnerable, but backed away from those of stronger disposition, resorting to other means to reach his goals with the more strong-willed. He was widely regarded as a coward who used his money and the legal system to force his way with those who would not accede to his domination.

Howard had apparently initially perceived Lillian as a compliant personality who would surely be grateful and adoring over his act of generosity in supplying a home for her and her children. He had tested her subservience by such acts as "playing up" to other women while she watched, coming home with lipstick fully visible on his shirt collar, stroking Vicki's leg in her presence, and forcing Vicki to sleep with him when Lillian had refused to do so.

In the earlier years of their marriage Howard had succeeded in reducing Lillian to a state of submissiveness. Although unofficially separated several times, she had always come back to Howard, each time with an apparent hope that her husband had changed. As she continually returned to Howard it was easy for him to assume that that would always be the case, and that she did not have enough fortitude to make the ultimate break. Thus, it must have been a shock to him when Lillian, after six years of disappointment and despair, took legal actions against him. One of Howard's closest friends, Peggy Alston, recalled that when someone pushed on Howard, "he pushed back twice as hard."

It was apparent that Howard would not accept being kicked out of his house, paying $800 per month to Lil, and suffering the accompanying indignities without some kind of response. The expectation in Guthrie Center was that he would use his standard approach: a bevy of lawyers using every conceivable legal approach to win his way. At the very time of Lillian's death Howard was indeed using that approach in two cases before the Iowa Supreme Court, cases that he won later that summer.

Between the separate maintenance decree and the restraining order, Lillian had a position of advantage over Howard that few, if any, people had ever held. Howard's options for legal retaliation were limited. In effect, there had been a role reversal. Lillian now had considerable control over Howard, rather than vice versa. That was a new and unhappy circumstance for Howard. He had been forced to give up his home and pay Lillian a substantial monthly sum. If he tried to re-enter his house, Sheriff Peterson and his deputies could enforce the restraining order at Lil's instigation. If Howard refused to pay for the monthly support of Lillian and her minor children, his vast property holdings would be vulnerable, something he could not risk. Moreover, Lillian governed Howard's access to his "two little princesses," Wendy and Vicki.

Lillian controlled Howard's house, a sizeable amount of his money, visitation with Wendy and Vicki, and exhibited her new-found independence by driving about Guthrie Center in her new Dodge. The wife that Howard had dominated so thoroughly now had important controls over him. Power over others, an exhilarating and common experience for

Howard for many years, was now being used against him. He was trapped, stymied, controlled—and very angry.

Howard stood to gain a great deal if Lillian were no longer alive, as proved by the aftermath of her death. The home she was living in, and to which he held title, would be returned to him. For his purposes it could not be quickly enough. He even tried to regain possession of the house on the day of Lillian's funeral. He was denied entry by Deputy Sheriff Roger Brown, who told him that the restraining order was still in effect. A few days later, however, Howard moved back into his house.

Howard's monthly payment of $800 to Lillian ceased at her death, an annual savings to him of $9,600. Des Moines Police Department detectives estimated that the cost of hiring two hit men at that time would be perhaps $10,000. Thus, looking at the circumstances as a cold business transaction, as Howard viewed almost everything, he could recoup his "investment" in one year.

With Lillian gone, she could no longer interfere, as Howard saw it, with his relationship with Wendy and Vicki. "His" daughters would then belong to him without the bickering and problems, as he saw it, that he had encountered in trying to arrange visitation through Lil. As it turned out, Howard did not gain custody of the two girls. But at the time of Lillian's death, he, as their legal father, anticipated that he would regain custody of them. When Hank and Peg Randolph sought legal custody of Wendy and Vicki, Howard fought for his fatherly rights in court, but lost. With Lillian gone, he could no longer blame her for the lack of an affectionate relationship with Wendy and Vicki. He then turned that blame towards A.B. Crouch, the girl's attorney. Howard sued Crouch for $4,000,000 for his "alienation of affections" of Wendy and Vicki.

Because Lillian did not have a will and Howard Randolph was her legal husband, he became the executor of her estate and the beneficiary of her assets. Indeed, Howard moved aggressively in that connection. Her Dodge had been impounded by the BCI as evidence and was in the custody of Sheriff Peterson. After being named as the executor for Lillian's estate, a standard outcome for a legal spouse, Howard then petitioned the District Court to have the car released to him. Judge S.E. Prall signed the release on July 26, 1965. Howard then had the trunk of the car steam-cleaned to remove the residual odor, and sold the 1965 Dodge Coronet, only six months old and with only 3,661 miles on the odometer, at an auto auction in Mason City, Iowa. Howard was back again in control, and had gotten rid of the despised automobile. He also had the sweet revenge of the proceeds of its sale in his pocket.

The motives for murdering Lillian and the ensuing advantages to Howard Randolph were clear to Special Agent Stump and Sheriff Peterson. But were there others who might also have motives for killing Lillian?

During the time of Lillian Randolph's disappearance Howard provided Stump and Peterson with the names of a number of people who might have an interest, in his words, of "detaining Lillian." Heading his list were her attorneys, A.B. Crouch and Paul Steward. (Apparently Howard was unaware that Steward had died prior to the abduction of Lillian, and could not have had anything to do with it.) Howard told the officers that Steward and Crouch "might be in it too deep" and that they "might have abducted her to keep her from returning to him." He went on to tell the disbelieving officers that Steward and Crouch were "using Lillian to get his money." In the process, he suggested, they might have done "illegal things that Lillian might divulge."

The accusation that Paul Steward, a man who had been fighting a losing battle with cancer, would use the last days of his life to arrange for the murder of Lillian was preposterous. Howard's lack of knowledge of Steward's fatal illness and death had trapped him into a totally implausible accusation.

A.B. Crouch's personal reputation was not sterling, but his legal repute was sufficient to be appointed later as an Iowa District Court judge in Des Moines. Moreover, it was Steward who had gained the separate maintenance decree for Lillian and had collected the attorney's fees connected thereto. (Note: Howard's notion that Lillian *wanted* to return to him was typical. He seemed to believe that others wanted to love him, but there was always someone else who kept it from happening. In this instance it was Steward and Crouch. With Wendy and Vicki it was first Lillian, and later, Crouch.) Since that time, and after Crouch took responsibility for Lillian's legal affairs after Steward became ill, there had been no further legal actions and, *ipso facto*, no basis for legal fees of any magnitude. Although Howard was a wealthy man, Lillian and her attorneys had made no claims against his extensive properties, except for providing a home for her and her children.

Thus the money that Steward and Crouch had "used Lillian" to get would have amounted to no more than normal attorney's fees. No doubt Howard did not like to pay them, but they hardly rose to the level of "extortion," a word he used in discussing the case. The primary beneficiaries of the costs to Howard were Lillian and her minor children, to whom Howard had legal and moral obligations, and not to attorneys. Stump and Peterson never took Howard's accusations against Steward and Crouch seriously.

Howard also told Stump and Peterson that Lillian "had several affairs both during (our) marriage and after." Presumably with the thought that any one of her "lovers" might have a motive to murder Lillian, Howard gave the astonished officers his list of possible suspects. It included a local friend and business associate of his, K.H. "Kenny" Buttler; a local attorney and nemesis of Howard's, Bob Taylor; and the very out-of-town friends and associates that Howard, in anticipation of a divorce and child custody battle, had induced to sign false affidavits saying that they had had affairs with Lillian. In other words, in the most Machiavellian of tactics, those who had agreed to sign false statements saying Lillian had committed adultery with them were now being set up by Howard as murder suspects!

Warren Stump and the other officers working on the case could find no one except Howard who would benefit by the death of Lillian. She had no enemies. No evidence has ever surfaced that would indicate that anyone other than Howard Randolph had a motive to murder Lillian. Law enforcement investigators did not take Howard's roster of supposed suspects seriously. Indeed his eagerness to implicate others only deepened their suspicions of him.

Howard certainly had a long list of motives for wanting Lillian out of his life. But did he have the means and the opportunity for having her murdered? Police estimated the cost of hiring the two hit men at $10,000, a relatively small sum for a multi-millionaire. Howard was used to dealing in large amounts of cash, sometimes carrying as much as $100,000 in a brief case on business trips. And he had employees and business partners with criminal records, not to mention a number of contacts with underworld figures in Chicago and Kansas City who would certainly know how to hire hit men. Indeed, Howard's existence was so insecure that he often took a bodyguard, Ed Bealow, on his business trips to large cities.

Investigators were also looking for evidence that directly connected Howard with the specific circumstances of Lillian's abduction and murder. By the time they knew that a homicide had taken place, they had already talked to a witness, Roger Anderson, who had seen Howard talking to the two strangers in the white Cadillac early on the morning that Lillian had disappeared.

Roger had not initially gone to the sheriff with his account of what he had seen. He had thought it strange that Howard was up so early on a Sunday morning talking with two strangers in the middle of Third Street, and it had lodged in his mind because he thought it unusual. But that was before he learned later the next day that Lillian had disappeared. By then word had reached Sheriff Peterson that Roger had seen Howard with the two men.

Lester went by the A & G Farm Supply to see Roger, and told him he had to come by his office and make a statement. Roger did as Lester asked, gave a full statement, and later provided a description of the driver of the car to an artist who was attempting to draw a composite picture of the two strangers. Lester recalls that Roger's assistance was invaluable to the investigation, and that he "was a good witness."

Agent Stump knew the *modus operandi* of "hit men." Such criminal activities were unusual in Iowa, but experienced detectives knew the steps involved in hiring professional killers, and why someone who employed them would likely meet with them. The first step in the process of employing professional killers was to locate someone who was capable of murder for money. Such an evil person might be found in a city the size of Des Moines, but Chicago or Kansas City were more likely. The initial contact would probably be made through a third party because someone living in a small Iowa town would be unlikely to know someone of the ilk of a hit man. That was why the BCI was interested in the extent of Howard Randolph's personal contacts. There was no difficulty tracing Howard's business connections to Chicago, Kansas City, and several other large cities, and to people who had connections with the underground.

In the course of a normal business contact, by phone or in person, it would be possible to make a hint—that could later be denied as a "joke"—of looking for a hit man. If the potential intermediary took the hint and the other party, in this instance Howard Randolph, felt comfortable with the intermediary, then the details of money and location could be discussed. Since the intermediary and the instigator would have normal business relations, such contacts are hard to identify as being out of the ordinary. Both parties would have a good reason to deny such conversations, because it would constitute a criminal conspiracy for both and possible prison time.

The typical arrangement for payment is one-half down and the other half to be paid after proof that the evil deed has been accomplished. The intermediary is unlikely to want direct contacts with the killer for fear of being implicated later by the instigator as the actual employer of the hit man. Something of the sort happened in the 2001 trial of Delfino Ortega in Colorado Springs. Ortega was the intermediary in a hit man killing, and was convicted on evidence supplied by the man who had hired him!

It is common for the instigator to make contact with the hit men in order to explain what he wants done. The hit men need a description or photo of the potential victim, information on the likely whereabouts and habits of the victim, arrangements for the final payment, and any other details. For example, the instigator may want to make sure that no one else is harmed, or perhaps that the victim's face is not disfigured. And thus it was important to connect the chief suspect, Howard Randolph, with the two strangers in the white car. Roger Anderson provided proof of that contact.

It did seem strange to investigators that Howard would make contact with the killers on a downtown street during daylight hours. That, of course, may not have been his preference, and it might not have been his first contact with them. Professional killers, by definition, are dangerous and unpredictable. They may have been "shaking down" Howard for more money or putting pressure on him to make sure they received their final payment. In other words, the meeting might have been at the initiative of the hit men rather than Howard.

It was also possible that the early morning meeting on a public street was the brazen act of an arrogant individual. Many of the details of the case were of that nature. Perhaps the meeting between Howard and the two men was another such instance. John Quinn, the agent now responsible for the case, believes that Howard Randolph was an egotistical individual who also had a motive of intimidating the people of Guthrie Center. Quinn's view is that "Howard didn't care if he was seen with those killers. He just didn't give a shit."

The last connection between the instigator and the killers is the final payment. Typically the one who has hired the hit men will want proof that he is getting what he paid for, i.e. that the murder actually took place. The hit men want the final payment as quickly as possible so that they will have lead-time on the police and can leave the area as quickly as possible.

Henry Buche, a long-time acquaintance of Howard Randolph, saw Howard at the Des Moines airport five or six hours after Lillian was abducted and slain. Her car was parked only thirteen spaces to the north of the front door of the terminal. The keys were in the ignition. Her white purse was under the driver's seat. The doors were unlocked. Howard could have, if he so chose, opened the trunk and discovered for himself that the evil deed had been accomplished. That would have been foolhardy, given the fact that it was still daylight, that he might leave personal evidence at the scene, and that it was a busy area near the front door of the terminal. Seeing her car there with the 39-2449 Iowa plates and her purse under the front seat would seemingly provide sufficient basis for making the final payment. Moreover, it would be dangerous, given the nature of the occupation of hit men, not to make the final payment. Howard was notorious for making initial payments but refusing to make the final one. This would be one instance when he surely did want to make the final payment.

Howard had ample opportunity to make phone contact with the hit men. He had spent the afternoon of Lillian's disappearance at the Veteran's Auditorium in Des Moines watching the Shipstad and Johnson Ice Follies with Wendy and Vicki. They reported that he had spent considerable time on the telephone at the Auditorium, and that they had observed his "serious nature" while doing so. It would have been easy for Howard to contact the killers at a designated time and at a designated number in order to find out if the murder had been accomplished, where Lillian's car and body were located, and how they might arrange to get together for the final payment.

Howard spent the night of May 2 in Des Moines at the Howard Johnson Motel on Grand Avenue. His overnight stay in Des Moines was not lengthy. He checked into Howard Johnson's at 6:59 p.m. on May 2, and was in his office in Guthrie Center, an hour's drive from Des Moines, the next morning shortly after 7:00 a.m. Thus he had ample time during his quick trip to Des Moines to make the final contact and payment to the killers, after viewing Lillian's car at the airport. Howard needed a reason for being at the airport, particularly after he had been seen there by Hank Buche, which he supplied by saying he was there to make arrangements for a flight to Cincinnati. He had been in Des Moines earlier that day and could easily have gone by the airport then, if he so desired, or could have called United Airlines either from the Veteran's Auditorium, a local call for a money-conscious man, or by long-distance from home. The overnight stay he claimed to have spent with Peggy Alston "to comfort her" was actually a short period of time over a cup of coffee. That provided Howard with an excuse for being in Des Moines. He had dropped Vicki off at the Lutheran Church about 5:30 p.m. and checked into the Howard Johnson Motel at 6:59, as metered by the motel clock. That gave Howard ninety minutes to drive to the Des Moines airport, supposedly arrange for a flight to Cincinnati, and arrive at the motel. The trip to the airport would take about seventy minutes and the onward travel to the motel another ten. That would leave only a matter of minutes that Howard could be at the airport. It would be long enough to verify the presence of Lillian's car and to make a quick pay-off connection with the hit men, but nothing more. Whatever Howard's explanation for the trip might be, it was very hurried. If it was for his stated reason, there was no reason to hurry. Indeed, there was no good reason to make the trip at all. For a man who was extremely conscious of the odometer reading on his car as an indicator of the connected costs, it does not seem plausible that he would make a hurried, 110 mile round trip to the Des Moines airport for something he could have done while in Des Moines earlier that day or by phone, or to have a cup of coffee with a friend. That there was a larger reason is highly plausible. Two of the hallmarks of Howard's personality were an extreme cost-benefit consciousness and a void where human compassion was concerned. A more plausible explanation for his hurried trip to Des Moines was to verify that Lillian had been murdered and to make the final payment to the killers he had hired.

*****

Solving crimes is hard work. But matters seemed to be progressing well for Stump and his BCI colleagues in the days following the discovery of Lillian's body. They had a good suspect with powerful motives and could place him in a scenario, with eyewitnesses, whereby he had, or could have, made contact with the killers before and after the homicide. They had a large number of witnesses, albeit many of whom were frightened and reluctant, who had seen the two killers in Guthrie Center and Stuart. Tony Weibel had added important and irrefutable evidence of Howard telling him that Lillian had been murdered before her body had been found. The next step was to identify the killers.

The two swarthy men and the white Cadillac had disappeared. A search of passenger manifests at the Des Moines airport, motel records in Guthrie Center and Stuart, and credit card receipts at Don Bates' Midway service station had been of no value in tracing the hit men. The composite drawings of the suspects, constructed with the help of witnesses, were unsatisfactory and never released. It was important that the witnesses who had seen the two hit men reach a consensus on the composite drawings. The artist's efforts were unsuccessful in that respect. The investigators even wondered, given the reluctance and tardiness of several frightened witnesses, if they were being thoroughly conscientious in their efforts. Perhaps they were concerned about identifying the hit men and endangering themselves. Apparently some people with information about the case approached Lillian's minister, the Reverend Donald Lutz, and expressed their apprehensions. He later recalled, "Fear of that kind of person who would commit such an act … kept people from volunteering information." Warren Stump echoes Reverend Lutz's memory, recalling, "There was a lot of fear (in Guthrie Center) all right."

Another logical explanation for the discrepancies in the composite drawings lies with the perceptual block in identifying facial details of people who are different from the local norm. With the decidedly non-cosmopolitan nature of Guthrie County, an area populated almost exclusively by people of northern European heritage, the witnesses seemed only to see two men with dark complexions and wavy black hair. There was great consistency on those features, and even more so on identifying the white Cadillac. Indeed, the luxury automobile seemed to have dazzled many witnesses to the point of distracting them from a more specific identity of the occupants and the car's license plates. Four of the witnesses identified the car plates as being from Illinois. None of them recalled the plates as being from Guthrie County, an identity that would surely have endured in their minds. No one, with the exception of Sheriff Peterson, had been sufficiently suspicious to note the license number of the white Cadillac, and that important information written on his palm disappeared in the sweat of his hand before he could locate a tablet.

Twenty-one witnesses had seen the two men in the white Cadillac in Guthrie Center and Stuart the weekend that Lillian disappeared. They were seen several times on Saturday and again on Sunday. They had disappeared with their white car at the same time as Lillian. There was no doubt in the minds of investigators that the two strangers were hit men who had been hired by a third person to abduct and kill Lillian. Seventeen witnesses had seen the two men in a car and sixteen described it as a white Cadillac. Two of the witnesses thought that the year of the Cadillac could be as early as 1959 and three thought it could be as late as 1962. But the most common year mentioned was 1960. All of the witnesses, except for Nita Couch, were males. Knowing the identities and features of automobiles was a common trait among local men, especially for a luxury car like a Caddy. There was no doubt that the hit men were driving a white Cadillac of recent vintage. Indeed, it seemed to be the car rather than its occupants that drew the most attention from witnesses.

Thirteen of the witnesses had no recollection of the car plates. Four remembered them as from Illinois, one thought they were Iowa plates from Polk County (Des Moines), one was sure they were not Guthrie County plates, and the other two said that they were "out of state."

The witnesses, without exception, described the two men as having dark complexions and dark hair. Some added that the hair was "wavy" or "combed straight back." Those who saw them more closely thought they looked similar, with one being a slightly taller and having a heavier upper-body build. Few witnesses saw the men standing, making an estimate of height difficult, but the larger man was described on the average as about six feet. There was a considerable range in the witnesses' assessment of the age of the two men, but the most common estimate was in the late twenties or early thirties. Those who had a perception of their ethnicity called them "Italian," "southern European," or "Latin." One described the larger man as being "a Fernando Lamas type," after the famous Latin movie star of the time.

The witnesses' description of the larger man immediately caught the attention of Des Moines detectives and BCI agents stationed in Iowa's capitol city. The image that the witnesses had provided was quite similar to a man well known in Des Moines police circles: "Raul." He was of Mexican heritage, had dark black hair, a muscular build, and was 5'11".

Raul had been born in Lebanon. His family later moved back to Monterey, Mexico, where Raul had spent most of his life. He had eleven brothers and one sister, all of whom lived in Mexico, except for one brother who lived in Edinburg, Texas.

Raul moved to the United States in the mid-1950s, living for one year in Miami and three in Los Angeles before moving to Des Moines in 1960. His immigrant status and fourth grade education had limited his employment to menial jobs. He had a growing police record.

Between 1961 and 1965 Raul was arrested eight times by Des Moines police on charges ranging from having an open can of beer in his car to "assault with the intent to do great bodily injury." In the latter instance he had threatened a man by placing a loaded gun to his head. He then struck the victim with the gun, causing it to discharge and leave powder burns on the victim's neck.

When Raul was stopped for a traffic violation in 1962 he boasted to the arresting Des Moines policeman, "I have a long record." In a March 1964 arrest for intoxication at Chase Tap in Des Moines the arresting officer made two notations. The first was that Raul fit the description of a man involved in an armed robbery that had occurred in Des Moines two weeks before. The other notation was that he was "reported to carry a gun in the glove compartment of his car."

Kenny Moon, a long-time detective with the Des Moines Police Department, remembers Raul as a "bad hombre." Ray Steiner, a retired Des Moines detective who was involved in the initial investigation of the murder of Lillian, recalls Raul as a "tough guy who was capable of murder." Indeed, he had boasted to others, including Steiner, of shooting people. He even claimed that he was wanted for murder in Mexico. No one who knew him doubted that his boast could be true.

According to Detective Steiner, Raul was also an informant for both the Des Moines Chief of Police, Wendell Nichols, and the Polk County Sheriff, Wilbur Hildreth. He knew both of them personally, and had passed along information to them that had been useful in preventing or solving crimes in the Des Moines area. Nichols and Hildreth valued the information that Raul provided, even though he was suspected of being involved in gambling, burglary, and "running a few girls." If he was wanted for murder in Mexico, that was someone else's jurisdiction and problem. In the meantime, he was useful to law enforcement officers in Des Moines. Raul may have sensed that his informant relationship with law enforcement officials gave him a certain "cover," and that may have been the case. If so, it did not extend to homicide.

A check of automobile registration records in Polk County did not indicate that Raul owned a Cadillac. The car registered under his name was a 1958 Mercury with Iowa plates "77-95129." If he had been one of the hit men, he was driving someone else's car.

When investigators attempted to find possible connections between Raul and Howard Randolph they struck pay dirt. He had been employed as an egg breaker at Des Moines Foods, a business owned by Howard. Hank Randolph, Howard's adopted son, also worked at Des Moines Foods. BCI investigators, Warren Stump and Dan Mayer, went to see Hank.

Hank told the officers what he knew of Raul. He had boasted to Hank of murdering a man in Mexico, apparently in retaliation for the murder of one of his brothers. Hank had found Raul's story persuasive and believable. Raul had shown Hank a small handgun that he carried with him. Hank also told Stump and Mayer that Raul had also worked for a few months at Howard's produce station in Harlan, and had visited the Randolph house in Guthrie Center in 1961 while Lillian was visiting relatives in Minnesota. Thus Raul knew the location of the Randolph house and something of its internal configuration.

Was it possible that Howard had been planning the murder of Lillian for several years? There were those near her, including her daughters, who felt after the fact that Howard had plotted the murder for a considerable length of time.

The BCI was convinced that Howard Randolph had hired killers to murder Lillian. They were heavily inclined to believe that Raul was one of the hit men. And they had a good suspect for the second man: "Gordon."

Gordon had a prison record and a considerable resemblance to Raul. Witnesses had said that the two men looked alike, with one being smaller than the other. Gordon, of Italian extraction, was also swarthy with dark black hair. He was a few inches shorter than Raul and less muscular. Those features were a good fit to the description of witnesses.

Gordon was known to Des Moines police, according to former DMPD detectives Ray Steiner and Bill Fitzgerald, as a safe cracker. He lived on the south side of Des Moines, not far from Raul. Raul and Gordon were not known by the local police to "work together," but Gordon did have a reputation for "doing anything for a buck." Although his criminal record involved primarily safe burglaries, he had participated also in at least two armed robberies. Detectives Steiner and Fitzgerald are uncertain about Gordon's capability for murder. Steiner thinks "probably not" and Fitzgerald thinks "probably yes." Both agree that if the two were the assailants in the Randolph case that Raul would have been the "trigger man."

Warren Stump took pictures of Raul and Gordon to show witnesses in Guthrie Center and Stuart. Several of the witnesses had been reluctant to help with the formation of composite drawings of the two hit men. There was even more reluctance to identify Raul or Gordon as one or both of the men that had been seen, as closely as three feet by some witnesses. It seemed that fear might be inhibiting the recollections of many of the witnesses. Stump was certain that Howard Randolph was behind the murder of his estranged wife. The connection between Howard and the hit men was critical. Raul had worked for Howard and knew him. He had been to Guthrie Center and visited in the Randolph home. Roger Anderson had witnessed Howard talking to the two strangers in the white car. Twenty other witnesses had seen the two men. Stump needed a witness to identify a photo of Raul or Gordon as one or both of the swarthy characters they had seen on the weekend of May 1 and 2.

Instead of the "that's him" that Stump was seeking, he was getting "it looks something like him," or "maybe," or "I'm not sure." The BCI had a few other potential suspects, but none as strong as Raul and Gordon. A critical link in the case that might make it possible to prosecute all three men—Howard Randolph, Raul, and Gordon—for murder was missing without positive identification by some witnesses. Agent Stump was discouraged that day when he did not get the identifications he sought from witnesses in Guthrie Center. He returned to Des Moines on the narrow and familiar Highway 64. It had been a frustrating day.

Investigators continued to follow leads, making trips to Chicago and Kansas City in the process, but were not gaining much additional information. In late May, a police informant in Des Moines, Merle Little, told police that he had been approached in the spring by a man who wanted to hire him to kill his wife. Little was in the Polk County jail at the time, and apparently looking for ways to gain leniency from the police. Detective Steiner took Little to Guthrie Center to see if he could identify Howard Randolph as the man who attempted to hire him. Little could not identify Howard as that man.

Steiner had wasted an afternoon, not a surprise to him based on previous experience with Little, and Merle had received a joy ride and some fresh air. Because of Little's uncertain mental state, the Des Moines police always questioned the information he provided in any case. Sometimes he was right, but more often he was wrong. Some months after his visit to Guthrie Center his mental health deteriorated further into a deep depression. Merle Little took his own life while still in his twenties.

The investigation into the murder of Lillian Randolph, which had shown great promise initially for solving the crime, soon reached a plateau. The investigating officers were absolutely convinced that Howard Randolph had hired two killers to murder Lillian. They thought that "Raul" and "Gordon" were the likely hit men, but could not get witness confirmations. If there was an intermediary involved, his identity was totally unknown. The white Cadillac had disappeared. A search of Howard Randolph's phone records and bank account had produced nothing out of the ordinary. A thorough

131

search of the Randolph house had not provided any useful evidence. Lucy Clark, who lived on a farm south of the Des Moines airport, reported that "a person" came to her house the afternoon Lillian disappeared and asked to use her telephone to report to police screams she had heard coming from a white car. A policeman was sent to the area and found nothing but hair curlers with fragments of blond hair. The autopsy performed by Dr. Leo Luka revealed little that was useful. Dr. Luka was in the twilight of his career as a pathologist and his autopsies were increasingly disappointing to police officials. All the detectives could determine from Luka's report was that a right-handed assailant had stabbed Lillian to death with a thin-bladed knife. Lillian's Dodge Coronet had a smudged, unidentifiable finger print on the left wing window. There were a number of items found in the trunk that were sent to the FBI for analysis. That list included:

1. .25 caliber slug
2. .25 cartridge casing
3. Blouse, sleeveless, white with floral design
4. Slacks, black pedal pusher
5. Shoes, black flats
6. Brassiere
7. Floor mat from trunk
8. Organic plant material
9. Blood samples
10. Hair samples
11. Paper, small fragment

The FBI laboratory analysis was prompt, detailed, and disappointing to the investigators in Iowa. A report from J. Edgar Hoover, Director of the FBI, to T.A. Thompson, Director of the BCI, dated June 17, 1965, described what FBI technicians had discovered in their examination of the submitted items of evidence. The information, except where quoted, is paraphrased below:

1. .25 caliber slug: The bullet is jacketed with six land and groove impressions. Some land impressions are deeper than others, indicating an older or cheap barrel. There was no flattening to the slug, "indicating that it had not struck a bone."

2. .25 caliber cartridge casing: The cartridge is of the W.R.A. brand and used in auto-loading weapons. There are not sufficient microscopic markings remaining to identify the weapon from which the cartridge was fired. (The cartridge had been found under the

body of the victim. Acidic body fluids had seriously corroded the cartridge casing.) The rifling impressions on the cartridge were "like those found in many makes of weapons."

3. Blouse: A hole was discovered in the blouse. However, "the absence of residues around the hole precludes the possibility of determining whether or not the hole was made by a bullet."

4. Brassiere: Eight cuts of three-tenths inch each were discovered in the left cup. The FBI concluded that the cuts "appear to have been made by a bladed instrument," but "could not determine if the instrument was single or double-bladed."

5. Floor mat: Five holes were discovered in the floor mat that had been taken from the trunk. The holes were not caused by a knife.

6. Hair samples: All were uniform and came from the victim.

7. Blood samples: All were Type O-Positive, consistent with the blood type of the victim.

8. Paper fragment: A form of wrapping paper as used in commercial packaging.

9. Organic plant material: Reedy, bamboo-like, fragment. Nothing found on it.

10. Slacks and shoes: Nothing found.

The FBI report greatly reduced the possibility of solving the case with physical evidence. However, there was still important circumstantial evidence implicating Howard Randolph, even if the two suspected killers could not or would not be identified with certainty by witnesses. Would Howard Randolph be prosecuted for the murder of Lillian? The person primarily responsible for making that decision was Coral Greenfield, the Guthrie County Attorney.

Chapter VIII

The Case Against Howard Randolph

"We all thought Howard guilty, and I don't mind making
any bones about that."
Gary Hopkins

Coral Greenfield, the Guthrie County Attorney, was a tall, slender man whose heavy smoking habit had left deep lines in his face that gave him the appearance of being much older than his fifty-three years. The investigation files on the murder of Lillian Randolph, one prepared by Sheriff Lester Peterson and the other by Iowa Bureau of Criminal Investigation agents, troubled Coral as he thumbed through the hundreds of pages of interviews, evidence, and related materials in the late summer of 1965.

Like Lillian Randolph, Coral and Margaret Greenfield had four children. The Greenfields were about the same age as Lillian. The thought that four children and five grandchildren were now left without their mother and grandmother weighed heavily on Coral. Police files can be gruesome, and he was not used to looking at them. The photos of the decomposing and bloated body of the victim, so swollen that it had ripped her clothing, made Coral sick to his stomach.

In his twenty-nine years as a lawyer, the last five of which he had also served as County Attorney, Coral Greenfield had never been involved in anything so horribly brutal, so out of character with the normal tranquillity of the area. There had obviously been hired killers in the community who abducted and murdered Lillian Randolph. It was almost too much for Coral to believe.

Coral Greenfield was the quintessential small town lawyer. He had established his law practice in 1936 in Bayard, a town of less than 500 at the time, located fifteen miles north of Guthrie Center. He was the only attorney in Bayard, which gave him an important local role, but one that did not extend much beyond the city limits until he became the Guthrie County Attorney in 1960.

Coral served as the Secretary for the Bayard School Board; as Secretary-Treasurer for the Bayard Care Center, a home for the elderly; and as City Attorney for Bayard and Coon Rapids, another small town a short distance to the west. His various administrative positions, considerable tax work, and other local legal matters provided Coral and his family with a comfortable, middle-class existence.

Coral was known in his community as a gentle, soft-spoken, honest, and hard-working man. Indeed, he was considered a workaholic who spent most evenings and weekends, especially during "tax time," laboring in his office. The exception was Wednesday nights when he bowled in Coon Rapids as a member of the Bayard Lion's Club team.

Friends and family were surprised when Coral accepted the appointment as Guthrie County Attorney in 1960. He was already very busy and the new position would require thirty-mile roundtrips to the courthouse in Guthrie Center. After twenty-four years of practicing law without the assistance of a secretary, Coral now decided that his expanded responsibilities required some help. He hired Clara Rosenbeck McClellan as his secretary. For the next thirty years Coral and Clara worked side-by-side, day or night or weekends. They were a team and friends.

On Mondays and Thursdays Coral and Clara made the trip from Bayard to Guthrie Center to conduct the county's legal affairs. Coral, who died of emphysema in 1990, never became fully comfortable and content with his new position, one he held simultaneously with his several other appointments. Clara recalled: "He didn't find the County Attorney office his favorite job." When Coral was preparing to leave the position in 1978, after eighteen years of service, he told a reporter that "sometimes the office gets to be a pain."

But like the position or not, the decision on filing murder charges against Howard Randolph was in Coral Greenfield's lap. Although the position of County Attorney involves the responsibility for prosecuting cases on behalf of the State, Coral had little of that experience. Lack of crime in the county was one reason. Another was that Coral, known in attorney circles as a "pussy cat," avoided the courtroom scene as much as possible. Sheriff Peterson recalled Coral as "a pretty slow piece of property" whom he often "had to work around," even taking matters up with judges when Coral failed to act. But a homicide case, something that Coral Greenfield had never faced, could not be ignored.

It would have been possible for Sheriff Peterson to determine that there was "probable cause" that Howard Randolph had committed a crime and to arrest him. That was certainly consistent with his line of thought. But there were several reasons why Lester did not make that move. First, he was concerned that if he made an arrest and the case did not proceed to a conviction that Howard and his bevy of attorneys might sue him in a civil case. Although such a suit is rare, Lester was chastened by any such prospect. Second, when the Iowa Bureau of Criminal Investigation, now

"Division" of Criminal Investigation, enters a case, it does so in a big way, sending a team of agents into the local area and, in effect, taking charge of the case even though it is formally the jurisdiction of the county sheriff. Lester was happy to defer to the BCI agents. They had the numbers, the technical resources, and the experience to deal with a homicide case. Lester had but two deputies, and they had their normal workload to fulfill. Thus, the police function of the case was primarily in the hands of the BCI and its lead investigator, Warren Stump. The third factor in Sheriff Peterson's decision to forego arresting Howard Randolph was the lack of urgency for his apprehension. There were no indications that Howard, who was going about his business as usual, intended to flee. And thus by the force of circumstances and personal preference, Sheriff Lester Peterson was not a major factor in the pending decision about arresting Howard Randolph and bringing charges against him for the murder of Lillian Randolph. On the police side of that decision was Warren Stump who was acting in consultation with his supervisor, Robert Voss, and the head of the BCI, Tillman Thompson. Handling the responsibilities of prosecution was the reluctant Guthrie County Attorney, Coral Greenfield.

In cases where a county attorney feels required to disqualify himself from a case because of a personal relationship, conflict of interest, or lack of specific experience, it is possible to seek assistance through the Iowa Attorney General or ask another attorney to prosecute the case. The latter was a preferred option of Coral Greenfield. He readily stepped aside when asked to do so by the Iowa Attorney General, Lawrence Scalise, and allowed an experienced prosecutor to assume responsibility for the case. Scalise requested Bob Taylor to accept the assignment.

Robert Yancy Taylor was a Guthrie Center native. He had returned to his hometown to practice law after serving in the Navy on a PT boat in World War II, and then earning a law degree at Drake University on the GI Bill. The name "Taylor" and the practice of law in Guthrie Center were nearly synonymous. Bob's father, Charles Taylor, was a local attorney who died when Bob was a boy. His older brother, C.H. "Buck" Taylor, had an ongoing law practice which Bob joined in 1949. In the meantime, and to further add to Bob's connections with the legal profession, he married Marge Vincent, also a native of Guthrie Center and the daughter of Judge Earl Vincent.

Soon after joining his brother's law firm, which was re-named "Taylor and Taylor," Bob sought election as County Attorney. His initial bid fell short by the painful margin of one vote, but a year later he was appointed to the position and then elected twice to two-year terms.

The position of County Attorney provided Bob Taylor with valuable trial and criminal law experience, but it was a part-time position with a small stipend. When his private practice grew to the point that Bob no longer felt he had time to be the County Attorney, he decided not to run for a third term.

By the end of Bob Taylor's tenure as the Guthrie County Attorney his reputation as a first-rate prosecutor had expanded far beyond Guthrie County. In 1964 he was approached by Iowa Republican leaders about running for the position of State Attorney General. Bob gave that possibility serious consideration, going so far as acquiring the necessary filing application, before deciding, with his wife's earnest encouragement, not to run.

When Attorney General Scalise asked Bob Taylor to review the investigative file for the Randolph case and make an assessment on possible prosecution, he had placed the case in the hands of a highly-qualified prosecutor who knew the prime suspect, Howard Randolph, personally and well. Bob and Howard had lived together in the same community for many years. Howard's manner of using his intelligence, money, deceit, and the law to take advantage of people aggravated Bob. Bob and Howard had squared off in the courtroom before. Indeed, Bob had represented Lillian against Howard in an earlier civil case in which Howard was accused of endorsing checks belonging to her. And thus there was an abundance of hostility between Bob and Howard. Marge Taylor, Bob's widow, recalled their feelings succinctly: "They hated each other."

Bob Taylor had to ask himself the central question: "Was Howard Randolph capable of murdering Lillian?" It was doubtful that Howard would commit the act himself. He had a reputation for hiring others to do his dirty work, and this seemed to be the ultimate test of that proclivity. He had a business reputation for being ruthless. Bob had faced him in the courtroom and knew of his cunning and merciless ways. The file that Bob was reviewing contained a number of statements from business associates, acquaintances, and even family members who said they thought Howard was capable of hiring killers to murder Lillian.

Perhaps the best evidence of Bob's conclusions about Howard's capacity for murder was his new practice of keeping a rifle beside his bed at night. His emotions and personal opinion of Howard Randolph had already convinced him of Howard's capabilities, long before he was asked to review the investigative file for possible prosecution. Yes, Bob Taylor believed Howard Randolph capable of committing murder, at least second-hand, but was there sufficient evidence to convince a jury that he had done so?

Public opinion in Guthrie Center had immediately and nearly unanimously convicted Howard Randolph for the murder of Lillian. Ted Allen, the former owner of the Garden Theater who was known for his tart tongue, had been stopped on the street by Howard and asked, "Ted, what are people saying about me." Ted looked Howard squarely in the eye and replied without hesitation, "Randy, we think you did it!" That was a concise summary of local opinion. Roger Wickland, one of the golf course witnesses, voiced the same opinion at a later date: "Everyone figured he did it."

The legal standards under which Bob Taylor would function as a prosecutor were much higher than those of public opinion, which require neither logic nor legality. He would have the *burden of proof* of convincing each member of a jury of Howard's guilt *beyond a reasonable doubt*. And, very importantly, he knew that he would have but one opportunity to make the case. If a jury returned a verdict of "not guilty," then the constitutional protections against *double jeopardy* would preclude ever again bringing Howard to trial for the murder of Lillian. Any prosecution of Howard would thus be a one-time opportunity. It was imperative that Bob get it right.

The standards for making an arrest are lower than those required for a conviction. To make an arrest a policeman must have *probable cause*, that is the belief that the suspect committed a crime and that there is more evidence than not of that fact. Probable cause was sufficiently strong to arrest Howard Randolph, but no good purpose would have been served by doing so. He was unlikely to flee. He had not done so when he had the opportunity. He was not likely to commit a criminal act since he was not believed to be the actual murderer of Lillian and was under constant surveillance. And it makes little sense to arrest someone unless charges are going to be filed. Indeed, the writ of *habeas corpus* places considerable limitations on that possibility. In effect, a prosecutor must anticipate the higher legal requirements of a conviction before assenting to an arrest.

To gain a conviction a prosecutor needs solid evidence of the guilt of the defendant. When there is no confession by the defendant, the prosecutor must present direct and/or circumstantial evidence to the jury in an effort to prove the guilt of the accused. *Direct evidence* proves a fact without any need for inference or additional information. Eyewitnesses and fingerprints fall into that category. *Circumstantial evidence* proves a fact from which another fact can be logically inferred.

Direct evidence typically makes a stronger case for the prosecutor than does circumstantial evidence. For example, if ten people saw a defendant shoot a victim to death and testified accordingly, a conviction is probably assured. On the other hand, if ten people heard shots and then saw the defendant run past them, on that information alone there is no direct evidence that the accused fired the shots. The prosecutor would have to prove with additional information that accusation to a jury, a harder assignment than having eyewitnesses who observed the shooting.

In his preliminary review of the thick file of interviews, evidence, and other details, Bob Taylor concluded that the State did not have a strong case against Howard Randolph.   There were an abundance of motives on Howard's part to have Lillian murdered, but motives would not be evidence that he caused her death.   Howard's motives had pointed to him as a key suspect from the very beginning.   But evidence that he had acted on his motives was necessary.   There was no direct evidence that he had done so. There was persuasive circumstantial evidence, but Bob was aware that a good defense attorney could make effective counter arguments.

If Bob prosecuted Howard on the basis of the information contained in the investigative file, he could explain to a jury that Howard had the motives, the means, the opportunity, and the will to have Lillian murdered. He could also describe, based on Howard's own acts, a plausible scenario that pointed to his guilt.   But evidence supporting any of the foregoing was weak.

The scenario that Bob could present would be of a man who was a wife batterer—there was plentiful evidence of that.   He could show that Howard had stooped to a variety of dirty tricks in an attempt to force Lillian from his house and to prepare a divorce case against her.   He could also show that Howard had a ruthless element in his behavior, as indicated by his business operations.   And Bob could call several key witnesses with damaging information concerning Howard.

There was the IRS agent, Tony Weibel, who had recorded notes of Howard telling him that Lillian had been kidnapped and murdered before her body was found.   That would certainly suggest to a jury that Howard had prior knowledge of her abduction and murder.

Roger Anderson had seen Howard talking to the two strangers early on the morning that Lillian disappeared.   Bob Taylor could tell a jury that Howard's conversation with the killers included information on Lillian, such as her appearance, her habits, and her plans for the day.   Indeed, he had helped establish her schedule for the day by making arrangements to take Wendy and Vicki to the ice show in Des Moines.   In the meeting with the killers Howard could have arranged to verify later by telephone that they had accomplished their evil deed and to make arrangements for the final pay-off. And why else would Howard be talking with the two killers? They had talked very little with others in the community when they had the opportunity.   Roger Anderson said that Howard and the driver were preparing to shake hands, as though they knew each other or were preparing to meet.   In either case there was a heavy suggestion that theirs was an arranged meeting.   Why had Howard arranged to meet with two killers? What possible reason could there be, other than a plan to have Lillian murdered?

Hank Buche, a long-time acquaintance of Howard's, had seen him at the Des Moines airport where Lillian's car and corpse were found. There was evidence that Lillian had been murdered on the day of her abduction and that the car was parked at the airport soon thereafter. Bob Taylor could explain to the jury that Howard went to the airport to verify the presence of Lillian's car as evidence that she had been murdered and, possibly, to make the final payment to the hit men. Howard had no logical reason to make the hurried trip to Des Moines, and he seemed intent upon creating equally non-plausible alibis, such as arranging for a flight to Cincinnati and to be by the side of Peggy Alston in a moment of need. He had never taken the flight and his sensitive treatment of Peggy was totally out of character for him. Moreover, his timing and explanation about her surgery were not consistent with the facts. Bob would certainly point that out to a jury.

Bob Taylor would explain that Howard had made an obvious effort to clear the Randolph house of everyone but Lillian so that she would be alone when the killers arrived. The day before her abduction he had told an employee, Gary Hopkins, to move his work away from near the house and to another field that was several miles distant. That same day he had called Vicki at home twice, at noon and 2:00 p.m., showing an interest in what was scheduled at the house for the weekend. Later that afternoon he called Lillian's son, Hank, to ensure that he would not be at the house on his birthday, May 2, the same day as her abduction. Howard had invited Ann and Harry and their family to accompany him to the ice show. That would also remove them from the area. Howard had said that Harry could take the day off, an unprecedented act of generosity by him, particularly during the planting season. When Ann said that they could not go because their baby was ill, Howard created a pretense for going to the Shackelford home and locking them in place while the hit men were abducting Lillian. Howard told Wendy and Vicki that he needed to go to the Shackelford farm to "check some machinery," but he never did so. When he talked with Ann at the farm he asked about Harry's whereabouts and made small talk when the schedule was already tight for arriving at the ice show by 2:00 p.m. When Howard finally left the Shackelford farm he started to turn by habit towards the Randolph house and then, realizing what he had done, swung abruptly in the other direction and towards town. He explained to the girls that he had forgotten the tickets and needed to go by his office to pick them up. Howard was an extremely organized and careful man. Forgetting something was unusual for him.

After picking up the tickets and while proceeding up Tank Hill, Howard made a point of observing highway patrolman John Novy's house and the presence of his patrol vehicle. As they proceeded further and passed the Randolph house, Howard watched the house from the corner of his eye.

When the girls saw the white car and mentioned it to him, he denied that there was a white car in the driveway, even though both Wendy and Vicki saw it and discussed whom it might belong to.

At the Shipstad and Johnson ice show at Veteran's auditorium, Howard had talked on a public telephone. His call at intermission occurred between 3:00 and 3:30 p.m., allowing enough time for the hit men to abduct Lillian, stab her to death, drive her body and car to the Des Moines airport, and take a phone call from Howard at a pre-arranged public phone number. By that call Howard could find out how to verify the deed of the hit men and to make the final payment to them.

Bob Taylor, like any good prosecutor, needed to measure the strength of his case against the abilities of a good defense attorney, and there was no question that Howard Randolph could afford the best. A prosecutor has the burden of proof of satisfying each member of a jury that the defendant is guilty beyond a reasonable doubt. But because the American criminal justice system is heavily balanced on the side of protecting the lives and liberties of the innocent against unwarranted punishment by the State, the defense attorney is not required to prove the defendant's innocence. Indeed, the dominant principle of a criminal trial is the *presumption of innocence* of the defendant. The defense attorney is not required to call any witnesses or to present any case. All the defense attorney has to accomplish to win an acquittal is implant a reasonable doubt in the mind of a single juror. Moreover, a defendant, under the provisions of the Fifth Amendment of the U.S. Constitution, is not required to testify. This means that the defendant does not have to explain his actions or deny the accusations and evidence against him. His demeanor and words on the witness stand can only be weighed by the jury if he chooses to testify. Otherwise, he is just another spectator in the courtroom.

Bob Taylor had to anticipate the potential tactics of a defense attorney. If the case were tried in Guthrie Center, where Howard Randolph was known and despised, a guilty verdict might be within reach. But given the local climate in which Howard had already been convicted by public opinion, a defense attorney would no doubt ask for a *change of venue*, a change of the trial location to a city where the defendant is unknown and opinions of potential jurors have not been formulated. The likelihood that such a request would be granted by the trial judge would be high. In the process, the advantage to the prosecutor of a hometown jury would be lost.

And how might a defense attorney deal with the star witnesses that Bob Taylor could present? In the case of Tony Weibel, the IRS agent who had notes indicating that Howard had information about the murder of Lillian before her body was discovered, the defense attorney might ask Weibel if taxpayers ever made excuses to delay meeting with him. After receiving an affirmative answer to that question, the defense attorney might call Sheriff Peterson to the stand and ask if he and others had suspected that Lillian had been kidnapped and perhaps murdered by the time that Howard and Weibel had talked on the telephone on May 7. With the sheriff replying affirmatively, the defense attorney could then tell the jury that Howard Randolph's statement concerning Lillian's disappearance was no different than the suspicions of law enforcement officers.

After Roger Anderson had completed his testimony about seeing Howard with the two strangers, the defense attorney would likely ask him if he had heard any of the conversation between Howard and the two men. Roger would have to respond, "No." The attorney could then say that it would be normal for strangers to ask for directions and ask Roger if it were possible that the strangers had simply asked Howard for assistance. Roger would have to respond, "Yes."

In rebuttal to the testimony of Hank Buche, the defense attorney could point out to the jury that Howard Randolph used the Des Moines airport frequently and, indeed, had a plaque on his wall from United Airlines that commemorated his 100,000 miles of travel with that company. In two interviews with investigators Buche had reported two different clock times for when he had seen Howard at the Des Moines airport. The earlier time would have been impossible since Howard was still with Wendy and Vicki. A defense attorney would jump on that inconsistency in an effort to discredit the witness, perhaps going so far as telling the jury that Buche was confused and had not seen Howard at the Des Moines airport.

The defense attorney could also tell the jury that neither the murder weapon nor the white Cadillac had been found, and that the identification of "Raul" and "Gordon" as the hit men was only a hunch on the part of investigators who thought they fit the descriptions of eyewitnesses. The eyewitnesses, however, could not agree on a composite drawing and could not identify photos of "Raul" and "Gordon" as being the two men they had seen. Moreover, neither "Raul" nor "Gordon" had ever owned a Cadillac. The fact that "Raul" had worked for Howard, the defense attorney could say, was a coincidence that the prosecution had seized upon to incriminate Howard, and showed how weak the case against him really was.

Bob Taylor could see that the physical evidence, as described in the BCI report, was practically nil. There were no fingerprints, the ballistic tests on the slug had not indicated a specific weapon, and all the blood evidence was that of the victim. Phone records did not connect Howard with either of the suspected hit men, and there was no money trail in his bank records that indicated anything unusual. If Bob were to build a case against Howard, it would not be on the basis of solid physical evidence.

Available circumstantial evidence and connected witnesses were vulnerable to a skilled defense attorney. Indeed, Bob was not certain how many of the 21 eyewitnesses would be willing to testify and how steadfast their testimony might be. A number of them had already said that they would not testify in a public trial, and others had been wobbly in their cooperation with law enforcement officers.

What was missing in the file that Bob Taylor was reviewing was a psychological profile of Howard Randolph. A psychologist could have revealed that Howard's complex personality was a good fit for the "narcissistic personality disorder," a personality deficiency which is characterized by a number of traits, including pre-occupation with fantasies of power, brilliance, beauty, and ideal love.[1] A good psychological profile of Howard Randolph might have provided a useful key in resolving the case that Bob Taylor was reviewing.

The initial impetus to the narcissistic personality disorder usually occurs in childhood and commonly involves the loss of someone who has provided love and affection to the child, such as a parent. If the child has had difficulty relating to the surviving parent, the trauma is deepened, making the youngster feel abandoned and desperate for affection. The child may then develop a psychological defense, which becomes the key to his future behavior.

At the age of twelve, Howard Randolph suffered the death of his father, Richard, a man he worshipped and who supplied his third son with an abundance of affection. In later years Howard recalled how he would stand side-by-side with his father as they ground grain, and how much he enjoyed their hunting and fishing ventures. Howard's mother, Bessie, a crusty and stubborn woman, was very strict with her son. She was a disciplinarian and a penny-pincher who struggled to eke out an existence for her four young sons, while living in the upstairs of her parents' farm home west of Guthrie Center. Later Bessie turned her attention and affections towards a new man in her life, John Eaton. John and Bessie married and moved to a new location at Monteith, Iowa, a few miles south of Guthrie Center.

The relationship of Bessie Eaton with her third son, Howard, was never warm and loving. Peggy Alston, Howard's companion of many years, recalled that the two "fussed" at each other. Leona Applegate, a secretary in Howard's office, remembered that when Bessie came by that "he had no time for her" and was "rude and short." Sue Christianson, a grandniece of Howard who lived with him while she was in high school and was later a

---

[1] Otto Kernberg, *Borderline Conditions and Pathological Narcissism* (New York: J. Aronson, 1985). James F. Masterson, *The Narcissistic and Borderline Disorders* (New York: Brunner/Mazel, 1981).

live-in caretaker for Bessie, recollects that Howard would "fly in and fly out" of the house, delivering beef neck bones for his mother to eat. "He was not real involved with his mom," Sue recalled. And Vicki, his youngest adopted daughter, remembered that Howard "treated his mother mean."

The nature of Howard's relationship with his mother is well illustrated by an incident that involved a plumbing problem at her home. Howard *loaned* her the money to repair the sewer line. When she discovered that the repairs were not needed, she refused to return the money to her son.

Bessie Eaton spent her last years on public assistance at the New Homestead, a care center in Guthrie Center. From the window of her room at the New Homestead she could view Howard's splendid house and acreage a short distance to the southeast.

Many of the specific features of the narcissistic personality disorder were a good match to Howard's idiosyncratic character, such as a grandiose sense of self importance, a need for attention and admiration, a lack of empathy, and inter-personal relations which result in the exploitation of others. Such personalities are typically arrogant and consumed with the work that they hope will lead to wealth and power. Howard had succeeded in that goal and developed a reputation for being a workaholic in the process.

Those of the narcissistic personality disorder, because of their high interest in beauty, are usually obsessed with their personal appearance. Howard fit that pattern. In a rural, agriculturally oriented community where formal appearance was not common, he wore suits and ties. Even in casual weekend circumstances Howard preferred suits to informal dress. When Hank Buche saw Howard at the Des Moines airport the day of the disappearance of Lillian, the visual impression that endured was Howard not wearing a suit. Over the many years that Hank had known Howard, he had never seen him wear anything but a suit.

In contrast to the attention the narcissistic personality pays to personal appearance, such people are commonly lax on personal grooming habits and hygiene. Howard also followed that pattern. He bathed infrequently, as those who lived with him noted, and when he did bathe it was often in water that he had asked a previous bather to leave for him. Howard's lack of attention to personal hygiene resulted in a powerful body odor that was noticed by anyone in his proximity. In Guthrie Center it was something of a trademark of Howard's that was the subject of many comments and jokes.

Of more significance than the poor grooming habits of the narcissistic personality are behavioral factors which cause harm and grief to others. One such quality is an obvious cool indifference and lack of empathy, even in situations that beg for sensitivity. This lack of empathy is often viewed by others, and appropriately so, as cruel, self-centered, and sadistic.

Howard often acted in that manner. When Wendy and Vicki were grieving and crying over the news of the death of their Uncle Clarence, Howard first asked them what they were "fussing about," and when told of Clarence's death, callously told them "to get over it." At the time of the assassination of President Kennedy, when the entire nation was in mourning, Howard's reaction was one of "good riddance" and commented to others watching his funeral on television that he was glad that "another Democrat was gone." Jim Belluci, who worked for Howard for a number of years and was his brother-in-law, recalled that Howard "liked to see people suffer" and reported that he had "seen a lot of cases where he got a lot of enjoyment out of it." Even Marion Messersmith, who was a friend of Howard's for nearly fifty years, recalled that he was "ruthless" and sometimes acted sadistically towards employees.

Several features of the narcissistic personality of a man can be connected with "womanizing," a feature of Howard Randolph's existence throughout his adult life. Women represent beauty to the male narcissistic personality, provide an opportunity to attract admiration, and may lead to love and affection, all of which are goals of that personality type. Howard's pattern of maintaining intermittent relationships with a number of widely scattered female friends fulfilled quite well the needs of the narcissistic personality.

Extensive lying, which serves inner demands for omnipotence, is another feature of the narcissistic personality. False promises are nothing more than lies, and Howard made enough false promises to fill a phone book. Business partners, employees, family members, and many others were the victims of Howard Randolph's failure to keep commitments. He had a talent for luring unsuspecting people into business and personal relationships in which he would gain an advantage and emerge the victor. Most local people avoided being manipulated by Howard by shunning sustained business relationships with him. There was a long list of outsiders who moved to Guthrie Center as "partners" with Howard Randolph, only to leave town broke and disgusted. Sometimes the dissolution of the partnership ended in the courts, sometimes it resulted in physical violence or threats thereof, but it always concluded with more bitterness and hatred directed at Howard.

Lillian Chalman was one of the outsiders who fell into the pattern of being lured by Howard's false promises. Lorraine Belluci, Lillian's sister who knew Howard for nearly fifty years, recalled that Howard promised Lillian "the moon" in wooing her into a quick marriage. So far as Howard's veracity was concerned, Lorraine summed up her thoughts candidly: "My, he lied to everyone about everything!"

145

Howard had specifically promised Lillian to send her two oldest children, Hank and Ann, to college; to treat her two youngest daughters, Wendy and Vicki, as "princesses;" to take the entire family on a vacation to Hawaii; and to buy Lillian a new car and fur coat. When Lillian realized that Howard had lied to her, their marriage began to deteriorate. But because Lillian's relationship with Howard was bound by the contract of marriage, he could not conclude the relationship at his own instigation and without penalty, as he had done so many times before in business relationships.

People with the narcissistic personality disorder have difficulty with intimacy and close relationships. Such relationships interfere with their primary coping mechanism, the "narcissistic defense," and are avoided. Thus, those with this personality disorder are likely to have few close friends. That was true of Howard. They are likely to have unreasonable expectations for personal nurturing from those few who are close to them. Lillian's letters and Howard's diary are filled with comments to that effect. And they are likely to be attracted to those who are unavailable by perhaps marriage or distance. Howard had a long-time affection for Lorraine Hedman Belluci who was married most of those years. Other lady friends were married or far away, such as one in Chicago and another in Los Angeles.

Those of the narcissistic personality disorder "groom their victims," that is they perceive what others want and then make the appropriate promises to provide those needs. Lillian Chalman had a need for financial security for her family and an interest in improving her standard of living. Howard Randolph correctly perceived Lillian's needs, made extensive promises to her, and convinced her to marry him. Her view of him was soured when his promises were not kept. His view of her was embittered when she could not satisfy the peculiarities of his psychological needs.

It seems evident that Howard's interests were directed more towards Lillian's children, particularly her then seven and nine-year-old daughters, than towards her. Children are easy targets for the needs of a narcissistic personality. The interests of a child are comparatively simple and easy to perceive, involving perhaps nothing more than an ice cream cone or a candy bar. Likewise, a child's satisfaction and gratitude with the gift are easily conveyed to and received by the provider. The request to "give me a hug" or "give me a kiss" is more likely to result in the desired response from a child than from an adult, who would better understand the complexities of such a request.

Howard's attention to Vicki and Wendy was apparent from the outset of his marriage to Lillian. Vicki was younger, a more compliant personality, and an easier target for Howard's extreme need for affection. There was a time, after an argument with Lillian, when he forced Vicki to sit on his lap and commanded her to kiss and hug him. He occasionally forced his tongue into her mouth, sometimes stroked her leg, and required her at one point to sleep with him. But however inappropriate such behavior is with a child, Vicki, by her own account, was not subjected to greater sexual abuse.

Lillian had apparently sensed Howard's keen interest in maintaining a hold on Wendy and Vicki, and expressed her concerns in a message to her oldest daughter, Ann. Lillian's premonition of her own death was also expressed in the letter in which she told Ann: "I can't bear to think of what a future faces Wendy and Vicki in the event of my death and they were left alone with Howard." As her "last request" she asked Ann to contact Roy, Wendy and Vicki's father, "in the event of my death," and ask him to do "everything in his power to get the girls back."

Lillian's fears that Howard wanted to gain control of Wendy and Vicki were amply proved by his actions following her murder. The day he took Lillian's three daughters to the Beidelman Funeral Home to select a casket for her burial, he tried to convince Wendy and Vicki to come to his house and live with him. He even added a coercive measure by suggesting that if they did not agree to do so, he would not allow their mother to be buried in Minnesota, as she had requested to family members on many occasions.

Another common feature of the narcissistic personality disorder are feelings of sadistic rage that are often directed towards animals. Animals are easily manipulated and marginally protected by the law. Thus the killing of animals as an outlet of rage is a common feature of the narcissistic personality disorder

Lillian and her daughters, all of whom were fond of animals, learned soon after moving into Howard's house of his sadistic behavior towards animals. Sometimes it was stray dogs he shot, and sometimes it was their pets. Sometimes he killed animals in front of them, and sometimes he just told them about it. The most painful of Howard's destruction of animals involved a succession of Wendy and Vicki's pet dogs. There was "Tip," then "Spot," then "Baby Doll," and finally "Eva." "Joey" was Wendy and Vicki's pet dog at the time of the murder of their mother. They rescued their pet from the house before Howard resumed occupancy out of fear that Joey might suffer the same outcome.

Envy is another powerful emotion of the narcissistic personality disorder and can take a highly destructive form. Indeed, it is possible that Howard Randolph killed the pets of Wendy and Vicki because they were receiving the love and affection for which he yearned.

The rage and hatred emanating from narcissistic envy can be strong and unforgiving. It has a reciprocal feature in that the narcissistic personality can feel justified in treating others as he feels he is being treated.

Associated with the narcissistic personality's pronounced feelings of envy is a *conviction* that whatever his needs, most commonly love and affection, will be withheld from him. His reaction to those circumstances is an urge to destroy whatever is interfering with his needs.

The narcissistic personality has a perpetual fear of abandonment. When faced with that prospect the reaction is severe, and commonly involves such emotions as suicidal depression, panic, hopelessness, helplessness, and *homicidal rage*. Howard envied the love that Lillian received from Wendy and Vicki, and constantly complained to her that she was interfering with the girls' feelings for him. He was apparently fearful of being abandoned by them.

The marriage of Lillian Chalman and Howard Randolph went through four stages, all of which had the heavy imprint of his complicated personality. In the first, Howard lured Lillian into a hasty marriage with an extensive list of false promises. The marriage fell apart in the second stage, and Lillian filed for separate maintenance and a restraining order to keep Howard away from his house. In the third stage, Lillian gained considerable control over Howard's existence, particularly his desire to spend time with Wendy and Vicki, and threatened his wealth. It was a new experience for Howard to be controlled. It made him very angry. In the fourth and last stage of the relationship between Lillian and Howard, she was brutally murdered. Howard then reoccupied his house and, with the threat to his business empire and wealth eliminated, turned his attention to developing a closer relationship with his minor stepchildren.

Wendy and Vicki, having suffered through unhappy times when their mother and natural father were married, were initially pleased with the prospect of Howard Randolph becoming their new "dad." He initially wooed them, just as he had their mother, with gifts and promises of many more to follow. Thus, in the first stage of his relationship with Wendy and Vicki, Howard was hopeful that they would develop the feelings of love and adoration for him that he craved. But Howard was disappointed in that objective for two reasons. First, Howard's failure to fulfill his many promises and his other forms of inconsiderate, even cruel, behavior, caused the marriage and the connected relationships to sour. Second, the narcissistic personality seeks a love at such a level of perfection that it is unlikely ever to be attained. Thus, in the second stage of Howard Randolph's relationship with his new family, he was dissatisfied with the degree of love and affection he was receiving from Wendy and Vicki, and blamed Lillian for his lack of fulfillment.

In the third stage, Lillian took her daughters and went to her family in Minnesota, threatening to never go back to Howard. He begged her to return. He went to Minnesota and took her on a second honeymoon, and then immediately afterwards took Lillian, Wendy, and Vicki on a vacation along the shores of Lake Superior. Lillian decided to return to Howard's home, an ultimately fatal decision, and to make another effort to salvage her marriage with Howard. But within weeks the problems of the past again emerged. This time Lillian took the fateful step of filing for separate maintenance and obtaining a restraining order which forced Howard to leave his house.

Howard's opportunity to seek the love and affection of Wendy and Vicki was significantly hampered by being forced to move from the household they had shared. Even further hindering his quest was a growing disinclination for the maturing girls to spend time with Howard. And again an angry Howard blamed Lillian. Her policy, as supported by the document of custody, was never to coerce the girls to go with Howard on his legal visitations. She did, however, encourage them to spend time with him in an effort to reduce friction with him. The time, however, that Howard was spending with Wendy and Vicki was diminishing. He was feeling, no doubt, increasingly abandoned.

Then Lillian told Howard that she planned to take the girls and move to the Boone/Ames area. That would be an even greater abandonment of Howard. Wendy and Vicki would be living eighty miles away, making visitations even more difficult. To make matters worse for the miserly Howard, Lillian was demanding that he pay her $20,000 to help reestablish her in a home in Ames or Boone. A narcissistic personality might take that move as near total abandonment, and trigger the pronounced rage and hatred of which that personality disorder is capable. Sometimes the narcissistic personality's rage over abandonment becomes homicidal. It is conjecture that Howard Randolph suffered from the narcissistic personality disorder. It is certain, however, that the last stage of the relationship between Howard and Lillian was terminated by her murder.

*****

Ultimately Bob Taylor decided not to recommend that murder charges be filed against Howard Randolph. Bob had three choices available to him. One was to file murder charges against Howard. Another was to drop the case against Howard altogether. The third was to delay filing charges pending the discovery of better evidence. Bob chose the third option.

The case against Howard Randolph at that point relied on strong motives for wanting Lillian out of his life, suspicious behavior on his part, a plausible scenario of his involvement, and other circumstantial evidence. Direct evidence, the cornerstone of a strong case, was scant. The two swarthy men in the white Cadillac seen by many witnesses were *presumed* to have abducted and murdered Lillian. But there was no direct evidence via eyewitnesses or any other means that proved either element. The many eyewitnesses could not positively and uniformly identify the two prime suspects, Raul and Gordon, as the two swarthy men. Howard knew Raul, but there was no evidence of recent communications, by telephone or otherwise, between them, nor was there any evidence of money transfers between them. Neither the murder weapon nor the white Cadillac had been found. There were no fingerprints or other evidence that connected Raul or Gordon to the Randolph house or the victim's car.

It was quite possible that stronger evidence of Howard Randolph's responsibility for the murder of Lillian would be forthcoming. There had been considerable reluctance among witnesses to come forward. Maybe, Bob thought, there were other witnesses who would gain courage and supply important information.

Bob also knew that criminals make mistakes. They talk. And when confronted by police on another criminal matter, they may attempt to "cut a deal" by revealing information against suspects in other criminal cases.

Bob understood that, because of the protection against double jeopardy, there would be only one opportunity to prosecute Howard Randolph for murder. Bob was sure that Howard was guilty, but was equally sure that it would be difficult to prove the guilt of Howard beyond a reasonable doubt. There was a risk that no better evidence would be produced and the one opportunity to prosecute Howard would disappear with the passage of time. But in the late summer of 1965 Bob Taylor's professional conclusion was obvious. There simply was not enough evidence to successfully prosecute Howard Randolph for the murder of his estranged wife.

Chapter IX

A Long Epilogue

"I wish we could have nailed him for that."

Lester Peterson

While Howard Randolph was in Duluth attending the burial services of Lillian, Warren Stump and his colleagues at the Iowa Bureau of Criminal Investigation were still trying to collect evidence that would lead to Howard's arrest, trial, and conviction. Little progress was being made in that respect. Dozens of people were interviewed. Records of airport passenger lists, automobile registrations, motel guests, telephone calls, and bank transactions were thoroughly searched, but with no major breakthroughs. BCI agents traveled to Chicago and Kansas City to confer with detectives in those cities. The investigators needed a break to produce justice, such as one of the hit men being picked up on another charge and exchanging information on the murder of Lillian for a lighter sentence.

The composite drawing of the presumed hit men that witnesses helped a BCI artist construct was not useful. Although the many witnesses were near unanimous in their identification of the two men as swarthy, black-haired, and Latin or Southern European in appearance, they were not consistent in their description of other facial features. BCI agents even thought that some witnesses were intentionally unclear in their descriptions out of fear that they might actually identify the killers and bring harm to themselves. The BCI was also convinced that there were other witnesses who were too fearful to come forward with information. Ultimately, the composite drawing was insufficient for the purposes of the BCI. It was never released for media publication.

The first public indications that the case was growing cold came from law enforcement officials in November, six months after the slaying. Tillman "Tommy" Thompson, Director of the BCI, told the press that "we do not have any fresh leads." Sheriff Lester Peterson echoed Thompson's statement when he told a reporter, "A murder case is never closed, but lately we have no leads to run down."

The BCI continued to send an agent to Guthrie Center at least once a week for over a year. Little useful information was obtained in the process. On one of those trips Warren Stump happened to see Howard Randolph at the Midway Cafe where both were having lunch. Stump approached Howard and asked tauntingly if he had any new information on the case. Howard told the agent that he knew he was a suspect, but was irritated with Stump for telling Lillian's family he was guilty. Lil's family had needed no assistance in reaching that conclusion, and had done so long before. Stump was nonplussed that Howard would blame him for the attitude of Lillian's family. Her sister, Helen, had written to Stump to ask why murder charges had not yet been filed against Howard. Ann and Harry Shackelford had severed all ties with Howard and moved away from Guthrie Center. Jim Belluci, Howard's brother-in-law, had told BCI agents that Howard was fully capable of hiring the killers of Lil. Wendy and Vicki were forced into visitation outings with Howard, but did not conceal their contempt for him. Lil's son, Hank, had a pistol and gave thought to "evening the score" with Howard, but did not do so because he had two small children. Lillian's family was quite capable of drawing its own conclusions about Howard's responsibility for her death. They had reached a verdict of guilty.

On most of Warren Stump's trips to Guthrie Center he stopped to compare notes with Sheriff Peterson. At one such meeting, in the fall of 1966, Lester told him that workers he employed to build a fence on the property line he shared with Howard Randolph had inadvertently placed the fence four feet onto Howard's property. When Lester discovered the error he called Howard and informed him. Howard told Lester "not to worry about it," but Lester felt he should tell Stump of the unintentional business connection with Howard. The BCI had known from the beginning of some business transactions between Howard and Lester, and had also noted that one of Howard's out-of-town attorneys was also an attorney for Lester. But the BCI also knew that it was hard to avoid business contacts with Howard Randolph in a small town whose economy he so thoroughly dominated. Dozens of people in Guthrie Center had business connections with Howard Randolph. The BCI did not pursue the matter.

Proof that other witnesses existed who had not come forward surfaced in August of 1967, more than two years after the murder of Lillian. At that time, Glen Kunkle, a car salesman at Leonard Logsdon's Ford dealership across Highway 64 from Don Bates' Midway service station, went to Sheriff Peterson and told him that he had seen the white Cadillac with the two strangers pass by several times the weekend Lillian disappeared. Glen apologized for his tardiness, saying he was too frightened to say anything earlier and had been doubtful that he had seen anything that others had not reported. The latter was mostly true, but yet law enforcement officials were troubled by the possibility that other witnesses might have vital information, a concern that lingers to this day.

Stump's trips to Guthrie Center became less and less frequent as his efforts to solve the case became more and more fruitless. Finally, and reluctantly, Agent Stump wrote a memo on January 29, 1971, to Robert D. Blair, who had become Director of the BCI following the retirement of Tillman Thompson, asking that the Randolph case be "closed administratively" because "all leads have been exhausted." And thus the Lillian Randolph murder file was moved to the "cold case" category.

Warren Stump was thoroughly convinced that Howard Randolph was responsible for the murder of Lillian. The fact that he could not prove his conclusion troubled him deeply. A short time later he left the BCI for a position as a United States Marshal, a position from which he is now retired. Stump's successors, most recently Special Agent John Quinn, have continued to investigate the open murder case of Lillian Randolph, but with little cooperation from the embittered Warren Stump.

In 1991 the Randolph case was moved back to active status. At that time, David Bruner, the Guthrie County Attorney, issued a press release:

"The homicide investigation of Lillian Elizabeth Randolph is progressing as the Guthrie County Sheriff's Office and agents of the Division of Criminal Investigation continue the investigation.

"New information has been received by authorities and these leads are currently being followed up.

"The public's concern and cooperation has been very helpful in providing new information that is assisting the investigators involved in the case.

"Investigative technology has improved tremendously in the area of these types of investigations, with new and enhanced scientific methods that are very useful in the detection and prosecution of offenders.

"Again, anyone with information concerning Lillian's homicide are asked to contact the Guthrie County Sheriff's Office at 515-747-2214, or the Division of Criminal Investigation at 515-281-5138."

The law enforcement officials involved in the re-opening of the case included David S. Bruner, the Guthrie County Attorney who issued the press release; John Quinn, a Special Agent from the DCI; Tom Miller, an Assistant State Attorney General; and Stu Stringham, the Guthrie County Sheriff who succeeded Lester Peterson in 1980. Those initially charged with the investigation were either retired, such as Warren Stump and Lester Peterson, or deceased, as was the case of Coral Greenfield, the Guthrie County Attorney from 1960 to 1978.

Sheriff Stringham recalled that the 1991 effort was an attempt to "smoke out Howard," and perhaps induce previously unknown witnesses to come forward. Bruner's recollections are similar. He remembers that the DCI wanted to "take another look at the case," hoping that perhaps Howard in his twilight years "might want to get the matter off his conscience and confess." When Stringham and Quinn met with the elderly Howard Randolph—he was 84 in 1991—he seemed curious about their interest in talking with him. But as the questioning continued he became irritated and told them to "get (your) asses out." A second attempt to question Howard met with the same hostile response. Stringham had no great expectations that they could trick Howard into making a revealing move or statement, but thought it was "worth a try."

The recollections of John Quinn and Tom Miller of the 1991 investigation do not square completely with those of Stu Stringham and David Bruner. They say there was indeed an anonymous letter with information that prompted re-opening the case, although they cannot remember its specific content. The reactivated investigation lasted several months, and included discussions by Miller, Stringham, and Quinn with former Sheriff Lester Peterson.

If those officials' recollections of the events of 1991 differ in detail, they are all unanimous in the belief that Howard Randolph hired two men to murder Lillian. Stringham rails at the initial probe, and believes that "somebody screwed up the investigation." Using the salty language that is his nature, the sheriff reflected his frustrations by saying, "God damn it, we hated to see him get by with this thing."

Former Sheriff Lester Peterson also thought that Howard was guilty, largely because of strong motives and his earlier harsh treatment of Lillian. Lester recalled wistfully, "I wish we could have nailed him for that." Special Agent John Quinn also thinks that Howard was guilty, seeing the murder of Lillian as the bold and arrogant act of a man who was accustomed to having his own way. Quinn reflected emotions and certainty when he said, "Howard didn't give a shit." Tom Miller, reflecting the view of an experienced prosecutor, focused more on the possibility of a successful trial. Tom also believes that Howard was guilty, but is more hesitant about the possibility of a successful trial, only going so far as to say, "There may have been reason enough to prosecute the case."

The 1991 re-investigation, whatever its basis, was short-lived and non-productive. By that time one of the suspected hit men, Raul, had died and the other, Gordon, had moved from Des Moines.

Raul and Gordon were under continual police surveillance because of their lengthy criminal records. Raul ran a garbage truck business for a number of years before selling out to Des Moines Waste Management. He then supplied that company with Mexican laborers with whom he could converse in Spanish. Employees at the waste management company recalled Raul as "jovial" and "always laughing," but also a "rough cut guy who mouthed off a lot." They also recalled rumors that he "carried a gun" and "could get you a girl."

Raul was a suspect in another homicide case in Des Moines in which the body of Diane Schofield was found in the trunk of her car in a parking lot near the Des Moines airport. In that case, which took place in the summer of 1975, Raul was believed by police to have hired a hit man, a friend who was a bricklayer, to rough up the victim for holding out money from him in his prostitution ring. She died of strangulation in the process.

Raul died in August of 1988 after enduring the agonies of stomach cancer. People who knew him at the time recall how his stomach was bloated and how much he suffered. The Des Moines *Register* ran an obituary on him, including notification that services would be held at the Caldwell-Brien-Robbins Funeral Home. He was fifty-four years old at the time of his death.

Law enforcement officials were less certain that Gordon was the second hit man. Raul was the type and was apparently involved in other homicides, although never convicted of any. Gordon was a smaller version of Raul in looks and build, just as eyewitnesses had described the two. But he was not known to be violent or to "work" with Raul. On the other hand, he was known among Des Moines police as a career criminal eager to enrich himself in any conceivable way.

Gordon was primarily a burglar, although occasionally involved in other crimes. He had a long police record and had been in and out of prison, actually serving more time than Raul. Gordon used Des Moines as a base of operations for many years, but was involved in burglaries in other cities. He was thought by DMPD detectives to be one of a group of burglars who stole $5,000,000 in jewelry in a Phoenix, Arizona, theft. Des Moines police lost track of Gordon when he moved out of the area. They have reason to believe that he is deceased.

*****

While the criminal investigation lost momentum, the lives of Lillian's survivors continued. After the disappearance of their mother, Wendy and Vicki lived at the home of their half-sister, Ann Shackelford and her husband, Harry. Ann and Harry concluded immediately after the discovery of Lillian's body that Howard Randolph was responsible. They felt that they had been "taken in" by Howard and were very angry. They were also in a vulnerable position. They were twenty-three years old, had three young daughters, and were dependent upon Howard for their livelihood.

Howard offered the Shackelfords $200 per month for the support of Wendy and Vicki. That payment would confirm Howard's legal relationship with the girls and his interest in caring for them. But Howard had more in mind than providing financial support for the girls—he wanted them to live with him. He knew he was unwelcome in the Shackelford home. Thus he sent a letter to Wendy and Vicki, addressing them familiarly as "Vick and Wend." The letter was dated June 9, less than a month after the burial of their mother. Howard wrote: "I don't know how you are fixed for bathing suits and other clothes that might come in handy this summer. If you will let me know when you would like to go shopping, I would like very much to take you shopping in Des Moines." He concluded his letter by writing: "I miss you a lot and would like to be with you whenever possible."

Howard then sent a business associate who often did his bidding, Richard Loftus, to talk with Harry and Ann. Loftus told the Shackelfords that Howard Randolph was the legal father of Wendy and Vicki, Howard understood the burden that the girls' presence placed on the Shackelford household, and that he was willing and ready to accept them back into his home and to care for them. Howard hoped the Shackelfords would relinquish control of Wendy and Vicki to him. The response of Ann and Harry was quick and negative. Instead of turning the girls over to him, Harry quit his job as a farm manager for Howard and moved his family, including Wendy and Vicki, to Coon Rapids, twenty miles to the northwest of Guthrie Center.

Times were sparse for the seven people living in the new Shackelford home. Wendy, sixteen at the time, recalls how limited their food was and regrets complaining about it to Ann. Howard was unhappy to see Wendy and Vicki move away. He had hoped and planned for Wendy and Vicki to live with him. They dreaded that possibility. Ann had absorbed the message from her mother that she must not allow Wendy and Vicki to fall under the control of Howard. Hank had also been requested by his mother to "look after the girls."

It was an awkward and difficult time for the Shackelfords. They were trying to raise a family and make ends meet. Their limited housing was severely cramped with seven occupants. Harry was finding work where he could. They were constantly reminded of the grief of Lillian's death as law enforcement officials questioned them. And Howard was complaining that he was not able to see Wendy and Vicki. He continued to write to them, urging them to come back to Guthrie Center and live with him. He typically sweetened his plea with a ten-dollar bill apiece, and signed his letters: "Love, Howard." Changing tactics, Howard again offered to pay Ann $200 per month for the support of Wendy and Vicki, but this time in exchange for visitation rights only. The girls, who felt the burden that they were placing on the Shackelford family, were unhappy with the prospect of spending time with the man they were convinced was responsible for the death of their mother, but went along with the visitations of Howard as their contribution to the support of the household.

Howard's child support payments alleviated the financial crisis of the Shackelfords, but required some involvement with him at a time when they wanted to break all connections. No one was happy. Ann and Harry had financial burdens that strained their meager resources, and a painful and unwanted connection with Howard Randolph. Wendy and Vicki thought they were a liability to the Shackelford family. Howard was unhappy that the girls were not living with him, and was trying to force circumstances in that direction. None of Lillian's children wanted that to happen, and all were mindful of Lillian's request to Hank to "look after the girls." In August Wendy and Vicki moved to Urbandale, a suburb of Des Moines, to live with Hank, his wife Peggy, and their two children. Wendy enrolled at Roosevelt High School in Des Moines for her senior year and Vicki did likewise for her sophomore year.

Harry and Ann were freed from all connections with Howard Randolph and remained that way for the rest of his life. Howard voiced his disappointment to several people, including Harry's brother, Marvin, and sister, Marie, over no longer being able to spend time with Ann and Harry's daughters. Howard established bank accounts for each of the Shackelford girls, with the likely thought that he could pry his way back into their lives with his money. But Harry and Ann, in a form of personal justice that the formal system could never manage, deprived Howard of something he apparently wanted very badly—a continuing relationship with their daughters.

The Shackelfords made a few moves before eventually establishing themselves in northeast Iowa, where they now reside. In the process they raised four daughters who have no recollections of Howard Randolph. That is the way their parents wanted it. They only wish they could expunge from their minds the ugly memories of Howard Randolph and the death of Lillian.

Wendy and Vicki were happy to be in a new high school and fifty miles from Howard Randolph. They were unhappy with Howard's continuing visitation rights, but suppressed their feelings out of fear of defying a court order and having Howard gain legal custody of them. They did what they felt they had to, and no more.

On a visitation with Wendy and Vicki in the fall of 1965 Howard took them to a movie, "The Great Race," in Des Moines. Afterwards, they asked to be returned immediately to their home at Hank and Peg's. Howard, upset with their obvious lack of interest in spending time with him, instead drove to the Des Moines airport, saying he had business there. He parked his Buick very near the spot where Lillian's Dodge Coronet was found a few months before. The girls took Howard's act as cruel retribution for their request to go home immediately.

That incident, and others like it, made Howard increasingly angry over visitation problems with Vicki and Wendy. They preferred to spend as little time with him as possible, and Hank and Peg did what they could to support the girls' wishes. But Howard was paying $200 per month child support and wanted the accompanying privileges. In July, only two months after the burial of Lil and seemingly oblivious to the hatred that her family had developed for him, he suggested to Helen, Lil's widowed sister, that he and she take Wendy and Vicki on a vacation to Wisconsin. Helen never responded to Howard's invitation, but instead contacted Special Agent Stump. A few months later, in November of 1965, Helen again contacted Stump and asked why murder charges had not been filed against Howard Randolph.

In late October of 1965 Howard approached Peg Randolph and told her that he would no longer accept the arrangement of paying child support, but having to beg for visitations with Wendy and Vicki. He informed Peg that he wanted full legal custody of Wendy and Vicki. The next day Howard sent Richard Loftus to Hank Randolph's home in an effort to convince Peg and Hank to give him custody of the girls. There was an element of threat in Loftus' approach, but Hank and Peg did not agree to Howard's latest proposal.

Soon thereafter the persistent Howard paid a visit to the D-X service station in Des Moines where Hank was working. He asked Hank to encourage Wendy and Vicki to accompany him on a trip to Kansas City. There was a special "Mary Poppins" festival planned there in connection with the release of the movie that starred Julie Andrews and Dick Van Dyke. Howard had already contacted Margaret Priebe, a Des Moines housewife who was a former Mrs. America, about making the trip with him and "his two daughters." The very attractive Mrs. Priebe had a fifteen-year-old daughter. Howard had communicated to her his desire to fly the two adults and the three teenage girls to Kansas City in a private plane to attend the Mary Poppins festivities, apparently with the intention of developing a relationship with Mrs. Priebe.

Margaret Priebe was suspicious of the proposal from a stranger and contacted the Des Moines Police Department. Knowing that Howard was a suspect in the murder of Lillian, the DMPD passed the information to the BCI. Mrs. Priebe was not inclined to accept the proposal in any case, and Wendy and Vicki did not want to accompany Howard on an overnight excursion to Kansas City. The trip to Kansas City never took place, but Howard did mount a full legal effort to gain custody of Wendy and Vicki. As was his nature, he turned to the courts for a remedy, filing a petition with the Iowa District Court for custody of the two minor girls.

The hearing for the custody of Wendy and Vicki took place over a three-day period at the new Guthrie County courthouse in late December of 1965. Robert Taylor of Guthrie Center and A.B. Crouch of Des Moines acted as legal counsel for Wendy and Vicki. Presiding was Iowa District Judge H. J. Kittleman. Howard produced a number of character witnesses that testified to his high character and glowing paternal qualities. Howard's witnesses were known to Lillian's children, all of who were present, to be lackeys of Howard whom he frequently used. When the witnesses passed the bench where Wendy and Vicki were seated, several hung their heads, in what the girls perceived as shame. It seemed unfair to Wendy and Vicki that there was no opportunity for people to say nice things about their mother. But at least the girls were given an opportunity to express their personal feelings to Judge Kittleman in a private meeting. The girls emphatically told the judge that they wanted to live with their half-brother Hank, continue their education at Roosevelt High, and dreaded any prospect of being under the control of Howard Randolph.

A few days before Christmas, Judge Kittleman delivered the decision that Lil's children had hoped for. He awarded custody to Hank Randolph, required Howard to pay $200 per month in child support, and gave him visitation rights. In effect, Judge Kittleman had ordered a continuation of the status quo. Lil's children were elated that they had warded off Howard's latest and greatest effort to force Wendy and Vicki to live with him.

Unfortunately, life in Peg and Hank's home was not easy. There were money problems, space problems, visitation with Howard problems, and eventually marital problems between Peg and Hank that later led to their divorce. Wendy and Vicki felt in the way and, although grateful to Ann and Hank for their support and assistance, were disappointed that members of their mother's family had not offered more help. In retrospect, that attitude of relatives can no doubt be explained by a reluctance to become involved in any way with Howard Randolph. But at the time Wendy and Vicki felt quite alone. Howard stood ready to offer financial support, but always at the price of greater involvement with them. It was an awkward and difficult situation for two teenagers.

Wendy graduated from Roosevelt High in the spring of 1966. Because Howard had court-ordered responsibilities to assist in post-secondary education for the girls, Wendy was able to enroll at the Mankato Commercial College in Mankato, Minnesota, with his financial support. While Wendy was moving to Minnesota to continue her education, Vicki moved into the Des Moines home of Walter Brown, Howard's tax attorney. For the next two years Vicki lived with the Browns, a family for whom she grew very fond.

Howard was ill much of the time that Wendy was attending the Mankato Commercial College, but tried to maintain contact. Occasionally he sent a lady friend to look in on Wendy. Wendy recalls the lady's kindness, but not her name. When the woman revealed that she hoped to marry Howard, Wendy tried to dissuade her. She related that Howard had hired killers to murder her mother, and that she should severe all ties with Howard. The woman grew silent. She never returned.

But Howard did return. When Wendy saw him approaching she ran to a friend's room and locked the door. Howard talked to her through the door and asked her to go out to dinner with him. She told him to go away and never come back. He departed, and so did his financial support for Wendy. She took a job as a waitress and paid for the remainder of her education.

When Wendy finished her training at the Mankato Commercial College her thoughts turned to moving far away, and far beyond the reach of Howard Randolph. She called her biological father, Roy Chalman, who was living in California, and told him that she would like to move west and live with him until she could find employment. Roy agreed and went to Mankato to help move Wendy to his home in California. She did find employment and, within a year, a husband as well. She and Gary have raised a family of three children over the ensuing years.

The last time that Wendy saw Howard Randolph was when he came to her California home in the late-1960's to ask her assistance in his $4,000,000 suit against A.B. Crouch for "alienating the affections" of Wendy and Vicki. Crouch, who later became a judge in Des Moines, was Lillian's lawyer at the time of her death. He and Bob Taylor had provided legal assistance to Wendy and Vicki, and had asked Howard Randolph to pay for their services. When he refused, Crouch and Taylor sued Randolph for their fees. Howard then countered with a multi-million dollar suit against Crouch, claiming that he was responsible for the ill will that Wendy and Vicki held for him. It was ludicrous to think that anyone other than himself had alienated the girls, but as a legal ploy Howard's strategy worked. Crouch and Taylor never collected a cent from Howard Randolph for the legal services they provided to Wendy and Vicki.

After Vicki graduated from Roosevelt High she attended the Chicago Art Institute and the University of Oklahoma before Howard cut off his financial support to her. She later moved to Colorado and has lived there since. Vicki maintained peripheral contact with Howard Randolph for a number of years, including occasional visits in young adulthood to Guthrie Center when she was in financial difficulty. Vicki loathed Howard and held him fully responsible for the death of her mother. She felt that tapping him for occasional financial assistance was just retribution, and the only form of justice that ever occurred.

*****

People's actions are the best indicators of their interests and priorities. Applying that measure to Howard Randolph in the aftermath of the murder of Lillian, it is clear that he gave a very high priority to gaining custody of Wendy and Vicki. He continued relationships with a number of women, most notably Peggy Alston. His business interests changed focus, but still absorbed great quantities of his time and energy. In business and other matters, Howard continued to use unethical means and the judicial process to force his way, although the latter approach eventually backfired.

Howard's local reputation, never good, plunged to the lowest of depths. Public opinion is not restricted like the requirements of the judicial process. Opinion in Guthrie Center was nearly unanimous that Howard Randolph was guilty of hiring two hit men to murder Lillian. From time to time, usually in a fit of anger over a sour business deal with Howard, someone would confront him with charges of being a wife killer. Howard, who was of Quaker origins and claimed he never told a lie, never specifically denied responsibility for Lillian's death, nor did he ever confess to being involved.

Howard's health rapidly declined following the murder of Lillian. People near him noticed he was pale and drawn. He attributed his failing health to arthritis and began to make visits to the mineral springs of health spas in Claremore, Oklahoma, and Hot Springs, Arkansas, in an effort to alleviate his pain. Visits to those spas continued for as long as Howard was able to make the trip.

Peggy Alston, who moved into the Randolph home shortly after the death of Lillian, believed that Howard's health problems were the result of "nerves." She thought he had developed a nervous condition over the shock of losing his wife. Others, including law enforcement officers, thought Howard's nervous condition was the result of a fear of being indicted for the murder of Lillian or facing the killers who might try to blackmail him.

Richard Rash, an employee of Howard's who worked near him every day, thought that Howard's nervous condition had reached the point in the fall of 1965 that he might be suicidal. Peggy, who was with Howard almost daily at that time, does not agree with Rash's assessment, but does recall that he was "a very sick man." With perhaps health a major factor in his decision, Howard decided to sell his widespread poultry and creamery interests that autumn to Seymour Foods of Topeka, Kansas, in a million dollar deal. He then turned his attention to raising cattle, always his preferred business operation. He created a corporation for that purpose and named it "Rolling Ridges Ranch."

Howard's arthritis and nervous condition suddenly seemed less significant when he was diagnosed in early 1968 with colon cancer. Howard did not believe that he had an affliction of nerves. He drank cod liver oil in huge quantities in an attempt to thwart his arthritis, but never thought he would succumb to that disease. Cancer was another matter.

Howard asked Charles Joy, another of his attorneys, to prepare his last will and testament. He signed it in Joy's office in Perry, Iowa, on Valentine's Day of 1968. There was no valentine for Lillian's four children. They were all excluded from any benefits of his sizeable estate, even though he had legally adopted them and all had switched their names to "Randolph." Howard even had Wendy's Minnesota birth certificate changed, an illegal act accomplished by unknown means, so that he was listed as her birth father. Richard Randolph, whom Howard never claimed as his natural son, was also excluded from Howard's will. He did provide for his mother's care and burial if he should precede her in death (he did not). All else was left to his brothers, their children, and their grandchildren, many of whom Howard had never met. The Guthrie County State Bank was named as executor.

Howard's colon cancer was known to some Guthrie County law enforcement officials, but to few other locals. There was a thought among some who did know that God was rendering a verdict and justice for the murder of Lillian. Guthrie Center is Bible Belt country and locals have faith in the Lord's justice. It appeared that the Almighty had pronounced a death sentence upon Howard Randolph for the murder of Lillian. But if Howard was indeed guilty of hiring killers to murder his estranged wife, God's system of justice is just as flawed as that of mankind. Howard recovered from cancer and lived another twenty-six years.

*****

After Howard was initially rebuffed in his efforts to move back into his house the afternoon of Lillian's funeral in Guthrie Center, he received the legal clearance to do so two days later. He then contacted his long-time companion, Peggy Alston, at her Stuart home and asked her to join him. She soon arrived with three riding horses to be stabled in the new barn behind the house. Howard had replaced the original barn when it burned to the ground as the result of his "little princesses" and their Belluci cousins playing with matches, something Howard never knew.

Peggy Alston also maintained a home in Stuart and continued to commute to Des Moines where she worked as a secretary at the Grey Lake

Holiday Inn. Peggy was thoroughly loyal to Howard, something like the character "Honey" in the Doonesberry cartoon. She was a chauffeur to Howard, his hostess on social occasions, the manager of his household, and a traveling companion. Her 1959 Ford convertible with its pink bottom and white top was seen frequently at the Randolph residence by locals who were now keeping a watchful eye on Howard's house, business office, and every move. He was seemingly under the surveillance of the entire community. People were taking license numbers from cars at his home and business, noting descriptions of people seen with him, and giving the resulting information to Sheriff Peterson.

While Wendy and Vicki had resisted Howard's efforts to move them into his household, Sue Henningson, a grandniece of Howard's, ran away from her Minnesota home and asked to live with him. After being orphaned by a tragedy, Sue had lived with her grandparents, Donald and Virginia Randolph, the brother and sister-in-law of Howard. Sue remembered how Howard had bought her clothes and other gifts when she was a child, and thought he would make a good custodial parent.

In 1968, when Sue moved in, Howard was battling colon cancer, needed care, and wanted a family. Sue needed a home. It was a match. Peggy Alston was living with Howard and caring for him at that time. As Howard's health improved and Sue became a bigger part of Howard's life, Peggy moved out of the Randolph home and back to hers in Stuart.

Sue recalls the affection that Howard felt for Wendy and Vicki, being especially partial to Vicki. Howard even "threw Vicki up" to Sue, as she describes it, as an example she should emulate. Sue also remembers that Howard "worked me hard," never gave her gifts, made her account for every penny, and never allowed her to use his car. Nevertheless, she developed a sense of affection for Howard, going so far as to say she "loved" him. He supplied a home when she needed one. She is still grateful for that.

Sue was later the caretaker for her Great Grandmother Bessie and Great Uncle Earle, Howard's mother and brother. The three lived together on Main Street in Guthrie Center in a modest clapboard house. She remembers that Howard would "fly in and fly out," keeping an eye on his mother but not being highly involved in her life. On occasion he would bring them beef neck bones to eat. Sue recalls Bessie as a crusty and frugal woman who used a washbasin instead of a sink to save water. She observed Bessie's niggardliness and difficulty in expressing affection, and thought there were obvious parallels with the behavior of Howard.

While Sue developed a genuine affection for Howard during the two years she lived with him, she was also aware of his shortcomings. An apparent ambivalence marked her opinion on Howard's responsibility for

Lillian's murder as she stated, "I cannot believe that he had anything to do with it, but if he did he is in hell now."

When Sue left the Randolph household, Peggy Alston began to spend more time with Howard. They shared an interest in travel and visited Mexico City, New York, San Padre Island, and the World's Fair in Montreal. They also made numerous trips to Claremore, Oklahoma, and Hot Springs, Arkansas, where Howard sought relief from his arthritis in the warm mineral waters of spas. Wherever they went in Howard's most recent Buick, Peggy did nearly all the driving.

In 1977 Howard told Richard Randolph, with whom he was spending more time, that he planned to re-marry. Richard immediately assumed that the bride would be Peggy Alston. He was wrong. The new Mrs. Randolph would be Thelma Jacobs from Harlan, Iowa, some forty miles to the west of Guthrie Center.

Although Richard was surprised, Peggy was not. Howard had bought her a ring on a previous occasion, but she had declined to accept it. "We would not have lasted two weeks," Peggy recalls. "He liked to control and I would not have that."

Peggy was not surprised that Howard planned to re-marry, but she did not know Thelma or that Howard was seeing her. Peggy knew Howard from 1946 until his death in 1994. She knew him better than anyone else. They lived together several times and traveled together frequently. But she did not know everything about him. Peggy was surprised to discover after Howard's death that he had hired a private detective at one time to follow her and a gentleman friend.

The process by which Howard selected the third Mrs. Randolph was unknown to both Richard Randolph and Peggy. It was known to Marion Messersmith, a long-time friend of Howard's, who was visiting in Guthrie Center from her California home at the time Howard was calculating his next marital move. Howard told Marion that he was lonely and wanted to re-marry. He showed her a list of prospects. He was seeing several women, as usual, and he reviewed the pros and cons of each "candidate" with Marion. As was Howard's nature, it was all business. Howard kept returning to the name of "Thelma Jacobs," and mentioned each time that she was a registered nurse. That factor seemed to have a special appeal to him. He was suffering from a continuing battle with arthritis and, according to Marion, was drinking cod liver oil "by the gallon." Apparently he was thinking that it would be good for his health to have a nurse at hand. Howard had originally met Thelma Jacobs through her sister, Darlene Anderson, an employee of his in Harlan. Thelma was a widow and had told Darlene several times of her loneliness. Darlene assumed the role of matchmaker.

After Howard chose Thelma from his list of candidates for the position of Mrs. Howard Randolph he asked her to accompany him on a trip, presumably as a courting proposition. Thelma accepted, but the trip did not go well. Thelma refused to share a bed with Howard unless they were married, and he refused to rent a second room. Howard told Thelma, "OK, then you can sleep on the floor." She did.

When they returned Howard asked Thelma to become his wife. Thelma was ambivalent about Howard's proposal. But she had grown weary of being alone and he had made many enticing promises. Darlene recalled: "He promised her the world. He was going to take her everywhere. My God, what he promised her!" For those who knew Howard, including in particular Lillian's family, those words would have a sour familiarity.

Thelma knew of the murder of Lillian and that Howard was widely regarded as responsible for her death. What impact that had on Thelma's decision to marry him is unknown. She refused to talk about it. Whenever the subject was raised, Thelma had a ready and standard response: "I don't want to hear about it."

Although Thelma had quickly learned that Howard's initial charm was not his full definition, her loneliness and his promises won out. She married him. She was Catholic and considered marriage to be forever, for better or for worse. There were some of both in their marriage but the balance was heavily weighted on the latter. Thelma was an RN and had a number of grandchildren. Thus Howard had a live-in nurse and a family life, both of which were priorities to him. Thelma and Howard had both been lonely. They had that in common, but not much else.

When Thelma moved into the bedroom at the Randolph house that had been occupied twelve years earlier by Lillian and Vicki (Thelma and Howard never shared a bed), she discovered the closet was filled with Lillian's clothes. She also discovered that Howard was still using Lillian's dishes. Thelma insisted that Howard get rid of Lillian's possessions. Eventually he complied with her demand.

Thelma's sense of loneliness was not eliminated by the marriage. Howard traveled a lot and left Thelma alone on the farm. She was new in town and had to break into the local social network. She did have access to an automobile and became involved in the local Catholic Church. Howard was not keen on Thelma having visitors at the house, although Darlene and her husband, Chet, occasionally visited on weekends.

Thelma soon learned that Howard had forgotten the many promises he had made to her. She also learned of his miserly ways. He expected that their living expenses would be paid by their Social Security checks, in effect placing Thelma on a pay-your-own-way basis. She kept a separate checking account, from which Howard borrowed from time to time. His money, as he explained to Thelma, was for making money.

Howard, who had forbidden Lillian to drink coffee, did not seem to mind Thelma's coffee drinking. Thelma was, however, diabetic and had a heart condition. Howard told her diabetic foods were "unnecessary" and refused to buy them for her. Thelma needed estrogen for a heart condition that eventually caused her death. Howard likewise thought that estrogen was a frill and discouraged her purchase of that medication.

Thelma had her own means and did not have expensive tastes. After she married Howard she sold her house in Harlan for $20,000 and loaned the money to a son who was starting a grocery business in Elk Horn, a small town thirty miles southwest of Guthrie Center. When the business was sold a few years later, Howard claimed that $5,000 of what was repaid to Thelma belonged to him. Rather than dispute the point, Thelma gave Howard the money.

Thelma also "loaned" money to Howard from time to time from her bank account, money that was seldom repaid. She lived in a cold house in the winter because Howard kept the thermostat low to save on fuel. She spent time in the dark because Howard kept the lights off to save electricity. Eventually Thelma told her sister, Darlene, that she was unhappy in the marriage. Darlene went to Howard and told him of Thelma's unhappiness.

"I'm happy," he responded. "If she's not, that's her problem."

Darlene asked Howard what provisions he had made for Thelma if she were to survive him. "Whatever the law permits," he told her. But he never changed his will to include her or any member of her family.

Diane Yokum, a close friend of Thelma's, passed along to Darlene that Thelma was "afraid of Howard." Darlene already knew of her sister's fears and had told Howard, "If anything happens to my sister, I'll be by to see you with a shot gun."

Thelma also made her fears known to Carl and Mary Moeller, new farm tenants of Howard who had moved recently from Sheldon, Iowa. Howard invited the Moellers to dinner. Thelma called the young couple and asked that they come early and spend the afternoon with her at the Randolph house. When the Moellers arrived at 2:00 p.m. Howard was still at his office. Mary began to help prepare dinner when Thelma blurted, "Get out while you can. He had her murdered." Thelma began to cry. "You have to get out," she said. "He is Mafia."

The Moellers were dumbstruck as they sat through the strained circumstances of dinner with Howard. Afterwards they returned to their house, packed, and moved in the middle of the night. They said nothing to Howard Randolph about leaving and never communicated with him again.

When Howard built an apartment complex at the corner of Third and Prairie in Guthrie Center, and told Thelma that he planned for them to move into one of the six units, she began to think seriously about leaving him. The prospect of living in one of the windowless units after a number of years in the spacious Randolph house was a dreary prospect. She discussed the matter with her children and was dissuaded from separating from Howard. Besides, she was Catholic and took her wedding vows seriously. In 1986 Howard and Thelma moved into the west end unit of the new six-plex.

Howard's one-story apartment building was a conversion of the hatchery he constructed on that site in 1937. The rumor was that chicken feed had so permeated the structure that fifty years later it was part of the aroma of the building. Others who shared the six-plex and its common glassed-in veranda recall that it was not the residue of chicken feed that tortured their nostrils—it was the B.O. of Howard Randolph. Velma Covault, who lived in one of the units, recalls Thelma badgering Howard to "take a bath."

Howard Randolph seldom had a year pass without a court battle. During the 1980s he was engaged in a lengthy legal struggle with Lester Steckelberg. This case is particularly noteworthy because Howard lost, an unusual occurrence for him; because the size of the judgment against him was so large that it sent him into a fit of depression; and because many people in Guthrie Center where the trial was held found an element of retribution in the outcome. At last Howard Randolph had received a long deserved rebuke, and where it hurt most—in his pocket book.

Lester Steckelberg was a match for Howard in his enthusiasm for court trials. Howard had had great success when confronting adversaries with a host of attorneys and legal procedures. Many were intimidated by Howard's approach, and capitulated. Lester Steckelberg had the patience and interest in the legal process to persevere. After Howard managed to gain title to the Steckelberg farm by means that Lester thought to be illegal, he challenged Howard in the courts. The legal battle raged for seven years until it was culminated by an eight-day trial at the Guthrie County courthouse in the fall of 1987. The local jury of Howard Randolph's peers awarded Lester and Norma Steckelberg $1,100,000, including $178,500 for fraud; $250,000 for emotional distress; and $532,000 for punitive damages. Richard Randolph recalls that when Howard heard the verdict he went into an emotional funk that lasted for several weeks. It was a low point in Howard's business career.

Thelma and Howard lived in the Randolph Apartments from 1986 until she died in her sleep on September 20, 1992, at the age of eighty-one. When Howard discovered that she had stopped breathing he immediately called the sheriff, Stu Stringham, and Darlene, Thelma's sister. Howard was very cautious in his behavior, leaving the apartment and its furnishings untouched until the sheriff, the coroner, and Thelma's family had every opportunity to arrange official and personal needs.

Darlene and Thelma's family made arrangements for Thelma's burial in Harlan. Howard was largely uninvolved. Darlene, thinking that he would want to provide flowers for the funeral, asked Howard's preference for a floral arrangement. He coolly responded, "Her kids can pick out whatever flowers they want to pay for."

After Thelma's funeral and burial, Howard called Peggy Alston and told her to "get back up here." Howard had not seen Peggy frequently during his marriage to Thelma, but did occasionally take her out to dinner. Peggy was still working at the Grey Lake Holiday Inn in Des Moines and living in Stuart. She began to come by Howard's apartment more often. Peggy once again became Howard's "Girl Friday," but did not move in with him. The following year, 1993, Peggy quit her job in Des Moines and spent even more time looking after Howard. He was lonely and ill. He called Marion Messersmith in California often, and nearly always mentioned how lonely he was.

When Howard died on February 9, 1994, Peggy Alston and Richard Randolph put Howard's papers in order at the request of Roger Underwood, President of the Guthrie County State Bank, the Executor for Howard's will. The most important document, his last will and testament, included nothing for any of the women who had shared his life: nothing for Maxine, his first wife, or for her son, Richard; nothing for the children of Lillian, his murdered second wife; nothing for the children of Thelma, his third wife; nothing for Peggy Alston, Veronica Clark, Marion Messersmith or any of his long-time female companions. Howard had promised Neil Christiansen, one of his farm managers who had labored for him for many years, that he would leave him a farm. Neil was left nothing, nor were the several others to whom Howard had made similar promises.

On February 12, 1994, a small group of people gathered at the Beidelman Funeral Home in Guthrie Center to attend the funeral of Howard Fitz Randolph. Those present included family members of Howard's third wife, Thelma, who had died two years before; a few friends and business associates; and a few curious locals. None of Lillian Hedman Randolph's family was present.

Richard Randolph arranged for the services with the assistance of Peggy Alston. They paid Betty Sheeder to provide a lunch for the funeral attendees at the Farm Bureau Hall. Some locals scornfully said that Howard Randolph's pallbearers would also have to be paid. Serving in that capacity were Neil Christensen, Howard's long-time farm manager who was soon to be bitterly disappointed when Howard's promise of bequeathing a farm to him turned out to be a cruel hoax; Steve Sheeder, a long-time friend of Howard's who was with him when he died and also hoped to benefit from Howard's will. He would also be disappointed. The other six casket bearers were five of Thelma's grandsons and Ryan Randolph, Richard and Rosie Randolph's son.

*****

The death of Howard Randolph did not close the Lillian Randolph murder case—unsolved capitol cases are never closed. But it did eliminate forever the possibility he would be brought to trial for her murder. In the nearly three decades between the murder of Lillian and the death of Howard no other suspect surfaced. From the beginning to the end Howard was the one and only suspect as the person who hired the two hit men.

Many of the imperfections in the American criminal justice system are reflected in the Randolph case. A family was left to grieve and carry on. A community was ruptured and tormented with fears and rumors. There was no trial. No conviction. No justice.

Index

About the Author

Carroll R. McKibbin, whose hometown in Iowa is the setting for this book, is a professor emeritus now living in semi-retirement with his wife, Lynn, in San Luis Obispo, California. As a full-time or visiting professor, Dr. McKibbin has held faculty positions at the University of Kansas, Drake University, the University of Nebraska, Cal Poly, Iowa State University, and the University of Pittsburgh. Professor McKibbin is the author of many journal articles and books, including *Choices in American Government* and *In Pursuit of National Interests*.

Printed in the United States
1223500002B/204

9 781403 392534